Societies and Social Life

An Introduction to Sociology

Second Edition

James W. Russell
Eastern Connecticut State University

2009

SLOAN PUBLISHING

Cornwall-on-Hudson, NY 12520

Library-of-Congress Cataloging-in-Publication Data

Russell, James W., 1944–
  Societies and social life: an introduction to sociology / James W. Russell.--2nd ed.
    p. cm.
  Includes bibliographical references and index.
  ISBN 978-1-59738-020-1
  1. Sociology. I. Title.
  HM585.R874 2009
  301--dc22

                              2008043232

Cover art: "Red Jazz" © Didier Lourenço/Winn Devon Art Group
Cover designer: Amy Rosen

Two previous editions of this text were published by Pearson
Education under the title *Introduction to Macrosociology*

Printed in the United States of America

10 9 8 7 6 5 4 3 2 1

ISBN 978-1-59738-020-1

For my daughters,
Julia, Magdalena, Armida,
with love

Contents

Chapter Four
Past Societies   40

Chapter Five
Contemporary Societies and the World Economy   58

Chapter Six
Global Trends   77

Chapter Seven
Classical Sociological Theory   108

Chapter Eight
Power, Politics, and the State   145

Chapter Nine
Class, Race, and Gender   171

Preface

The classic nineteenth- and early twentieth-century founders of sociology began their quest for objective social knowledge by addressing the large questions: Where did their societies come from? What were their characters? Where were they going? Put more exactly, they sought out the origins of Western capitalism, analyzed its major economic, political, and social institutions, and tried to predict future developments. Sociology's original intellectual mission was thus to objectively analyze societies and social life. Its promise was that by doing so it could help people make collective sense of the social conditions under which they lived.

As we settle into the twenty-first century, understanding the large questions of social life has become even more important. Societies have grown more complex. People have become caught up in ever more intricate and extensive sets of economic, political, and social relationships that transcend national boundaries. New problems of social life have grown up alongside of old, unresolved ones. Despite spectacular technological advances in the past century, social contradictions abound. Astronauts travel in space but fear to walk crime-ridden streets. Stretch limousines crawl uneasily down New York City's crowded streets past legions of homeless people.

The text that follows was written to introduce sociology in a way that maintains the classic focuses of its founders—to provide conceptual tools for addressing the large questions of social life, such as, for example, making intelligent sense of changes sweeping Central and Eastern Europe and parts of the developing countries or the outbreak of wars in different regions of the world. The text therefore incorporates a historical and comparative approach that examines past and present societies and their major economic, political, and social features.

That orientation at the same time incorporates important classical contributions that have come from more social psychologically oriented concerns. Conceptualization of the relationship between individuals and societies—between psychology and sociology—is a necessary foundation for all social knowledge and research.

The logic of presentation of the text is to begin in Chapter One with an introductory description of sociology as a field of study. From there the text progressively builds up the conceptual apparatus of sociology. Chapter Two, Individuals and Societies, describes the basic terminology that sociologists use to conceptualize and analyze social life in all types of societies. Chapters Three through Six contain descriptions, analyses, and discussions of different types of past and contemporary societies. Chapters Seven through Twelve are devoted to discussions of major sociological units of analysis: power, the state, class, race, gender, organizations, the family, and population. The text ends with a chapter on techniques of social research.

I recommend that Chapters One through Six be read first and in order since they contain concepts and themes that build in logical order. Chapters Seven through Thirteen can then be read in any order.

In my experience, the best way to learn a new discipline is to study its basic concepts. For that reason, basic sociological as well as other social science concepts are progressively introduced, discussed, and defined throughout the text, with a complete glossary at the end. Chapter One introduces the idea that specialized social concepts—such as class, norms, state, and power—are human intellectual tools for making sense of social realities. In Chapter Two the most basic of concept—that of the human being—is discussed, including the idea that human beings are social beings. From there through Chapter Six, the text builds with concepts—such as the self, roles, and institutions—for analyzing micro and macro patterns of social relations, up to concepts—such as slavery, feudalism, and capitalism—for categorizing whole societies, both historically and comparatively. When a key concept is introduced in a chapter, it is boldfaced, and key concepts are listed in order of presentation at the end of each chapter for review purposes.

This text is the long-term product of my attempts to teach sociology in a manner that encourages historical, critical, and international thinking about contemporary social concerns. As such, it has developed out of the practice of teaching and learning from students at universities in San Francisco, along the United States-Mexico border, in the Pacific Northwest, New England, and Mexico City. Those students were the sounding boards and constructive critics for much of the modes of expression and explanation that follow. From a distance, I therefore express my gratitude.

Intellectual debts—some recent and some long-standing—are also owed to a number of individuals I have had the good fortune to encounter along the way. They include Hans H. Gerth, Maurice Zeitlin, Harvey Goldberg, James O'Connor, James P. O'Brien, Carolyn Howe, Jerry Lembcke, Martin Hart-Landsberg, Alexander Taylor, Angela Morales, Dennis C. Canterbury, Mary Erdmans, Shannon Latkin Anderson, Radim Marada, Csaba Szalo, and Levon A. Chorbajian. The manuscript also benefited significantly from the suggestions from reviewers of earlier editions: Robert K. Miller, Jr., of the University of North Carolina, Wilmington, and Saul Feinman of the University of Wyoming, for which I am grateful. Bill Webber of Sloan Publishing made this edition possible. He provided encouragement and skilled help in as close to an ideal working relationship with a publisher as I can imagine.

NOTE TO THE SECOND EDITION

Those familiar with the first edition will find that the chapter on contemporary societies and the world economy has been divided into two chapters: Contemporary Societies and Global Trends. In addition, former and present communist-governed societies are now labeled simply *former communist* and *communist societies;* in previous editions the term *socialist* was used. The change in naming is to avoid confusion—Western socialist parties, for example, never embraced the form of socialism that existed in the communist-governed countries—and to reflect the reality that China and most other communist-governed societies today have adopted substantial market changes while retaining their one-party form of government.

About the Author

Educated at the University of Wisconsin, James W. Russell has taught at universities in the United States and Mexico. He is currently University Professor of Sociology at Eastern Connecticut State University, and was formerly a visiting Fulbright professor at the Universidad Nacional Autónoma de México in Mexico City (1990–1992). His other books include *Class and Race Formation in North America*; *Double Standard: Social Policy in Europe and the United States*; and *Modes of Production in World History*.

Chapter 1

Sociology

Sociology is most commonly defined as the scientific study of societies and social life in general. The fundamental premise of sociological explanations is that most of human conduct occurs and is shaped within group and social contexts. Therefore, it follows that the social properties of societies need to be understood and studied because they are important determining factors of human conduct.

The promise of sociology is that it will help us to understand better our societies and the social life within them. Through such social awareness and understanding, it is hoped, humans will then be able to resolve social problems as they develop and design social programs and legislation to both prevent future social problems from occurring and enhance the social quality of life.

HISTORY

The word **sociology**—a hybrid of the Latin *socia*, or "society," with the Greek *logos*, or "knowledge"—first appeared in 1837 in a writing by the conservative French philosopher Auguste Comte (1798–1857). He called for the establishment of sociology as a new field of inquiry to counteract the value-laden claims of, on the one hand, socialist ideologists who criticized the social conditions in Europe's nineteenth-century industrial capitalist societies, and on the other, religious writers who evaluated societies on the basis of theological and moral concerns.

Comte believed that it was possible to develop a specifically scientific approach to the acquisition of social knowledge that would not be based on political, moral, or other types of values. This could be achieved, he believed, if social knowledge was acquired through the same value-free methods and techniques of research that were practiced in the physical and organic sciences such as biology, chemistry, and botany. He prescribed that the scientific methods developed in the physical and organic sciences be directly transferred to the social sciences, where they would presumably yield objective, value-free social knowledge.

Nevertheless, Comte's motives for establishing this scientific sociology were as much political as methodological. He used the term **positivism** to describe his approach to sociology because with it he sought to improve, rather than criticize or subvert, the structures of existing societies. Socialists and other revolutionaries, in Comte's view, were negativists who sought to destroy the existing structures. Despite these originally conservative origins, the concept of positivism is today more identified with Comte's methodological principle that sociologists follow the same general scientific approach to research as practiced in such physical and natural sciences as biology, chemistry, and botany.

Ironically, the types of socialist writers of whom Comte was most critical were also concerned with developing a scientific understanding of society. Karl Marx (1818–1883) and Frederick Engels (1820–1895) devoted an entire section of *The Communist Manifesto* to criticizing socialist writings that were based on religious and moral, rather than scientifically founded, criteria. They saw **socialism**—a type of society based on common, public ownership of businesses, cooperation, and social equality—as the inevitable and desirable next historical stage after **capitalism**, which is based on private ownership of businesses, market competition, and class inequality. But Marx and Engels never called themselves sociologists, in part because of the conservative connotations of the term in Comte's hands. They saw themselves rather as founders of scientific socialism, by which they meant socialist change based upon the discoverable laws of history.

Unlike Comte, Marx and Engels believed that there were unresolvable problems—such as class inequality and injustice, alienation, and crisis-prone economic tendencies—deep within the structures of capitalist societies. Only a thorough socialist restructuring would be capable of resolving these problems. According to their dialectical methodology and reasoning, there is a logic to world historical change in which rising new types of societies supplant declining old types. In this respect, they believed that capitalism would eventually decline and be replaced by a new socialist type of society.

In many ways Comte, the conservative and positivist, and Marx, the revolutionary and dialectical thinker, established the poles of Western sociology. They shared a common desire that the study of society be scientific. But they differed profoundly over how to develop a scientific study of society and the political implications of that endeavor.

Sociology, whichever its guise, Comtean or Marxian, emerged as mid-nineteenth-century Europe was undergoing rapid economic, political, and social transformations. The **Industrial Revolution**, roughly between 1760 and 1840, produced a surge in technological innovations in economic production, such as the inventions of the spinning jenny and power loom, which altered the physical and social landscapes of European countries by accelerating the growth of factory life and cities. Country peasants became urban workers. The slow pace and certainty of rural life gave way to the seeming chaos, long workdays, and uncertainties of urban life. At the same time, political revolutions swept across Western and Central Europe, continuing the trend set off by the 1789 **French Revolution**. Republican forms of government with constitutions replaced old autocratic governments ruled by royalties and aristocracies. Democratic ideals, if not their full practice, increased. Feudal aristocracies declined in wealth and power. Rational, secular, and scientific thinking challenged the near monopoly hold of religion over popular consciousness.

These rapid and dizzying changes, as well as their life-altering consequences for millions of people, caused many to question whether they truly understood their societies. If in the rural-based agricultural society of the past, where the pace of social change was very slow, one could with fair confidence predict the foreseeable future because it would not be that different from the present, in the new conditions, the certainties about the likely shape of things to come evaporated. Social knowledge could no longer be assumed. It had to be produced.

By the second half of the nineteenth century, the term *sociology* was in wide circulation. To some extent it was simply a catchall and convenient label for general writings about societies that did not seem to fit neatly into the existing and already defined academic categories of political economy, history, or philosophy. But it was also becoming a recognized and respectable academic discipline in itself. By 1900, universities in France, England, and the United States had established departments of sociology that awarded degrees.

Throughout the twentieth century, sociology expanded further, primarily as a result of two developments. First, as governments increased spending on education, welfare, and other social programs, they enlisted the aid of sociologists. Second, universities in the United States—the country with the greatest number of sociologists—expanded sociology departments in the aftermath of perceived social crises.

In the 1920s, as mass migrations from Europe and the American south caused rapid growth of northern and eastern cities in the United States to the point that elites feared that they would become ungovernable, universities expanded their sociology programs. Sociologists in that era turned out a number of now-classic studies of urban lower classes, ethnic minorities, and patterns of urban development. In the middle and late 1960s, when riots broke out in many black ghettos, universities likewise expanded their sociology programs, both because students sought such courses and because they thought that increased social knowledge could help to avoid future riots.

The growth of membership in the American Sociological Society (later renamed the American Sociological Association [ASA] to avoid the embarrassing acronym) reflected these developments. The organization began in 1905 with 116 members and grew to just over one thousand in 1920—a membership level that remained steady through 1940. In 1950 membership tripled to 3,241 as universities expanded to provide space for soldiers returning from World War II. In 1960 ASA membership doubled to 6,875, and then in 1970 more than doubled again to 14,156—a membership plateau that remained steady for the next three and a half decades (Rhoades, 1981, p.74) to the present. In 2007 it counted 14,763 members (Spalter-Roth and Scelza, 2008, p.1).

Today sociology is a recognized academic discipline in most parts of the world. As the discipline has developed and expanded, it has generated its own specialized fields, including demography, stratification, organizational research, family research, the sociology of development, the sociology of knowledge, the sociology of the family, criminology, and gerontology.

SPECIALIZED CONCEPTS

In common with all human work, sociological work uses a basic method or approach. All laborers use tools to transform raw materials into products. Carpenters, for example, use saws and other tools to cut and shape wood into cabinets. Sociologists use their own types of physical and intellectual tools to transform raw data or observations about the social world into social knowledge. Their physical tools include word processors, filing cabinets, computers, and calculators. Their intellectual tools are explanatory **concepts** that are used to organize and make sense of the data. The product of sociological work is presumed to be social knowledge that can range from simple self-clarification to books, articles, speeches, and social programs.

Concepts are the most important element of this sociological labor process. They are the fundamental intellectual tools for making sense of the social world. Facts rarely speak for themselves. They must be interpreted with the use of concepts, which are intellectual abstractions used to categorize and illuminate the essential meanings of real-world occurrences. Human language is built from concepts that symbolically represent objects of human experience. Water, for example, is a word that is a concept or symbol that represents not this or that particular body of water, but rather what all bodies of water share in common. The meaning of the word *water* thus is an abstract concept constructed from the common properties of all particular examples of water. Sociologists have their own particular concepts that they use to name and analyze aspects of social experience. Such concepts include social class, power, roles, and norms. As with any trade, in order to learn it, one must become familiar with its tools.

The conceptual tools of sociology, however, are not as straightforward as one might wish. The concept of social class, for example, has a variety of general connotations to people. Sociologists, on the other hand, have technical meanings in mind when they use the concept—*meanings* rather than meaning—because sociologists do not always agree on the meanings of such key concepts as social class. It follows that in order to be introduced to sociology, it is necessary to become familiar with the meanings of its key concepts. This is true even if there is disagreement among sociologists about which meanings are the most adequate. It is, after all, not unusual for workers to disagree over which tools are the most appropriate.

SOCIAL AND INDIVIDUAL EXPLANATIONS

Sociologists approach a number of society's problems from a perspective that is often different from that dictated by individual experience or common sense. For many social problems—such as alcoholism, unemployment, and crime—there is a tendency to assume that the individual alcoholic, unemployed person, or criminal is the source of the problem. Perhaps because we live in a highly individualistic society, we tend to assume individual causation of social problems. Most sociologists acknowledge this obvious reality, that there are individual factors involved in social problems. It would be difficult to treat the problem of a particular alcoholic without at least partially focusing on that person's particular characteristics.

But sociologists are more interested in investigating the less obvious social dimensions of such problems. In addition to describing the social consequences of the problem—alcohol consumption impairs driving ability and can lead to accidents, and alcoholism is a source of stress in many families that affects spouses and children—sociologists attempt to explain either why different groups have different rates of particular problems such as alcoholism, or how the structure of society itself may be responsible for part of the problem. To exemplify these less obvious sociological explanations, we will briefly look at two social problems—suicide and unemployment—and compare individual to sociological explanations.

Suicide, it is often said, is more of a tragedy for the families and friends than for the victim. The families and friends must continue to live with the tragedy for the rest of their lives. They quite reasonably attempt to explain the suicide by looking to the person and her or his problems to try to determine what caused the despondency. This manner of explanation is logical, and it goes a long way toward explaining the causes of the suicide, but it does not go all the way.

Emile Durkheim (1855–1917), a French sociologist, made the first systematic study of the social factors involved in suicide. He (1897) was struck by the fact that different countries had different rates of suicide, and groups within them had different rates. He reasoned that if different groups had different rates, then nonindividual social factors had to be involved in the causation of suicide.

His most famous finding was that Catholics had significantly lower rates of suicide than Protestants. He concluded that the cause of this difference lay not in the religious belief differences —both religions equally condemned suicide as a personal option—but rather in the different structures of the religious communities. Individual Catholics embraced and internalized a highly developed set of religious beliefs that left little leeway for independent thinking. The Protestant churches, on the other hand, had a looser hold on their members' beliefs because they encouraged each member to come to her or his own personal understanding. It followed that when Catholics suffered deep despondency, the suicidal impulses they might feel were held in check by the internalized moral authority of the church. But when Protestants suffered deep despondency, their church's moral authority was less binding.

Stated more formally, individual Catholics were more structurally integrated into their religious community than were Protestants. This greater integration meant that Catholics would internalize more completely the injunction against suicide than would Protestants and thus be less likely to carry out a suicidal urge.

Unemployment is another problem that people tend to explain in individual terms, seeing it as being caused primarily by personal defects such as lack of motivation to work, lack of adequate skills or education, or being fired for poor performance. Such factors may indeed explain why some people rather than others lose jobs or are not hired in the first place. But they do not explain why in market societies there always seem to be more people looking for jobs than available places, which gives employers the power to pick and choose among applicants and to dismiss those who do not work out.

Sociological explanations place greater emphasis on understanding the role that unemployment plays in the functioning of the whole economic and social system than on determining what individuals need to do to make themselves employable or to hold on to their jobs. The existence of labor surpluses (an economic euphemism for people out of work) have been a nearly constant feature of market societies since their origins in the sixteenth century. Hence, unemployment is more an unavoidable side effect of the structuring of market societies than the result of individual defects.

Seen that way, social explanations of unemployment hinge on determining the function or role that it plays in the overall economic organization of market societies. For that explanation, a lot of evidence indicates that the existence of unemployed populations is beneficial to employers. Competition for jobs allows employers to offer low wages, knowing that there is someone desperate enough to accept them. Fear of unemployment keeps workers working hard at the job. The presence of labor reserves in a country gives owners the flexibility to move existing businesses or open new branches.

Sociologists are also interested in tracing the social and physical consequences of unemployment. As unemployment increases, so too do a number of social problems, including family stress and strife, alcohol abuse, and even suicide. It follows that unemployment negatively affects both mental and physical health. Brenner (1976), in a pioneering and influential study, found that increases in unemployment rates are associated with increases in mortality rates in the United States and England; and Stefansson (1991) found that the long-term unemployed in Sweden had a 37 percent higher death rate than the employed population.

Personal problems, therefore, rarely are completely personal. There are social components in the causes and consequences of virtually all personal problems. It is the job of sociologists to ferret out those social components and, where possible, propose policy alternatives for alleviating them. It is the job of those who wish to understand sociology to employ what C. Wright Mills (1961) called a **sociological imagination** to trace the linkages between personal troubles and public issues.

RELATION TO OTHER DISCIPLINES

The very nature of its subject matter—society and social life in general—guarantees that sociology will often overlap with and sometimes be difficult to distinguish from other academic fields. There is no hard and fast line that separates it from other social science disciplines, such as political science, economics, or anthropology. The concerns and types of research pursued by sociologists also often overlap those of disciplines in the humanities, such as philosophy, history, and literature. Many sociologists hold that the existence of these overlapping concerns and approaches is beneficial because they believe that sociology must proceed on the basis of combining broad understandings from such fields as philosophy, history, economics, political science, and literature with the results of its own specialized researches.

The two fields that sociology is most closely related to are **anthropology** and **social work**. In many small colleges and universities, these three fields are often combined into a single department. Anthropologists share with sociologists the goal of understanding how the cultures and social institutions of total societies function. But while sociologists have concentrated on studying contemporary industrial-based societies, anthropologists have been primarily concerned with the cultures of preliterate and preindustrial societies. They have studied contemporary native peoples or those of the recent past in Africa, Asia, the Americas, Australia, and the Pacific Islands. The traditional boundaries between sociology and anthropology, however, are often overstepped. A number of anthropologists now apply their methods for studying the cultures of pre-industrial and preliterate peoples to studying subcultures in industrially based societies; historical sociologists, concerned with developing an understanding of the varieties of prehistorical and historical societies, venture into areas that have traditionally been the terrain of anthropology.

Sociology is often confused with social work, largely because both fields focus on society and its problems. The difference between the two is that sociology seeks a general understanding of the functioning of all aspects of society, while social workers specialize in understanding and treating the human casualties of concrete social problems, such as poverty, substance abuse, and domestic violence. Clearly, there are overlaps between the two areas. In some respects, social work is an applied form of sociology, but in other respects, social work includes its own specialized techniques for working with clients.

With respect to other social science fields, the focuses are also related but distinguishable. Economists focus on how goods and services are produced, exchanged, and distributed in contemporary societies. Many economists and sociologists believe that the nature of an economic system is the most powerful determinant of other institutional, including social, features of societies. Sociological understanding, therefore, requires economic understanding. Political scientists focus on the working of governments: how laws are made, elections won, budgets proposed, and so forth. For sociologists, the state or government is a basic institution of nearly all societies. Its character, like that of the economy, is a powerful determinant of other societal features. For that reason alone, knowledge derived from political science studies is useful to sociologists.

OCCUPATIONS AND USES

By far the largest occupation of people who call themselves sociologists in the United States is as university teachers. In a far distant second place are researchers employed by government agencies and private corporations. Many times those numbers, though, graduate with sociology degrees, and many times more pass through university sociology courses. This pyramid of numbers—from those who pass through courses, to those who major in sociology, to the much smaller number who become full professionals in the field—may appear unusual, but it is common in all the humanities and social sciences. Few history majors, for example, ultimately become historians. Sociology, thus, like other liberal arts fields, prepares students for a wide variety of occupations and careers apart from those directly associated with teaching or research in the field.

Through sociology courses students gain the skills that are necessary for all occupational positions that require abilities to think logically and creatively and to communicate well in written form. In addition, sociology programs expose students to contemporary social issues and problems, a preparation that is useful for legal, political, media, and social work careers.

The question of whether to major in sociology or take other courses comes down to the question of interest. There are no real differences in employment prospects or financial benefit of different humanities and social sciences degrees. All are of roughly equal value for entering those professional and managerial job markets and career ladders that require general rather than particular skills.

Key Terms and Concepts
(in order of presentation)

Sociology

Positivism

Socialism

Capitalism

Industrial Revolution

French Revolution

Concept

Sociological Imagination

Anthropology

Social Work

Chapter 2

Individuals and Societies

If concepts are the basic intellectual tools of sociology, as presented in the previous chapter, and if the focus of sociology is on understanding human societies and social life in general, then it follows that clarity about the conceptual meaning of **human beings** is a first step toward understanding the nexus between individuals and their social conditions of existence. While it may at first glance seem obvious what the meaning of "human beings" is, more reflection indicates that the concept has been the subject of rigorous debate in the life sciences, philosophy, and psychology. There is not even agreement on when human life begins—whether at conception, birth, or some point in between. In general, how one conceptually defines humans influences how one understands the workings of societies and social life.

Once the concept of human beings has been explored, we will then be in position to analyze and explore the relationship between humans and their social conditions of existence. In particular, we will be in position to conceptually describe the basic components of social interaction, entering into what has become the classic language of sociology.

HUMAN BEINGS

From an evolutionary and biological point of view, human beings are members of the subspecies *homo sapiens sapiens* that emerged from a long line of antecedents about 100,000 years ago. In defining their concept of human beings, biologists have tended to concentrate on those human features that are species-distinguishing: First, humans walk with an upright gait, as opposed to walking on all fours. The upright gait has social importance because it frees the hands for tool use, which in turn has allowed humans to advance technologically. Second, the structure of the hand allows for dexterity; that is, free movement of the fingers and thumb. This has given humans the capacity to grasp tools.

Third, and most important, the human brain has a capacity, centered in the cerebrum, for creative thought that no other species either has or has to the same degree; hence, *sapiens*, from Latin, means "capable of knowing." This human thinking capacity has enormous social importance. Humans are capable of learning, reducing that knowledge to symbols and concepts, and passing it on to future generations; therefore, human history is, at least in technological terms, developmental. The histories of other species are cyclical, composed of a series of birth, life, and death cycles whose only development is unwilled evolutionary physiological change.

Fourth, humans are capable of articulate speech, the social importance of which is self-evident, since it allows them to communicate in more complex manners than other species. Finally, twentieth-century biology has identified the species' unique genetic structure. That too has social importance, as gene splicing and other new technologies allow humans to treat one of their own species' conditions as variable.

Of these defining characteristics, the capacity for creative thought has dominated traditional philosophical discussions of the conceptual meaning of human life. If homo sapiens sapiens is the biological term, human being is the philosophical term. Philosophically, "being" means existing; human existence, though, means a thinking or conscious existence. In this respect, philosophy and psychology were originally merged, since both focused on the human thinking capacity.

The center of all attempts to define the conceptual meaning of human beings thus has been an emphasis on the species' unique thinking capacity. Humans are uniquely capable of thinking abstractly and creatively. They think abstractly when they use symbols, concepts, and language in general to name and group objects that they perceive into categories. Other species only see the objects concretely. A dog is familiar with his owner but unaware of the meaning of "owner." Because humans can think abstractly, they can labor creatively. Creativity is the two-step process by which humans first imagine something as an abstract possibility and then, second, proceed to concretize it. An engineer first thinks through the possibility of a dam and then proceeds to oversee its construction. A student first thinks about what he or she is going to write and then puts it down on paper. Other species labor, but they do not labor creatively. Beavers build dams, but only because the knowledge is instinctually encoded within them. They do not learn to build dams, nor do they improve dam-building designs over generations.

HUMAN BEINGS AS SOCIAL BEINGS

George Herbert Mead (1863–1931), one of the classic theorists of twentieth-century sociology, indicated that the capacity for abstract thought made a unique form of intersubjective social life between individuals possible. In Mead's view, much of human social communication occurs as a two-step creative process similar to that of creative labor. The communicator mentally evaluates and rehearses a message according to its imagined effect on the other and then delivers it. A student who misses an exam may mentally run through a menu of possible excuses, imagining the possible reactions of the professor, before approaching her or him. Job hunters strategize how they will talk to prospective employers. Much communication requires no such actual rehearsal, but only because what was once established creatively has become routinized. Other species communicate through gestures, as when a dog snarls, but they are incapable of refining their message after abstractly taking the role of the other. Human being thus implies **social being**, in the sense that humans have a capacity for a unique form of intersocialabilty.

Human beings are social beings in another sense too. Because of their unique ability to communicate, they can be greatly affected by other members of their species. Children learn and develop their personalities through the medium of language, which is itself a product of social inter-action. Words are, after all, labels for socially agreed-upon meanings. Hence, one's innermost thoughts are always couched in socially produced forms, that is, words. A dog may be subject to the negative actions of another dog but not to another dog's negative thoughts.

Beyond agreement that humans share these capacities, there is considerable disagreement over whether the species has other immutable qualities. Much of this disagreement revolves around the concept of **instincts**; that is, unchangeable in-born behavioral predispositions. On one side of the conflict are those who argue that nonhuman animals have instincts but humans do not. Their behavior is learned. On the other side are those who argue that there are instinctual bases to human and social conduct.

Undoubtedly, the most provocative and influential argument for human conduct being instinctually based is associated with Sigmund Freud (1856–1939). According to him (1930, 1933), each individual is driven by a contradictory bundle of instincts. One set—called **Eros**, or life—produces a need to have loving relations with others and self-preservation. The other set—**Thanatos**, or death—produces the need for aggression against others and self-destruction. Each instinct, if allowed to go to its logical conclusion, would be socially destructive. For that reason, societies must have structures to rein in human instincts. Those structures allow societies to survive and enable a modicum of order. But by inevitably frustrating instinctual fulfillment, they also ensure continuation of psychological frustration and misery. Freud thus pessimistically concluded that human misery could never be fully ended.

Herbert Marcuse (1955), in the most important and sustained critique of Freud's social conclusions, cast doubt on the existence of an immutable death instinct, while accepting as valid the existence of a life instinct. According to him, the way that societies are structured can curtail the expression and fulfillment of the life instinct, but they need not do that inevitably. Contrary to Freud, Marcuse concluded that it was historically possible for humans to construct societies that met both the needs of social order and psychological fulfillment.

Still others argue, as mentioned, that there are no instincts at all, that all behavior is learned, and that whatever psychological fulfillment might be, it will be what humans make of it. The good society in which individual and social needs harmonize remains a possibility, neither precluded nor advanced by innate human qualities, instinctual or otherwise.

However one might conceptualize the meaning of human existence, it is clear that humans have the unique species capacity to create their social conditions of existence, for better or worse. They can create concentration camps, genocide, and harsh dictatorships as well as love, solidarity, and freedom. But it is also clear that although humans have the capacity to create those social conditions abstractly, they are never free to create social conditions. Pre-existing social conditions, the products of previous generations, constrain what it is possible to socially create. One may abstractly believe in the superiority of free love, but tradition, custom, and institutions concretely weigh against it. Humans thus create their social conditions of existence, but within limits established by previous generations. For the analysis of whichever case— newly created or inherited forms of social interaction—early twentieth- century sociologists constructed a set of concepts, to which we now turn.

COMPONENTS OF SOCIAL INTERACTION

We can begin by defining as **social** any interpersonal situation or setting in which a person orients her or his actions to one or more others. The interaction may be initiated by the person or the others. Others may be physically present, as when a conversation takes place. But they need not be for social conduct to take place, as when a person dresses in anticipation of impressing or pleasing others later in the day.

Social life has both objective and subjective dimensions. The term **objective** denotes the observable actions of people when they interact with others as family members, labor force participants, citizens, and so on. The term **subjective** denotes how people think and feel about themselves and others. Objective and subjective are interrelated. Objective circumstances affect feelings; for example, the death of a close family member results in grief. Emotional states of being affect interactions with others; an emotionally distraught driver is a potentially dangerous driver. Quite clearly, most of what people do is objectively or subjectively socially influenced and oriented and therefore falls within social interaction patterns.

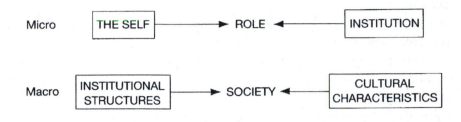

Figure 2–1   The Components of Social Interaction

Sociologists analyze these social interaction patterns from micro and macro sociological angles. The micro sociological tradition concentrates on the linkages between individuals and their social existence and experience. The macro sociological tradition concentrates on whole societies and how they function. Common to both is the premise that what makes individuals the way they are is a combination of both their unique characteristics as human beings and the social relationships that have influenced how they developed their character structures and personalities as they grew and matured within societies (shown in Figure 2–1).

Social surroundings and contexts therefore deeply influence the formation of men and women and the type of persons that they turn out to be. If it were possible with a time machine to have the same baby grow up both in the contemporary United States and in ancient Rome, the resulting adults would have distinctly different personalities, since they would have matured and formed their personalities within distinctly different social relationships. Key to understanding individuals sociologically thus is the specification of the social relationships that have influenced their development.

Settings and Positions

From the micro sociological perspective, social life occurs and is experienced in **settings** ranging from chance street encounters involving two people to ongoing societal interactions involving millions. Face-to-face social interaction takes place in families, classrooms, stores, workplaces, and on streets, among other settings. More indirect interaction takes place in larger social settings, as when legislatures approve new laws that affect citizens. In the analysis of patterns of social interaction, we thus first must specify the settings within which they occur that are of interest.

Once the setting of the interaction has been determined, the next step is to identify the **social position**—what sociologists often call the **status**—of the people involved. In a chance street encounter, there may be no distinguishable social positions; each person is an equal. There is social interaction among people occupying, at least for the moment, the indistinguishable social position of being a person-on-the-street. But street encounters also occur between people who occupy immediately distinguishable social positions, as between blacks and whites where racial discrimination exists, or between state troopers and stopped motorists. In these encounters, the differences of social position affect the quality of the interaction.

In most settings—including families, workplaces, classrooms, and whole societies—social positions are immediately distinguishable. Such differences are **horizontal** when they involve interaction among people who are equal in terms of power, wealth, prestige, or any other similar hierarchically based criteria, but whose positions are distinguishable, as when teachers of different subjects meet for curricula planning. Differences are **vertical** when they involve interaction among people who occupy positions that carry unequal amounts of power, wealth, prestige, or some other relevant resource, as between employers and employees or rich and poor.

Roles

Once the settings where the interaction takes place and the positions of the participants have been specified, we are then ready to identify **roles** and role behavior. Attached to each position in the setting is a socially defined behavioral expectation; that is, a role. People in particular positions are supposed to act in predictable ways. When we go to class we expect the professor to teach, not to start juggling, unless of course it is a course in juggling.

We learn to do what is expected of us as children in families. We learn how to be and perform as students. Later, we become workers, adult citizens, community leaders, and family creators. Social life does, indeed, as Shakespeare keenly observed, resemble a play in which we all learn to perform parts or roles. The analogy between a play and social life is so compelling that sociologists took their concept of the role directly from the theater. The theatrical concept of the role was a perfect metaphor for the patterned ways in which humans socially orient their conduct to meet the expectations of others. As different plays are structured around different roles, different types of social situations call for different roles. The role metaphor indicates that people may intentionally orient their conduct to the expectations of others. To some extent, their performances are just that—performances—for there is a human being behind the role who may or may not be comfortable with the role he or she is playing or how the performance is going.

People occupy different social positions and play different roles in different contexts—in the family, at work, as citizens, as members of voluntary groups—as they move between settings. The more complex the society, the more each person must play a multitude of different roles in daily life. They, so to speak, move from scene to scene or perhaps play to play: first awakening and interacting with family members, then leaving for work and interacting with people on the street, arriving at work and interacting with co-workers and those above or below in power, going out to lunch with friends, and so forth. The more modern the society, the more the individual belongs to multiple groups. He or she becomes, in the words of the classic theorist Georg Simmel (1858–1918; 1922, p. 150), "determined sociologically in the sense that the groups 'intersect' in his person by virtue of his affiliation with them."

In each frame or setting of interaction the person performs a role that is expected of the situation. As a newspaper buyer, he or she flashes the paper to the clerk so that the clerk will know which paper is being bought, then advances the money, and perhaps mutters a perfunctory "thank you" when change is returned. Such routine role playing as that of a customer in a store is so automatic and usually depersonalized that we literally think nothing of it.

However, some sociologists and social theorists worry that the routinization of much human interaction in modern societies has produced mass alienation, making it increasingly difficult to recognize the human behind the role. The newspaper vendor might as well be a coin-depositing machine. Many restaurant customers cannot remember who their waiter or waitress are when it comes time to request the bill.

In earlier, less complex societies, there were fewer roles that each person played in daily life. For peasants, the most populated social position in world history, human interaction was closely circumscribed both geographically and in terms of people encountered. Peasants rarely traveled out of the areas where they lived and tilled land. Their household was the unit from which they worked. They left the house and went directly to the fields. They did not, as in contemporary urban societies, leave home in the morning to go to another social setting to work. Aside from household members, the most social interaction that peasants had was with other peasants who either lived or worked close by. They on occasion had dealings with religious and political authorities, but in general these contacts were not numerous or complicated. Peasant human interaction thus involved far fewer people than that of contemporary urban dwellers. Whether that made it qualitatively fuller or less fragmentary than that typical in modern urban-based societies is open to interpretation.

The more stable the social situation, the more people take their roles for granted. But periods also occur when given role expectations cannot be taken for granted. For most of medieval feudalism, peasants assumed that they were born into their roles and that God had ordained it to be that way. But there were also times in which peasants revolted against the whole system of feudal roles. For much of the twentieth century, men and women in the United States assumed that in normal families the man earned a paycheck and the woman stayed home taking care of the house and children. But within the last generation those role expectations no longer match the reality of most families, where both adults now have to work outside of the household in order to make ends meet.

Norms, Sanctions, and Socialization

Roles incorporate rules for how they are to be played. The origins of those rules are **norms**, which are the values that specify how roles should be played. Professional norms, for example, govern how a professor should relate to students; he or she should concentrate on the pertinent subject matter, not wander off into irrelevant areas. Similarly, ethical norms dictate that the professor should treat students fairly and with respect. Other norms govern how students are supposed to act. Norms are a subset of the general values that exist within a society. They represent the application of societal values to the "shoulds" and "oughts" of role conduct.

Each role thus carries with it a set of norms for how it is to be played. Each family has its spoken and unspoken rules. Each work organization has rules. There are even rules governing how to buy a newspaper. Such rules vary from informal to highly formalized. Norms can be imposed by the powerful on the powerless, as in a prison or family, or they can be developed through general agreement, as in a small club.

The norms governing roles vary in how clearly defined they are. For many roles it is absolutely clear what you are supposed to do. You pay money to the clerk in order to take possession of the newspaper. But for other roles the rules or norms may be ill defined, ambiguous, or nonexistent. When parents disagree, children may find contradictory sets of norms in the household. During periods of rioting, ordinary norms governing citizen behavior evaporate.

Sanctions are social forms of approval and disapproval for role performances. They range from mild gestures and comments to outright rewards and punishments. The student who disrupts a class by talking indiscreetly to a neighbor may be glared at by the teacher, asked to stop, or in extremes, thrown out. The suburban homeowner who does not keep the lawn mowed may directly experience subtle to not-so-subtle gestures of disapproval of neighbors. The Roman citizen who did not pay his taxes or debts ended up in prison, and the insubordinate slave faced the whip. Laws ultimately enforce the conduct expected from the role of being a citizen. Legal sanctions range from warnings and fines to capital punishment.

Sociologists use the concept of **socialization** to refer to the processes by which people learn the norms and roles necessary for functioning within groups and societies. Socialization begins at birth. The newborn comes into the world as an unsocialized being who must continually learn and adopt values, norms, and forms of behavior if he or she is to perform as a member of society. Socialization continues throughout life as individuals learn to interact within new social environments, such as neighborhoods, workplaces, or, for that matter, delinquent gangs.

Institutions

Institutions are ongoing configurations of social positions, roles, values, and norms—patterns of social behavior—that exist to meet particular needs within societies. The most basic material needs of any society, around which economic and kinship institutions form, are production of food, shelter, and clothing necessary for survival and reproduction of the species itself. Most societies have also developed political and religious institutions. Secondary, often subsidiary, institutions develop around other social needs, such as health, education, recreation, sports, courtship, and science. Sociologists often use the term *institutions* to refer to both the abstract patterns of social behavior and particular organized manifestations of those patterns. General Motors, according to this usage, would be both an organization and an institution.

Economic institutions, such as farms, workshops, and multinational corporations, are concerned with the production and distribution of goods and services. They vary according to the complexity of their internal role differentiations. Hunting groups in early societies had simple role divisions of labor, with each member performing similar tasks. In contrast, contemporary industrial corporations contain highly differentiated role structures. There are vertical power and authority role differences from the top levels of management to the shop floor; and there are horizontal differences of specialization, such as engineering, production, sales, and advertising. In general, the earlier the society, the less the role differentiation and the simpler the division of labor within its institutions. The more modern the society, the greater the role differentiation and the more complex the division of labor.

Kinship refers to networks of people interrelated on the basis of common ancestry or marriage. Each family is a kinship institution within which members play different roles as wives, husbands, mothers, fathers, children, grandparents, or other relatives. Roles vary in terms of work expected, power, and authority accorded.

Political institutions include political parties, government bureaucracies, and military organizations that are involved in the struggle for and administration of territorial power. The government—the state in a more classical language—is the arena within or against which political institutions function. The state itself is an institution that attempts to pattern the ways in which its subsidiary administrative, military, judicial, and other institutions perform roles. In that sense, whole institutions can perform roles within encompassing institutions. Constitutions are the most formalized expressions of intended patterns of role interrelationships within states, their subsidiary institutions, and the institutions over which they have power. As with all other institutional areas, there are a variety of historical types of political institutions.

Religious institutions are based on belief systems about the ultimate meaning of life that are practiced within churches, synagogues, mosques, temples, and other settings. Religious institutions vary according to the nature of their role configurations and differences. The respective powers and degrees of authority accorded to leaders and members vary. In some, the spiritual leader is assumed to be omniscient; in others, to be merely a facilitator.

In sum to this point, objective observable social life takes place in a variety of different settings and institutions. Within each of them, people occupy different social positions for which they perform roles; that is, engage in socially expected behavior patterns. Norms are the values that govern the rules incorporated in the conduct of particular roles. Sanctions are forms of social rewards and punishments that are used to uphold the rules of role conduct.

Subjective Social Life and the Self

Subjective social life refers to how people internalize and react to their experiences with objective social life. Its most important analytical concepts are the self and character structure, or personality.

By the term **self** sociologists mean a person's concept of her or his own being, life, or inner identity: how one perceives one's own being. Sociologists have long noted that the sense of self is greatly influenced by interactions with others. Charles Horton Cooley (1864–1929) introduced (1902) the wonderfully evocative and metaphorical concept of "the **looking-glass self**" to indicate that how a person is perceived by others greatly influences how he or she perceives his or her own self. A shunned person will feel insecure if he or she desires the approval of those who are doing the shunning. A praised person will feel more secure, especially if she or he values the opinion of the person or persons doing the praising.

George Herbert Mead (1934) developed the most influential sociological concept of the self. Building on the work of the psychologist William James, Mead conceptualized the self as having two parts: the me
and the I. The **"me"** is the self as object, as formed by internalization of
the attitudes of others. The **"I"** is the self as subject, developed by the individual's own impulses and response to the attitudes of others. The
"me" is the socialized self, the "I" the unsocialized self. One's sense of
self is formed from both without and within, from both internalization of
others' attitudes and purely internally generated beliefs and reactions to
outside attitudes.

Cooley and Mead were classic exponents of what came to be known
as **symbolic interactionism**. This microsociological approach investigates the interaction processes between individuals and their social surroundings. Its key postulate is that social interaction is carried on
through symbols—language and gestures—and that individuals are involved in ongoing processes of interpreting and reinterpreting these social symbols. It follows, according to this school, that social reality is
continually being transformed through the changing meanings that individuals attach to the social symbols that they receive.

Social positions and roles affect perceptions of self and **self-esteem** in
a variety of ways. They usually, but not always, carry with them different levels of prestige or status. As the wary reader will have realized by
now, the concept of status is used in two not entirely consistent ways in
contemporary sociology. In the first case, it means any position within a
hierarchy. In the second, it means prestige. According to the first usage,
sociologists speak of statuses as the positions themselves within a hierarchy, such as the statuses within a particular corporate structure. In the
second, sociologists refer to status as an attribute—the level of prestige—which may be attached to a particular position, as in "the presidency is a high-status position," or person, as in "John Smith enjoys high
status because of his charm." We will follow the second meaning here.

There are low, high, and in-between status positions and roles in society. The status of janitor is relatively low, that of a professional is relatively high. A person who occupies a role that enjoys considerable status
may feel high self-esteem and satisfaction. A member of an oppressed
minority who is forced by racism and discrimination into low-status
roles may feel low self-esteem and, in extremes, personal dislike.

There is thus a relationship between the status attached to a person's role and self-esteem, but it is not necessarily direct in all circumstances. It is probable that roles with high status tend to enhance self-esteem. Respect and recognition for what a person does enhance self-image, but that is not always the case. A high-status position can be occupied, but the role may be performed or may be perceived to be performed badly. In that case, the benefits of status can evaporate quickly, as when a high public official is judged to be incompetent.

People who perform low-status roles may draw compensatory existential or spiritual meanings for their lives from elsewhere. A lower-class worker can see himself as first and foremost a good father. An oppressed peasant can have faith that there is a better world waiting to compensate for the misery and low social status in this one.

Character Structure

In between role and self lies the **character structure** of the individual. As in theater, a character represents a unique personality. To play a character in theater or film requires more than the playing of standard roles. It requires mastering and evoking what is unique about how a particular person performs in her or his social roles. Similarly, character structures in real life are determined by the unique ways in which people integrate innate physiological and organic capacities, psychological dispositions, and the social roles that they perform (see Gerth and Mills, 1953).

One becomes a person (from the Latin *persona*, meaning "mask") in society by playing a variety of roles. Roles make the person, but they do not completely define the individual. How people react to the roles they play, as well as the reactions of others, determines their concept of who they really are and the development of their unique character structures. A person can be proud and satisfied with the roles he or she plays or ashamed or dissatisfied. Others also react to how well they believe one is playing her or his appointed roles. How good a mother are you in the eyes of others? How responsible a worker? How much do these judgments affect your sense of being? If the person is playing the role badly enough and the persons reacting have power enough, sanctions come into play: the state can take children away from negligent mothers;

workers can be fired; a clumsy actor in a theater elicits yawns and perhaps boos from the audience; an inept social actor may suffer ostracism.
In the end, each unique character or personality emerges from the inter-
play of a wide variety of internal and external forces.

At the same time, there can be a disjuncture between public and private personalities. Who one appears to be in a position or role may be
quite different from who one really is. "What do you do?" is a useful
question for beginning to learn about someone. But if by it you only
mean, "What is your job?" you will not learn all there is to be learned
about that person. Behind the role at work is always a human being who
has beliefs, values, hopes, dreams, and experiences. There are quite extraordinary people who occupy quite ordinary positions. Many different
kinds of people can share similar positions and roles. What is behind the
role can also be disappointing. No man is a king to his butler.

In contemporary Western societies there is a public fascination with
the lives of those who occupy highly visible celebrity roles. Gossip magazines and tabloids endlessly and mercilessly pore over their lives to tell
the public "who they really are." The more scandalous, the better. As has
become clear from recent presidential elections in the United States,
candidates for the role of the highest office are not only expected to be
able to do that job well—to perform that position's role—but also to lead
a flawless private life. For the celebrity the boundaries of public and private life are increasingly fuzzy. Public religious personalities have
found that they too are fair game for hunters of hypocrisy and sensation-
alism. The disjunction between public role and private self is reminis-
cent of when the terrifying Wizard of Oz was unmasked to be a genial
showman.

STRUCTURE, SOCIETY, AND CULTURE

From a sociological perspective, a **society** is a historically bounded population that shares a unique configuration of institutional structures and
cultural characteristics. Specification of a society's institutional structures is important because they are the contexts within which social life
is molded. Specification of a society's cultural characteristics is important because societies with similar institutional structures can differ
greatly according to their cultural characteristics; the United States and

France share similar institutional structures but differ culturally. Specification of historical period is necessary because the characteristics of
societies change over time. The pre-Civil War United States is not the
same as the contemporary United States.

Institutional Structures

When sociologists speak of **institutional structures**, they mean configurations of institutions within given areas: the total of economic institutions in a society constituting its economic structure, all of the political
institutions constituting its political structure, all of the institutions reg-
ulating the class relations its class structure, and so forth. Institutions can
overlap and crosscut each other. The institutionalized class structure of a
society, for example, encompasses economic, social, and other relationships. The grand total of institutions within a society constitutes a society's overall social structure.

Individuals are born and exist within institutional structural contexts.
While they may conform to or challenge those structures, including the
ways that they are supposed to play roles, no one is immune from having
to take those structural contexts into consideration. Both law-abiding
and criminal citizens know what the law is. Conformists and nonconformists are aware of what is considered normal and abnormal. Structural contexts thus heavily influence individual behavior.

Many social thinkers have sought to conceptualize how structural
influencing occurs and how much of it there is. They have sough to conceptualize how much of and how human activity is structurally determined. This, in turn, raises the question of existential freedom: to what
extent is or can be human behavior free, if it must always in one way or
another adapt to structural conditions.

Discussions of **structural determination** fall into three broad categories: those that concern how history is made, those that concern how
individuals make choices, and those that concern social policy.

Humans inherit structures from the past that constrain the ways in
which they can make their own histories. In an often-quoted classic
formulation, Karl Marx wrote in 1859 (p. 298) that "men make their
own history, but they do not make it just as they please; they do not
make it under circumstances chosen by themselves, but under circum-

stances directly encountered, given and transmitted from the past."
People thus are free to make decisions that result in historical changes,
but they are not free to choose the structural contexts—the circumstances —within which those decisions occur. Because their decisions
do not occur in freely chosen structural contexts, they cannot be considered to be entirely free. The fiscal policy of a president, for example, may be severely constrained by public debts accumulated by
previous administrations. The president of a poor country may inherit
problems of corruption as well as poverty that constrain her or his ability to achieve other goals.

In its second application, structural determination has to do with how
individuals make choices. Recent sociological thinkers, such as Pierre
Bourdieu, Loïc Wacquant, and Henry A. Giroux, pose the matter in
terms of structure and agency, with *structure* referring to constraining
economic, social, class, political and other conditions into which people
are born and exist, and **agency** to the decisions that individuals make regarding their actions, whether those decisions involve adapting to or de-
fying structural conditions or are made independent of them. A constant
issue is the extent to which structural conditions determine human
thinking and actions and the extent to which human thinking and action
are not so determined.

Any concrete social situation may be thought of in terms of its structural conditions and the possibilities to adapt to, challenge, or overcome
those conditions. Individuals may be thought of in terms of whether they
are inclined to adapt to or challenge particular structural conditions.
There are possibilities for conformists and rebels in all social situations
and societies.

Third, the issue of structural determination underlies many social policy debates regarding how best to resolve particular social problems.
Are poverty and unemployment, for example, best addressed by reforming the economic structure so that more jobs are available and income is
more equally distributed, or by reforming the educational preparation,
motivation, and work habits of the unemployed and poor? The first assumes structural determination of the problem, the second that the poor
and unemployed are individually responsible for their condition.

Quite clearly, most situations of historical causation, individual
choices, or social policy issues exist somewhere between the poles of

complete structural determination and complete freedom of action, with the possible locations between the poles varying greatly.

Societies

The number of societies that have existed in world history is uncountable for two reasons. Modern human beings, in the evolutionary theory sense of that term, and their societies have existed for at least a hundred thousand years. The majority of those societies existed and then vanished without leaving a trace. Even if archeology were able to compile a complete record of all human social existence, there would still be a problem in determining the number of societies. If societies undergo social change and eventually pass away or transform into other societies, how do you determine when a society has so changed that it has become another? Is the United States of the 1970s the same society as the United States of the beginning decade of the third millennium?

What are countable are types of societies. Societies with similar institutional structures can be placed into categories that are marked off from societies of different structures. The units of analysis become types of societies—which we will outline and discuss in chapters four and five—rather than particular societies.

Culture

By cultural characteristics is meant that societies have their own particular ways of life. They have their own distinguishable material goods, such as food, buildings, and handicraft, and nonmaterial values, such as customs, myths, songs, and languages. Cultural characteristics infuse institutional structures, making it impossible to rigidly separate the two.

Nineteenth- and twentieth-century anthropology pioneered employment of the concept of **culture** as a way to describe and explain value differences between societies. Societies, in the words of the anthropologists, had different cultures. To understand how they functioned, it was necessary to determine the contents of their cultures. In doing so, it was important to avoid **ethnocentrism**—using the perspectives or biases of one's own culture to judge the values and practices of another.

Sociologists inherited the concept of culture from anthropology and proceeded to investigate the ways in which societies inculcated cultural values into their members. In studying the overall cultural dimensions of societies, sociologists, however, became increasingly aware of the need to distinguish the subcultures of different internal class, regional, and minority groupings.

The concept of **subculture** is particularly important in societies that contain different ethnic and racial peoples or minorities. Such multicultural societies show clear internal differences of customs, values, and general points of view between peoples. In the United States, being brought up in minority families (such as black, Mexican, Puerto Rican, or Native American) and neighborhoods results in socialization into values and lifestyles that overlap those of the majority, but still retain important differences. Such differences are manifested in language (Spanish rather than English, for example), dialects, forms of music with different beats and syncopation (salsa and soul music), and general values. The more a group leads a separate existence within a society, the more it develops its own unique cultural identity.

Sociologists also speak of class subcultures, as in working-class and middle-class cultures. If classes lead separate lives and lifestyles, then it makes sense to refer to them as having separate subcultures. People from working-class backgrounds share forms of speech—more pronounced in some countries such as England than others—values, and lifestyles that are different from those of the middle and upper classes. For that reason people tend to feel at least vaguely uncomfortable, of not really belonging, when attending social gatherings of classes above or below their own.

There are also regional subcultural differences. The less territorially or culturally integrated a country is, the more subcultural particularities of regions stand out. In the United States there are clear subcultural differences between southerners and northerners, Appalachians and New Englanders, and Californians and Iowans. These differences are marked by speech accents, values, and lifestyles. The same holds for regions within Mexico, where there are subcultural differences between norteños and sureños. In the extreme, regional subcultural differences can result in the fragmentation of countries, as when the Central American republics broke away from Mexico in 1823. But it seems likely, as roads and mass media reduce the physical and social distances separating regions within countries, that national cultures will develop more fully at the expense of regional subcultures. In the same respect, it also seems likely that globalization of economic relationships and communication networks will eventually undermine national identities themselves.

The concepts just described constitute the basic language of sociological analysis. They are applicable to descriptions and explanations of all societies. In the next three chapters, we proceed to classifying and discussing historical and contemporary societies according to their technological stages of development and dominant socioeconomic institutional structures.

Key Terms and Concepts
(in order of presentation)

Human being	Institutions (economic, kinship,
Social being	political, religious)
Instinct	Self
Eros and Thanatos	Looking-glass self
Social	"I" and "me"
Objective Social Life	Self-esteem
Subjective Social Life	Character structure
Setting	Society
Social position	Institutional structure
Status	Structural determination
Role	Social structure
Norms	Agency
Sanctions	Culture
Socialization	Ethnocentrism
	Subculture

Chapter 3

Technological Change

The societies of *homo sapiens sapiens*—the subspecies to which modern humans belong—began approximately 100,000 years ago. Over the succeeding millennia, countless numbers of societies have appeared and disappeared. For most of them there is no recorded information, since they existed before the relatively late invention and spread of writing, about 5,000 years ago. Indirect archaeological evidence has shed some light on how a number of those in the preliterate era functioned, but for the majority there is no information. They simply developed and disappeared, leaving no clues about how they lived for future historians and social scientists. Therefore, any understanding of the different social ways in which people lived over the millennia of world history relies of necessity on logic as much as it does on direct evidence.

Whether on the basis of logical possibilities or direct evidence or combinations of both, most sociologists classify the varieties of societies that have existed in world history according to two criteria: their technological capacities—the subject of this chapter—and their socio-economic structures—the subject of the following two chapters. The first yields a vocabulary of such terms as hunting and gathering, agricultural, and industrial societies; the second, a vocabulary of such terms as slave, feudal, and capitalist societies.

STAGES OF TECHNOLOGICAL DEVELOPMENT

Technology (from the Greek *techne*, or "technique" and *logos*, or "knowledge") means literally "knowledge of techniques." In our context, technology means knowledge of techniques of production. The degree of sophistication of a society's techniques for producing food, shelter, clothing, and other survival necessities indicates its stage of technological development.

There are three different ways in which social scientists classify societies according to their technological stages of development. In the first, they distinguish **historical** and **prehistorical** societies. *Historical societies* are those that developed the communications technology of writing, while *prehistorical societies* were preliterate. Writing first developed about 5,000 years ago in Sumer (in the Middle East). Thus, most of the 100,000 years of world history have been prehistorical according to this use of the term. For this work, though, we will use the term *world history* to cover both history and prehistory.

Second, archaeologists base classifications of prehistorical societies on the materials from which their tools and weapons were constructed. They use primary tool materials—stone, bronze, and iron—because those materials survived the ravages of time long enough to be found in the nineteenth and later centuries and thereby offer direct physical evidence that can be examined.

During the **Stone Age**, which lasted up until 2500 B.C., people shaped their tools and weapons, as literally indicated by the name, out of available stones. As technology increased over thousands of years, copper (beginning in 4500 in Mesopotamia) and then bronze, a combination of copper and tin, replaced stone as the main tool- and weapon-making materials. The first production of iron began around 1200 B.C. Use of metals indicated a tremendous technological advance over use of stone because it resulted in tools that were far superior in strength and precision to those fashioned out of stone.

The third approach, which is now conventionally used in sociological writings, classifies stages of development according to dominant types of production-oriented technologies. Sociologists and other social scientists now agree on a fairly standard vocabulary that classifies development into hunting and gathering, pastoral, horticultural, agricultural, industrial, and postindustrial types and stages (see Lenski and Lenski, 1982).

Hunting and Gathering

As the name **hunting and gathering** indicates, the earliest peoples survived by literally hunting animals and gathering ready-made nuts, vegetables, and fruit. It took tens of thousands of years for human societies to advance beyond hunting and gathering to more sophisticated production technologies. Hunting and gathering continues to be the major technology of only a few peoples in remote regions of the world today. Societies have also existed that resorted mainly to the related technology of fishing as their means of survival, and such societies continue today on many continents.

Pastoral

Herding, or pastoralism, and horticulture were the first technological advances beyond hunting, fishing, and gathering. **Pastoralism** is based on keeping and producing food from a herd of animals such as goats, cattle, and sheep. Pastoralism continues to be the main technological means of subsistence for peoples in several regions of the world. The best examples of recent or contemporary peoples who have subsisted on pastoral technologies are in East Africa, including the Borana, Maasai, Nandi, Turkana, and Jie peoples (Huntingford, 1953; Gulliver, 1955; Dahl, 1979). The Maasai are the best-known examples of pastoralists. They have had problems, though, maintaining their traditional way of life in the face of development pressure to use grazing lands more productively for growing food (Hunt, 1988).

Horticultural

Horticultural (from the Latin *hortus*, meaning "garden," and *cultura*, meaning "cultivation," thus literally "garden cultivation") technologies are based on people using hoes to cultivate small plots of land or gardens. The earliest evidence of horticulture being practiced is from about 9,000 years ago in Mesopotamia, Palestine, and Asia Minor (Lenski and Lenski, 1982, p. 137). Horticulture has continued to be the dominant technology of a number of peoples down to the present. Horticulture is often referred to as the lower stage of **agrarian societies**.

Box 3-1   Key Dates in Techological Development

10,000 B.C.	Prehistory, Stone Age, hunting and gathering
9000–8000 B.C.	Domestication of plants and animals; beginnings of horticulture and pastoralism in Near East
7000 B.C.	Farming villages between Tigris and Euphrates rivers
6500 B.C.	Copper use (Anatolia), beginning of Bronze Age
3100 B.C.	Pictograph writing (Sumer), beginning of history
2500 B.C.	Bronze ox-drawn plow, beginning of agriculture
2000 B.C.	Beginning of horticulture (the Americas)
1200 B.C.	Beginning of Iron Age
1750	Beginning of industrialization in Europe

Agricultural

The higher stage of agrarian societies is **agriculture** (from *ager*, meaning "field," and *cultura*, meaning "cultivation," thus literally "field cultivation"). It is a more advanced technology than horticulture for cultivation of the soil. Instead of human energy using hoes to cultivate small gardens, humans used animal energy (oxen, horses, cattle) to drive plows to cultivate fields. Mesopotamia and Egypt were the first sites of the agricultural revolution, about 4,500 years ago. Agriculture marked a tremendous technological advance over horticulture because humans employed nonhuman sources of energy to drive their tools. The later incorporation of wind and river power to drive mills was related to technologies of using readily available natural energy sources.

Industrial

Industrialization, dating from about 1750, represents both an advance in technological sophistication and a shift of populations away from the land; that is, an urbanization of populations. In industrial production, humans use fossil fuels, electricity, steam, and now controlled nuclear fission as energy sources and machines as tools. At the same time, industrial production takes place in factories around which grow city populations of workers and others. While the factory was the primary location of industrial production, the invention of tractors and other motorized farm machinery has also brought about an industrialization of agriculture. (Hoe, plow, and tractor are the most useful symbols of the technological development of growing food.)

Post-Industrial

Many social scientists argue that today most of the developed countries of Europe and North America have advanced beyond a strictly industrial technological base to their economies. In general developmental stages, as agriculture becomes more productive, fewer laborers are needed on the land, freeing up labor to be employed in industrial production. A society can be considered to be at an industrial stage of development when it has more industrial than agricultural employees, and when the two together constitute a majority of all employees. But these conditions no longer prevail for most of the European and North American labor forces, where service employees in health, education, recreation, and other sectors now constitute the majorities. Labor-saving productivity gains in industry freed up labor to be employed in services, as previously productivity gains allowed labor to be shifted from agriculture to industry. For that reason, a number of social scientists (see Chapter Six) now refer to most of Europe and North America as being at a post-industrial rather than industrial stage of development.

World technological development has been significantly uneven. Some regions and societies passed beyond the prehistoric stage sooner than others. In modern times there are still societies that have yet to industrialize. It is thus impossible to date technological classifications universally. The prehistoric stone and bronze ages lasted longer in some regions than others. While horticultural societies began in 9000 B.C. between the Tigris and Euphrates rivers, they did not begin until 2000 B.C. in the Americas.

TECHNOLOGICAL CHANGE AND SOCIAL PROBLEMS

There is no doubt that technological progress has been a central feature of grand historical development. But it is arguable whether that development has brought unmitigated human benefits. Many argue that there is no evidence that people in technologically advanced societies lead happier or more fulfilling lives than those in less advanced societies. The most that can be said is that technological advance has always brought with it the capacity for reducing misery. Development of technological means of producing more food has the potential to reduce malnutrition, starvation, sickness, and death. Increases in medical knowledge have a similar potential for reducing sources of misery. On the other hand, increases in the technological means of producing misery, such as military means of destruction, may have proceeded as fast as or faster than the means of reducing misery.

With scant exceptions, societies in the world economy today exist somewhere between the poles of the agrarian and industrial or post-industrial stages of development. Developing societies are closer to the agrarian pole, while developed ones are closer to the industrial and post-industrial poles. All are experiencing and adapting in one way or another to social changes associated with degrees of industrial change over the last two hundred years.

Industrialization affects the lives of people in different ways. Industrial technologies enable greater labor productivity; that, in turn, leads to increases in the availability of food, clothing, housing, and other material goods. There is a clear potential for industrialization to increase the material welfare of societies that benefits even the poorest members. Over the last half century, for example, average life spans have increased in the world, indicating that industrial change has had positive benefits for the species as a whole. Clearly though, those benefits have not been equally distributed, with the greatest share going to the world's higher-income countries and classes. Nevertheless, even the poorest have derived some benefits from industrial change. Despite continuing great hardships and health problems, compared to fifty years ago, their lives are materially easier and they are healthier, albeit again with far less positive improvements than those of higher income countries.

Technological development alters the distribution of labor forces and populations. Up until the industrial transformation, food production consumed most of the productive energies of societies, with most laborers toiling on the land. As farmers became more productive through employment of better tools and other techniques of production, they produced increasing surpluses of foods that could be sold to city dwellers. This was the vital condition that allowed urban factory economies to develop. In the industrial stage proper, the proportion of farm laborers in labor forces declined as their overall production of food increased, allowing food supplies to get to the now-increasing proportion of factory workers. In the most advanced societies, technological innovations in industrial production resulted in the proportion of factory workers in the labor force declining, while their overall production of physical goods increased. This allowed relatively more laborers to be devoted to producing services such as education, health care, and administration—the post-industrial condition.

However, technologically induced shifts in labor force distribution rarely occurred without leaving considerable social problems in their wake. Industrialization spawned social uprooting, with individuals and families being squeezed off the land and driven into urban areas where they faced a host of new social problems. When industrialization occurs, more people come off the land than can be immediately absorbed in factory jobs. Unemployment is the inevitable consequence, which then spawns other social problems, including poverty, crime, and family breakdown.

The shift out of rural into urban locations produces social instability and stress. Uprooted people—some forced to migrate internationally in search of jobs—have difficulty adapting to new conditions. Families find that they are cut off from the social support networks provided by extended family members (aunts, uncles, grandparents) and traditional communities. In such conditions, parents find it difficult to maintain control over their children.

Sociology textbooks in the United States during the 1940s, reflecting the experience of still fresh rural-to-urban migration, contained long discussions of the differences between rural and urban forms of social life. In American popular culture, Country and Western music plaintively and nostalgically continues to sing, literally, the virtues of rural life in the face of urban alienation.

Across the developing world, cities are mushrooming as it becomes less possible to survive economically in the countryside. Most of the poor in those cities are recent arrivals from still poorer rural conditions. As in the experience of the United States and Europe earlier, they find that there are more of them than available jobs in factories. At the same time, workers in developed societies find that their jobs are vulnerable too, as corporations continually seek to use new technologies to save on labor costs.

This unrelenting drive for technological innovation in industry and other areas produces pressure on the natural and social environment. Increasing demands for energy to power production threaten to deplete natural resources. Greater levels of production result in waste disposal problems, including disposal of radioactive and toxic materials. Expansion of industrial areas creates urban sprawl. Advances in biochemistry, including gene splicing, raise ethical issues.

The human drive to invent new technologies—in part driven by competitive market forces and in part reflecting the human need to find creative solutions to existing problems—while unquestioned in the past has come under question today. Should technological innovation proceed as quickly as possible regardless of ecological and social impacts? Should there be public regulation of the direction and rate of technological innovation as well as social programs to support those who suffer negative consequences, such as displaced workers?

These are important questions since we are living through a period of exceptionally rapid technological change. Medieval peasants could rest assured that very little would change during their lifetime in how they worked and lived. Today the opposite condition prevails: technological change is continually altering how jobs are done and where and how people live.

Technology, then, both in terms of its stage and direction of development, must be taken into consideration when analyzing societies of the past and present. However, technology does not develop abstractly in a vacuum. It develops in, and is greatly influenced by, social and economic contexts, the subject to which we now turn.

Key Terms and Concepts
(in order of presentation)

Technology	Agrarian
Prehistory	Horticulture
Stone, Bronze, and Iron Ages	Agriculture
Hunting and gathering	Industrialization
Pastoralism	Socioeconomic structure

Chapter 4

Past Societies

Analyzing past types of societies in terms of their types of social and economic structures is important to contemporary sociology for a number of reasons. At a bare minimum, we need to understand these societies in their own rights, in order to have an accurate account of the social ways in which humans have lived over the long span of world history. In addition, part of the logic of world capitalist development from the sixteenth century forward has been determined by its encounter with state societies in the Americas (the Aztec and Inca empires), absorption and destruction of communal societies in many areas, struggle with feudal institutions in Europe and other areas, and initial articulation with slave modes of production. The encounters and articulations of rising capitalist societies spreading outward from Europe with precapitalist ones in other areas has been a significant thematic element of the construction of modern world history.

SOCIOECONOMIC STRUCTURES

Socioeconomic structures are composed of the institutionalized ways in which societies carry out the production of their necessities. These institutionalized ways, called modes of production in some accounts, contain typical economic and social role configurations.[1] The first type of socioeconomic structure in world history incorporated essentially equal social roles; all subsequent ones have incorporated unequal class roles. The history of types of socioeconomic structures, beyond the first, has thus been largely the history of different types of **class structures**.

Socioeconomic classifications shed light on the different institutional characteristics of societies. Societies at the same stages of technological development can have very different socioeconomic structures. Agriculture can be practiced under conditions of both slavery and free labor. Industrial societies in this century have functioned with both capitalist and socialist socioeconomic structures. Used together, the technological and socioeconomic forms of classification create a complementary whole in the identification of a given society, as, for example, industrial capitalist.

COMMUNAL SOCIETIES

At the beginning of world history, humans lived in small **communal societies**, bands that roamed over territories in search of food and other means of survival; that is, practiced hunting and gathering technology. Because of their ability to adapt creatively, they were able to improve their survival skills and tools. Unlike other animals that were unable to accumulate and pass on technological knowledge to succeeding generations, humans have been able to make developmental technological progress a unique feature of their historical experience.

The communal nature of these societies is beyond doubt. Virtually all anthropological, archaeological, and prehistorical studies confirm that they were composed of people who cooperated in their production tasks and shared what they produced. The vertical role differences that existed were not enough to produce class differences, and there were little horizontal role differences or the development of different specialized production tasks. No one worked for anyone else. Instead, each worked for the survival of the whole community, and no one received a larger share of the communal product.

Equality was thus the primordial social condition of humanity. They were equal products of nature, equally weak before nature's awesome storms and harsh living conditions, and equal among themselves as they tried to eke out usually meager existences. If they were equal among themselves, no one was richer or poorer than the others. The common-place saying that there have always been rich and poor in societies is simply wrong.

The first of these communal societies began with the final evolution of the subspecies homo sapiens sapiens, approximately 100,000 years ago. For tens of thousands of years, up until the advent of class-based societies—which came relatively late in world history, and when it was possible to begin to distinguish rich and poor—these were the only types of societies in existence. Communal societies have therefore predominated for well over 90 percent of world history.

After the beginning of class-based societies in some regions of the world, communal societies continued to exist in other regions. Down to the nineteenth century they were still numerous. The Americas were home to large numbers of communal societies of indigenous peoples. Such societies exist today in remote areas of Ecuador, Botswana, New Guinea, and elsewhere, but their numbers are rapidly dwindling to the point of near extinction. It is doubtful that they will survive this century.

The early prehistoric societies were **nomadic**, moving from area to area, in a continual search for better hunting and gathering possibilities. Over generations, nomadism became migration as peoples wandered thousands of miles in search of easier living conditions. The luckiest found lands with temperate climates, lush vegetation, and bountiful game. There is now reason to believe that some of these fortunate early communal peoples led lives of relative ease. Because of the favorable conditions in which they lived, they could produce their necessities in a short amount of time and devote the rest of their days to leisure and cultural activities. Studies (see Sahlins, 1972) of some Australian aborigines indicate that despite having working days far shorter than those commonplace in contemporary developed societies, they managed to secure enough to enjoy a relatively healthy diet.

But these were exceptions. Most early communal societies led unenviably poor existences. They were by no means utopian societies. Most were at the technological stage of hunting and gathering and materially poor. Their tools and knowledge of production techniques were primitive, enabling them to produce only a miserable subsistence standard of living. Most children did not survive infancy, and adults died at early ages.

What stands out economically about these societies is that there was equal access to **means of production**: land, tools, raw materials, and other necessary prerequisites for producing. Each member was free to hunt and gather in surrounding forests and plains. Land, the central means of production of societies that subsisted through hunting and gathering, was the property of no one. Land was a means of production in the sense that it was where animals existed to be hunted and wild plants to be gathered. Without land on which animals and wild plants existed, there could be no production of food through hunting or gathering.

What also stands out economically about communal societies is the subsistence character of production and lack of accumulated wealth. Virtually all that was successfully hunted or gathered was consumed, with nothing left over for storage or that could be turned into wealth for accumulation. Personal items may have been prized, but there was no wealth in the economic sense of that word. Nomadism itself precluded wealth formation, since there was little possibility of carrying more than a few light-weight personal items from place to place.

Socially, equality reigned in the communal societies. There could be status differences—as between leaders and followers, medicine men and ordinary members, and elders and others—but those differences were not so great as to become economic class differences. Leaders, medicine men, and elders were workers like everyone else. All that was different about them was that they were looked up to. They did not have privileged access to or ownership of means of production.

Politically, the earliest societies were undoubtedly small-scale democracies. Their small size made it possible for everyone, or at least adults, to participate in decision making. Since there were neither economic nor social differences, it is unlikely that there would have been sharp differences between political decision makers and those whom they dominated. They were prestate societies in the sense that they had no permanent group of full-time governing officials. Nor did they have standing armies. When fighting was required, the adults temporarily suspended their economic roles as hunters and gatherers and assumed military roles. When the conflict was over, they returned to their usual roles. The existence of full-time governing officials and armies would not have been possible in subsistence societies, since there was not enough surplus production to support them.

There was thus governance in the sense that people met and agreed upon rules and courses of action for their common affairs. But there was no state apparatus in the sense of an identifiable group of full-time governing officials. There may have been chiefs or head persons, but they worked and participated alongside of everyone else in producing the collective subsistence. Only in relatively late history, after tens of thousands of years of communal stateless existence, were chiefs able to begin to devote their full time to governance.

What is known from the earliest societies from which there has been accessible evidence is that at some point blood relationships became very important in their institutional ordering. As they grew larger and transcended being small bands, kinship units differentiated themselves. Why they differentiated, causing the origins of the family, remains an area of mystery and great dispute.

One of the leading hypotheses was endorsed and spread widely by Karl Marx's collaborator, Frederick Engels (1820-1895), in *The Origin of the Family, Private Property and the State* (1884). According to it, the origins of the family and private property were interrelated. Once private control over property in land or herds of animals became important, men who had accumulated such property wanted to be able to pass it on to their biological offspring. They could only do that if they had their own exclusive wife from whom they could be sure that births were their own progeny; hence, the origin of monogamy. But, as Engels observed, it was monogamy only for the woman because prostitution correspondingly arose as an institution available to the man.

Whatever their origins, once kinship units were established, they began to play key roles in the institutional ordering of societies. Through these kinship units, property was accumulated and passed on, and primary identities formed. As societies grew, they divided themselves into clans of interrelated families and individuals. **Clans** included those who could trace their biological descent to a common individual. Mates of biological clan members became members also, as their offspring would add to the pool of biological descendants. In clan-structured societies, the clan itself was a political structure within and through which decision making occurred.

It is impossible to know the beliefs of the early communal peoples. What is known, or at least what can be reasonably assumed, is that they quickly developed explanations for the mysterious and awe-inspiring natural conditions that surrounded them. Magic and animism were among the first forms of religious explanation.

In **magic**, supernatural means are used to control natural phenomena. The communal practitioner of magic invoked a chant or used an object assumed to be invested with supernatural powers to attain a naturalistic end—to ensure success in a hunt, to make it rain, or to cure a sick person. The more often the end was achieved, the more the practitioner was believed to have access to supernatural powers. If the practitioner failed to achieve the end often enough—if the medicine man could not cure the sick or the rainmaker not make it rain—then he or she lost the presumption of having that power. In such societies, magic existed as a potentially available means for controlling a natural world in which humans with their primitive means of production and knowledge were largely powerless. Magic represented wishful thinking, a compensatory belief in potential power for humans who, at their stage of technological development, were quite weak in the face of the thundering powers of nature.

In **animism**, all elements of the physical world—humans, animals, rocks, trees, and so on—are believed to have indwelling spirits that gave them life. In some cases, the spirits were all different, with each having a separate identity. In others, the spirits were all emanations from one source that united every human and other creation in nature.

Animism, like magic, arose in conditions where the low state of technological development condemned humans to little knowledge of and feeble control over the natural world that surrounded them. Instead of being able to gain knowledge of what constituted a tree, for example, myths were invented and then believed about the indwelling spirits of trees. Animism and magic outlived the social and technological conditions that gave rise to them and continued as secondary thought currents within later social formations.

FORMATION OF SURPLUS PRODUCTS

From a technological point of view, the great watershed of world history occurred when humans domesticated plants and animals, which gave birth to farming and pastoralism. From an economic and social point of view, it occurred when early societies began to be able to produce surpluses beyond their subsistence needs. Both watershed developments were interrelated. The technological advance of domestication made it possible for societies to produce regular surpluses.

An **economic surplus** is production in excess of subsistence necessities. Since the earliest societies had to immediately consume all that they produced to avoid starvation, they had no surpluses. Without surpluses, they could not develop economically. It is like contemporary people who must spend all of their income on food, clothing, rent, and other necessities. They do not have money to advance their lives by taking education courses, putting a down-payment on a house, or investing in a business. The earliest societies did not even have access to credit, as do contemporary people, to use as a fictitious surplus. There was no such thing as credit in the earliest societies because, for it to exist, there would have had to have been a surplus somewhere from which it could be drawn.

Production of regular economic surplus products enabled societies to become more complex. If food producers had surpluses, they could trade them to nonfood producers, such as toolmakers, for their products. The more food surpluses there were, the more they made possible the development of specialized production roles within a widening horizontal division of labor. The more specialization of production roles became possible, the more time laborers had to devote to particular tasks, the more skill they developed, the more technology advanced, and the more overall production increased. Food surpluses made possible the development of vertical class role differences. Dominating classes could live off surpluses that they expropriated from dominated laboring classes.

Development of regular surpluses brought with it population growth. They made possible the support of non-producing children, old people, and the incapacitated. The more surpluses there were, the more people could be supported. Early subsistence-based societies had of necessity practiced infanticide, since they were unable to support all of the children born. The production of regular surpluses also created more reliable and better diets for producers, resulting in healthier and longer lives. As death rates decreased and people lived longer, overall population increased.

Surpluses made state apparatuses possible. In one way of defining it, a **state** is an organization of officials and employees who devote full time to the various activities of governance. In order to be able to devote full time to those activities rather than to producing necessities, they must have available taxable surpluses from those who produce necessities.

Engels, in *The Origin of the Family, Private Property and the State* (1884), drew all of these developments together into a classic theory of the relationships between formations of private property, internal class divisions, the family, and the state. At some point, according to his account, communal ownership of the means of production broke up, with individuals and households appropriating for themselves exclusive control over herds and lands. In time some individuals accumulated more herds or land than others. These herd- or land-rich individuals required a specialized organization of armed men to protect their wealth from the rest of society. Thus was born the state.

Its birth indicated the definitive end of communal life. The community was now internally alienated. The rich needed and had the power to protect themselves and their wealth from the poor. The formation of private property made the emergences of class divisions and the state both possible and inevitable.

In Engels's account, the formation of regular surpluses, individual appropriation of means of production as private property, and the consequent development of class divisions between rich and poor were the necessary prerequisites and historical steps that led to the development of the first state apparatuses. States thereafter were simply a necessary facet of class-based societies. Their essential function was to protect the privileged from less privileged classes. To protect the privileged, states had to concentrate in their hands the military means of control and repression—arms, soldiers, and jails. The core of state apparatuses was thus essentially military.

This is not to say that relations between communal societies had necessarily always been peaceful. Raids and plunder among neighboring peoples were common in many regions and periods, necessitating formation of communal militaries. But these were not full-time military forces. Communal warriors were also hunters, herders, and farmers. They were only part-time warriors whose fighting abilities were called upon when necessary. The military skills of communal warriors were directed against outsiders. They were not used at the behest of an internal class of rich people because such a class did not yet exist. Communal warriors were warriors of whole peoples. Therein lies the difference between them and later state military forces. Only when class divisions forced the development of states would warriors be put to the service of privileged classes as opposed to whole peoples, and only then would they serve on a full-time basis. Warriors would now be used both against foreign peoples and internally to maintain control over peasants, slaves, and other domestic lower classes.

Engels's theory remains the most provocative account of early state formation. Other theorists may not accept one or another of its features, or they may reject entirely the way in which he tied it to general Marxist theory, but its hypotheses continue to be points of departure in anthropology and the social sciences in general as an attempt to explain the formation of early states.

There is broad consensus that state formation followed private appropriation of herds or land. There is less agreement over how and why that appropriation occurred. There is also little agreement over whether state formation was a function primarily of the development of class divisions, as Engels held, or more a natural function of growing population sizes and the evolution of complex divisions of labor.

The production of regular surpluses thus was the economic prerequisite for the giant step out of the primordial communal past. It was in many ways, though, a mixed blessing. It opened up the possibilities of extraordinary technological development in all areas. With the production of regular surpluses, the pace of technological innovations quickened greatly. There was now collective time available for thinking about and creating innovative solutions to production problems. But, on the other hand, regular surpluses also enabled the formation of wealth, which could be and was privately appropriated, and which was divisive of collective unity. Regular surpluses became the foundation upon which developed class divisions and alienation of humans from each other.

PEASANT COMMUNITIES AND STATE SOCIETIES

As early peoples learned the techniques of horticultural planting, they could abandon the nomadic way of life and settle into small **peasant communities**. Many parts of the world at different time periods show this pattern: in the Near East farming villages existed by 7000 B.C., in

China and Southeast Asia by 3500 B.C., in Scandinavia and Britain by 3000 B.C., and in Mesoamerica by 2000 B.C.

In time the increasing value of land for production caused the first incipient class divisions in world history to arise within these communities. The practice of horticulture changed the relationship between humans and the land. Instead of land being merely a surface on which to hunt and gather already existing food and other necessities, it became the irreplaceable direct means of production along with seeds and tools. Its rising importance in production provoked the disintegration of communal relationships. Class divisions emerged between large and small landowners, between relatively rich and poor. In a parallel fashion, the same process of private property formation occurred among pastoral peoples and led to class divisions between herd-rich and herd-poor households.

Regular surpluses, as in the form of stored grain, were available to be taxed by outside authorities. Villages were drawn voluntarily or through conquest into nets of taxing relationships that central authorities, most often institutionalized as royalty, cast over far-reaching territories. Out of taxes collected from the peasant communities, state authorities supported their households, armies, and the tax collectors themselves. The clearest examples of these types of **state society** formation in ancient history occurred in Mesopotamia, Egypt, Northern China, the Indus Valley, and Persia in Asia, and among the Aztecs and Incas in the pre-Columbian Americas. These early state officials were a dominant economic class that expropriated and lived off taxes collected from the peasant village communities.

A long and controversial literature identifies these state societies as Asiatic modes of production. Karl Marx (1858) introduced the concept somewhat in passing, touching off debates over its validity and usefulness, which continue today in both Marxian and non-Marxian circles. For approaches that use the concept of the Asiatic mode of production, see Godelier (1969, 1978) and Krader (1975). For an interpretation of pre-Soviet Russian society as an example of an Asiatic mode of production, see Kagarlitsky (1988). For an analysis that rejects the validity of the concept of the Asiatic mode of production, see Anderson, (1974b). The term used here, *state society*, confers the same general meaning but has the advantage of not being geographically restrictive.

By most accounts, the peoples of the ancient state societies were deeply religious. Temples dotted the land, their priests being parts of religious bureaucracies that rose up to the very top of societal power. In many cases the head of state was simultaneously the head of religion—both emperor and high priest. Hence, political governance and institutionalized religion were organizationally fused at the top, indicating the importance of religion as a component of overall social control. The fusion of the pinnacles of Aztec religious, military, and political hierarchies is an example.

One of the explanations for the depth of **religiosity** in these societies was that, while they were centralized politically, they continued to be decentralized economically, producing the need for a strong unitary religion as an arm of state power. The more people held common fundamental beliefs, the easier it was to govern them. Common and deeply held religious beliefs compensated for the lack of economic ties binding people together.

It was within these state societies that the first large cities grew, often around the royal centers of power, and within these cities the first systems of writing were invented, often for the purpose of keeping track of tax collections.

In many areas state authorities performed a clear economic function of overseeing the construction and maintenance of vast irrigation and river-control systems, such as around the Nile, Tigris, Euphrates, and Yellow rivers. This led to their identification in some writings (see Wittfogel, 1957 for the classic treatment) as **hydraulic civilizations**. In some areas they developed to oversee the common defense needs of confederations of villages. In other areas they emerged strictly out of the prerogatives of conquest and empire. In all areas, once established, state rule became institutionalized and intergenerationally reproduced.

SLAVE SOCIETIES

Production of a regular surplus was the absolutely essential prerequisite for the development of **slavery**. Not even marginal slavery could exist without it. Slaves had to be able to produce both enough for their own maintenance and a surplus amount that was exploitable by their owners. Otherwise there would be no incentive to own slaves. If the slaves produced only subsistence necessities, expropriation of products from them would result in their death.

Technically, a slave was a person whose labor was owned by another. Slaves were not free to sell their labor to employers who offered the most favorable wages and other conditions of work, as are modern workers. Nor were slaves free to quit and change employers.

Conditions of work did not have to be harsh for slavery to be in force. Oppressiveness of working and living conditions was a correlative of slave systems that was present in varying degrees. To be sure, there is no more accurate symbol of slavery than the whip. But there were also favored slaves—house slaves in the southern parts of the United States—whose treatment was more benign if none the less degrading; and there were owners who, as their descendants endlessly recount, "treated their slaves well." But a well-fed slave was still a slave.

Chattel (meaning property) **slavery** was the purest and most literal form of a slave labor system. In it, the owner possessed the slave unconditionally for life or until sale to another owner. The clearest examples of fully developed chattel-slave societies were in the ancient world (Greece and Rome primarily) from the sixth century B.C. to the fifth century A.D. and in the Americas (Brazil, the Caribbean islands, and the southern areas of the United States) from the sixteenth to nineteenth centuries. The institution of chattel slavery existed in other societies, but alongside of and subordinate to other labor systems that accounted for greater proportions of the total surpluses produced.

Chattel-slave societies, as opposed to other types of societies in which there is marginal use of slave labor, existed when slaves produced the bulk of societal surpluses. In order to do that, slaves did not necessarily have to be the majority of the population. Slaves were minorities of the populations of ancient Rome, the antebellum United States south, and eighteenth- and nineteenth-century Puerto Rico, but they produced most of the surpluses. The majority populations were made up mainly of free subsistence peasants who did not produce surpluses.

Ancient Slavery

Paradoxically, ancient Greece is known as both the world's first democratic and first full slave republic. Democratic privileges were enjoyed only by the free population; the slave population had no democratic rights. Estimates of the proportion of slaves in Greece vary considerably from one-third to 80 percent of the population (see Westermann, 1955; Andrewes, 1967; Anderson, 1974a; Vogt, 1975; and Finley, 1980). Most of the slaves were spread out in small numbers among many free families.

Most researchers agree that there were proportionately fewer slaves in the Roman Empire than in Greece, but the scale of the institution was much larger (see Brunt, 1971). The Roman Empire covered a much greater area and included more people than did the Greek city-states. Where slavery was practiced in the Roman Empire it tended to be on a large scale. Ownership of slaves was concentrated among the rich, not spread out among many free families, as it had been in Greece. Large-scale Roman plantation slavery, for which there had been no precedent in Greece, became the prototype for slave production systems in the Americas.

New World Slavery

Capitalism drove slavery in the Americas from its sixteenth-century beginning (for the classic discussion, see Williams, 1944). Slaves produced a number of the early commodities that built early international capitalist trade. Sugar was the first ,and for many years the most important, slave-produced commodity (see Klein, 1986). Slave-produced sugar from Madeira and other areas had been imported to Europe for some time before Columbus made his voyages to the Caribbean. Favorable soil and climatic conditions made the newly discovered Caribbean islands natural sites for the establishment of plantation economies to supply the international sugar market. At first, the local indigenous (Indian), peoples were enslaved by their Spanish conquerors. But they dwindled as a labor supply within a generation due to disease, being killed resisting enslavement, or overwork on the plantations. At least one million Caribbean Indians perished during the period of establishment of the plantation slave economies. With sources of labor diminished to almost nothing, plantation owners turned to Africa as a more reliable source of labor, thereby stimulating the international slave trade that continued for three centuries more.

The economic effects of slavery were far reaching. In many ways slaves built the foundations of the modern capitalist economy. Profits gathered from the slave trade and slave production contributed to the accumulation of capital that helped to finance the Industrial Revolution. Slave-produced raw materials such as cotton fed the early textile factory systems in England and the northeastern United States. Slavery thus benefited capitalist development in the West. But the effects of the slave trade on Africa were disastrous. At least ten million members of West African societies were kidnapped, causing a continual drain of those societies' youngest and strongest laborers and condemning those parts of Africa to long-term structural underdevelopment and poverty—conditions that still exist today (see Rodney, 1972). Slavery also left a continuing legacy of racism and racial tensions in the areas where it was practiced.

Peonage, Indentured Servitude, and Contract Labor

Aside from chattel slavery, there were other systems in which the slave condition was either hidden or not imposed as severely or permanently. **Peonage** was a system of debt slavery that existed in a number of historical societies, including ancient Greece, Mexico in the nineteenth and early twentieth centuries (Turner, 1910; Meyer and Sherman, 1987), and in the post-bellum ex-slave areas of the United States south (Daniel, 1972). In peonage, creditors claimed the future labor of debtors as payment for an incurred debt. In some cases the debt was so high that it could not be paid off during the lifetime of the people who incurred it. The creditor or succeeding generations of the creditor's family then laid claim to the labor of succeeding generations of the debtor's family.

Indentured servitude and **contract labor** are semi-slave systems in which labor is owned for a defined period of time. Approximately half of the white colonial working class came to British North America as indentured servants. Ship owners and other labor suppliers paid their passage from England in return for an agreement that that would be sold upon arrival as temporary servants (usually for a period of seven years). After that they were freed. Most of the early Chinese population that migrated to the United States in the late 1840s and 1850s came as contract laborers, having had their passage paid for in return for future labor obligations.

The labor of modern prisoners may also be analyzed as having a slave-like character. They are paid minimally, if at all, for their labor. They are neither free to quit nor to change employers for better working conditions. Whether they deserve to be in prison is irrelevant to the analysis of the economic type of labor they perform.

FEUDAL SOCIETIES

The classic examples of **feudalism** developed in Europe between the decline of the Roman Empire in the fifth century and the beginnings of capitalist development in the thirteenth and fourteenth centuries (for the classic account, see Bloch, 1933, 1940). Feudal societies, or at least semi-feudal characteristics, have also been noted in Asia (Japanese history offers the closest examples), Africa, and Latin America.

European feudal societies had military origins. As the Roman Empire disintegrated, leaders of military bands took control over areas. They institutionalized their control by granting land to subordinate officers in return for loyal past deeds and the promise of loyal future service when needed. These land grants, or **fiefs**, included the peasants who were living there. Loyal subordinate officers were essentially granted income-producing estates in return for pledging military support to the grantor in times of conflict or other need. The bond between grantor and grantee was intensely personal. The grant could be revoked at any time for acts of personal disloyalty.

Landlords controlled their estates, but not as private property. Paradoxically, they had almost complete control over the peasants who worked on the estates, but they were not as free to do with the land as they pleased. They could not, for example, sell the land, since it was not ultimately theirs to sell.

The largest part of feudal surpluses took the form of rent payments peasants made to landlords for being able to use land for their own subsistence needs. Historically, there have been three ways in which these rent payments were made. In the first—the predominant form during medieval European feudalism—they paid with their labor. They met their rent obligations by working on land set aside for providing for the landlord's household. This system, called **corvée labor**, usually had the peasants working three days a week on their own plots and three days on the landlord's. In the second form of rent payments, **quitrent**, or payment in kind, peasants delivered to the landlord a set quantity or proportion of the harvest. In the third, the peasant paid the rent directly in money.

There was very little actual buying and selling of products. These were essentially pre-commodity economies. Most of what peasants produced was either directly consumed by their households or turned over to landlords as rent payments. Very little took the form of commodities; that is, goods that were sold through markets. For sure, there could be village markets and traveling merchants, but their merchandise represented only a small proportion of total societal production.

Strict hierarchy, ascription, and rigidity characterized feudal class relations. Landlords, through their control of the key means of production for agriculturally based societies—land—were able to dominate majority peasant classes. Landlords saw themselves socially and ideologically as nobles and aristocrats (from Latin and Greek *aristos*, meaning "best," and *kratein*, meaning "rule," hence, "rule of the best"). The contemporary identification of aristocratic attitudes with snobbery is a

Box 4–1   Key Dates in Socioeconomic Change

1000,000 B.C.–7500 B.C.	Communal societies in all inhabited areas
7000 B.C.	First village communities (Near East)
c 6000 B.C.	First surplus products (Near East) First development of class divisions (Near East)
3500 B.C.	First state societies (Near East)
1150 B.C.	Beginning of Olmec state society (Mesoamerica)
700 B.C.	First standardized coins (Anatolia)
500 B.C.–500	Greco-Roman slavery
500–1500	Medieval European feudalism
1500–	Capitalism
1500–1888	New World slavery
1917–	Socialist societies—major examples
1989	Collapse of socialist societies in Eastern and Central Europe

carry-over from feudal days of landlords' self-rationalization for their class domination.

Feudal ideologists assumed that people were born (ascribed) into their class positions, whether high or low, due to natural differences of superiority and inferiority, and that there they should remain. Our contemporary notions of achieved class mobility from humble to exalted positions or of the virtue of becoming a self-made millionaire were completely absent in feudal societies. Born a peasant, die a peasant was the rule. It was exceptional for people to move out of the class position into which they were born. The attitude that lower classes are innately inferior is a feudal carry-over that continues in areas where feudal traditions are still strong.

Decentralization and personal loyalty characterized feudal political relationships. There could be centralized states that nominally covered large territories, but substantive political authority was seated and exercised locally by landlords who often organized their own private armies. The complete hegemony of local over central authority included legal affairs. Each feudal estate and area had its own law, which was made, interpreted, and enforced by the local landlords.

The Roman Catholic Church monopolized the religious terrain of medieval European feudalism. Church doctrine was essentially conservative, advocating peasant docility and acceptance of the social order as natural. It placated their earthly misery with the promise of better things to come in the next life. In many ways, the organization of the church—with hierarchical levels for priests, bishops, archbishops, cardinals, and the Pope—paralleled the hierarchical social and political organization of feudal society. The church also was a great landlord. One of the intended or unintended consequences of priesthood celibacy was that there were no heirs other than the church itself for the property that accumulated or otherwise fell into its hands.

Feudal societies were the context out of and against which capitalist societies developed. As such, it is not possible to understand how capitalism originated without an understanding of the European feudal past. For long periods of time, feudal and capitalist regions existed side by side within and between countries. Within countries, capitalist development took place first in cities—the locations of markets—while estate economies dominated the countryside. Capitalist development proceeded at a much faster pace in some countries, resulting in uneven development. Today there are still countries with semi-feudal institutions. Class relations in most parts of Latin America, for example, have a much more feudal character than do those of the United States.

Key Terms and Concepts
(in order of presentation)

Socioeconomic structures	Religiosity
Class structures	Hydraulic civilizations
Communal societies	Slavery
Means of production	Chattel slavery
Nomads	Ancient slavery
Clans	New World slavery
Magic	Peonage
Animism	Indentured servitude
Kinship	Contract labor
Economic surplus	Feudalism
State	Fief
Peasant communities	Corvée labor
State Societies	Quitrent

ENDNOTE

[1] I have discussed the concept of modes of production as well as of types of modes of production more substantively in *Modes of Production in World History* (London: Routledge, 1989).

Chapter 5

Contemporary Societies

In the half-millennium since 1500—the year marking both the entrance of developed capitalist socioeconomic structures on the world stage and the beginning of modern world history—two large-scale socioeconomic dramas have taken place. In the first, rising capitalist societies overcame the obstacles and resistance of precapitalist orders. In the second, Western capitalist societies led by the United States confronted and ultimately prevailed over the challenge posed by European communist societies during the twentieth century.

ORIGINS AND SPREAD OF CAPITALISM, 1500–

Capitalist societies are market societies in which a private class of individuals and families owns the major means of production—including factories, banks, land, and retail outlets—and employs laborers for wages or salaries, with the primary goal of reaping profits. In capitalist societies the elements of production processes—including raw materials, tools, land, buildings, and products—take the form of **commodities**—goods that are bought and sold in market transactions. The growth of commodity markets of all types was and continues to be central to capitalist development.

Elements of capitalistic organization existed on the margins of precapitalist societies for thousands of years. Ancient Greece and Rome had some market trade and employment for wages of laborers in urban workshops. But in precapitalist societies, the majority of products were not sold or exchanged through markets. They were, instead, consumed by their producers or simply handed over as payment to landlords or tax collectors. The majority of labor was not performed for wages.

The first societies that were substantially capitalist emerged in the sixteenth century in Europe after a protracted and successful struggle to transform feudal conceptions of labor, land, and production. Peasant labor under feudalism had been tied to particular estates. Peasants neither worked for wages nor were free to change landlords. Feudalism, hence, knew no markets for peasant labor. Land, the central means of production of feudal societies, was not considered private property that could be bought or sold. It was rather a grant or fief from an over-lord that had to be continually renewed. The landlord was not free to sell it. Finally, with most goods being directly consumed by peasant households or turned over to landlords as rent, feudal economies saw little distribution of products through markets. For capitalism to become entrenched as a way of life, peasant labor would have to be released from the estates and become available for employers to hire for wages, land would have to become privatized and available for sale, and goods would have to be distributed through markets. Put more succinctly, labor, means of production, and goods would have to be commodified.

For several centuries capitalist development proceeded unevenly in Europe. Cities were its strongholds, while the countryside remained backward and feudal, resulting in a European social landscape that was a patchwork of capitalist cities surrounded by feudal rural estates. The cities formed at port and crossroads locations. Some were completely new, arising around commercial activities that began to increase in the late feudal period. Others were revived old Roman cities that had declined greatly in size and importance in the feudal period. In time, city-based commercial, productive, and financial activities gained enough hegemony to pull the countryside into the vortex of capitalist development. By the sixteenth century, many European countries could be described as having predominantly capitalist socioeconomic structures.

But at the same time, the political structures of these early European capitalist societies were still largely feudal. They had been formed during the feudal period and were occupied by the landed aristocracy, producing a contradiction between rising capitalist and old landed interests over state policies. Further capitalist development required transformation of the state, which was accomplished through revolutions and civil wars in England in the seventeenth century, France in the eighteenth century, and Germany in the nineteenth century.

Externally, the capitalist world market took shape by the early sixteenth century and pulled into its controlling influence widely disparate countries and regions. Its centripetal pull was felt far and wide. Western Europe was its original center. As capitalist production and market activities developed there into a solid system, traders, explorers, soldiers, and missionaries ventured into Asia, Africa, and the Americas, establishing peripheral markets and production sites. The world capitalist system thus developed at first with Western Europe as its center and Asia, Africa, and the Americas as its periphery. By the early twentieth century, the United States and Japan had joined Western Europe as centers of world capitalist development.

Today, capitalist societies continue to be based on commodity-producing economies in which the dominant class exercises power by owning and controlling the most important means of production, including factories, mines, banks, software production, media outlets, and stores. Wealth invested or available for investment in the means of production is *capital*. Those who own significant shares of capital are capitalists. The major part of the labor force of developed capitalist societies is made up of workers who are obliged to work for private or state employers because they do not own their own means of producing an income. Aside from the class positions of capitalists and workers, which arise from the central class division of capitalist societies, other class positions have been occupied by peasants, small-business owners, and employed professionals and managers (see Chapter Nine).

There seems to be no necessary political form of the state for capitalist economies. Historically, they have functioned under governmental systems that have ranged widely from highly autocratic to relatively democratic. The most essential task of the government of a capitalist society is to have economic policies that protect and promote the general business climate. Whether that is done through autocratic or relatively democratic means is secondary.

In a parallel sense, the economic policies and programs of the governments of capitalist societies have varied widely depending on the parties in power. Conservative parties, such as the Republican Party in the United States and the Conservative Party in Great Britain, use capitalistic means as much as possible. Their primary goal for government policy is to improve the operating conditions for private businesses. Liberal parties, such as the Democratic Party in the United States, and social democratic parties, such as the Socialist Party of France, use semi-socialistic means. That is, they have at times adopted policies leading to state ownership of some industries and the establishment of publicly financed services, such as socialized health care systems.

In reality, there are no purely capitalist countries, since in all of them the government, to one degree or another, participates in economic planning, ownership, or provision of services. Countries where state participation is relatively high, such as Sweden, can be justifiably classified as having, to some extent, mixed economies. But so long as private interests own and control the largest share of a society's major means of production and state ownership is secondary, the society retains a predominantly capitalist economic structure, albeit mixed with significant state ownership and economic participation.

The universal market is a central characteristic of predominantly capitalist societies. The more capitalism developed initially, as we have seen, the more it transformed the fundamental elements of production—labor, means of production, and produced goods—into commodities, resulting in the eventual institutionalization of the labor, capital or stock, and goods markets that are now central features of all capitalist societies. This **commodification** of all central economic activities has had far-reaching cultural consequences. Many critics argue that consumerism has become a central feature of daily life, reducing all other life goals to secondary importance. Massive advertising campaigns inflate consumer desires and divert attention from more substantive life questions.

Capitalist firms have two primary goals: to make as much profit as possible in the short run, and to grow through accumulating capital in the long run. The two goals are related since profits are the immediate source of capital formation. Corporate executives may be personally concerned about the public interest, but they believe that they can only serve it if their companies are profitable. But it is not necessarily clear that, as Charles Wilson, secretary of defense for the Eisenhower administration and a former top corporate executive, once put it, "What's good for General Motors is good for the U.S."

Class and social inequality are structural principles of all capitalist societies. Some, such as Durkheim (1893) and, more recently, Herrnstein and Murray (1994), argue or imply that such inequality simply reflects natural inequalities among people. Others argue that unequal distribution of income and wealth functions to stimulate labor productivity. The most cited sociological analysis that defends income inequality is by Davis and Moore (1945). They argued that societies needed highly educated professional skills. In order to motivate individuals to attain them—which involved investing extra years of education during which incomes were deferred—societies had to offer as a reward the realistic prospect of ultimately receiving significantly higher-than-average incomes. For criticisms of Davis and Moore's analysis, see Tumin (1953) and Szymanski (1983).

Inequality as a motivating force, by implication, means that one strives to become rich both for its own sake and also to avoid the penury of being poor. It is a competition that in the extreme encourages each man or woman to be out ultimately for himself or herself alone. Inequality and individualism thus come together as guiding capitalist principles.

The more relative income and wealth the upper classes receive, the less relative income and wealth the lower classes receive. It follows that upper-class standards of living are, to some extent, gained at the expense of other classes' standards of living. In the United States, the richest 10 percent of households receive more income than that of the combined bottom 56 percent. The distribution of income for the total world population is even more unequal. The richest countries, with about 10 percent of the world's population, have more income than do countries that contain all of the rest—90 percent—of the world's population (calculated from World Bank, 2007a, Table 2.7).

Despite inequality being a firm principle of capitalism, individual capitalist societies vary considerably in the actual extent of inequality within them. In therm of the distribution of income, Namibia, where the richest 10 percent of the population take 65 percent of all national income, is the most unequal society. By way of contrast, in Denmark, the most equal, the richest 10 percent, take only 21 percent of the national income, less than a third of what their Namibian counterparts take. In the United States, the top 10 percent take 30 percent of national income.

THE COMMUNIST CHALLENGE, 1917–1989

By the nineteenth century, opposition to capitalism coalesced in major ideological alternative movements such as **socialism** and **anarchism**. The basic socialist critique of capitalism was that private capitalist owner- ship of the means of production was undemocratic since it gave capitalists inordinate power to economically (and indirectly politically) control soci- eties at the expense of majority populations; the structure of capitalism was built on class exploitation and inequality; and the culture of capital- ism encouraged the antisocial values of individualism and greed, as op- posed to solidarity among people. In place of capitalism, socialists advocated creating societies based on common public or government ownership of the means of production that could be democratically con- trolled, equality, and the promotion of solidarity among people.

Anarchists shared the socialist critique of capitalism but disagreed with the socialist solution of building up the state through public owner- ship of the means of production. Anarchists viewed large state structures as being at least as responsible as capitalist economic structures for hu- man misery and injustice. In place of building up state ownership, they advocated small-scale decentralized societies with small cooperative ownership and control of the means of production. Of the two anticapi- talist movements, socialism and anarchism, the former has had much greater historical influence.

Socialism as an ideological movement received its greatest intellec- tual development with the epochal works of Karl Marx and Frederick Engels (see Chapter Seven). By the late nineteenth century, Marxism was firmly established in Europe as a major ideological and political al- ternative. Marxist ideas and political parties struggled openly or clan- destinely everywhere, as circumstances dictated, against the capitalist organization of society. By the early twentieth century, large socialist or socialist-oriented opposition parties had developed in Germany, France, England, Italy, and other countries.

In Russia, V.I. Lenin (1870–1924) led the Bolshevik Party through two decades of a mostly illegal and underground existence against the decrepit and highly repressive czarist state to the successful 1917 revolution. The Bolshevik Revolution inaugurated development of the world's first society with a socialist organized economy.

The eruptions of the 1917 Bolshevik and later 1949 Chinese revolutions, in the world's largest and most populous countries, respectively, challenged the continued development of the capitalist world economy. The subsequent spread of **communism** to other countries in Asia, Africa, and Latin America further constrained capitalist development. Through the 1950s, those countries largely developed outside of the parameters of international capitalism, leading to the sharp demarcation of separate capitalist and socialist worlds.

At the same time, socialism as an ideological movement divided into many rival camps. The two most prominent were communism, which was the ruling ideology in the Soviet Union, China, and other countries led by communist parties—referred to here as socialist countries because of their economic features—and **social democracy**, which was an anticommunist ideology embraced by leading socialist parties in Western Europe and elsewhere. To make matters terminologically confusing, the social democrats referred to themselves as democratic socialists, while the communists in the Soviet Union, China, and the other similarly organized countries referred to their economic structures as socialistic. We shall refer to the Soviet Union and other societies with one-party communist governing systems as communist societies, while at the same time classifying their economic structures as socialist.

In communist societies the state, rather than a private capitalist class, owned and managed most of the major means of production, such as factories, banks, and large stores. It pursued policies directed in the short run toward narrowing the range of social inequality, and in the long run toward establishing full social equality. In the mixed economies of the Western European societies where socialist parties were strong, both the state and private corporations played important roles. In sum, the social democrats or socialists operated in multiparty societies with mixed public and private-controlled economies, while communists operated in single-party societies with state-controlled economies.

Since 1917, revolutions in China, Cuba, Vietnam, and other countries were either led by Marxists or adopted Marxist ideas in the aftermath of their triumphs. Following World War II, the Soviet Union used its military power to dominate Eastern Europe and ensure that those republics would be both allies and socialist. After their devastating experience in the war, in which upwards of thirty million of their citizens were killed during the Nazi invasion and occupation, the Soviets sought to create in the Eastern European countries a buffer zone between themselves and the hostile NATO (North Atlantic Treaty Organization) countries.

A large body of literature, mainly in the Western countries maintains that the communist countries that identified themselves as having socialist economies were not socialist at all. Trotskyist-influenced writers claimed that the Soviet Union was a state capitalist society in which workers were rendered powerless by bureaucratic domination. Others, such as Sweezy (1980) and Kagarlitsky (1988), held that the Soviet Union was neither capitalist nor socialist, but rather a different, as yet to be fully understood, postcapitalist class formation. Still others maintained that these societies did not conform to Marx's notion of socialism. All of the above types of criticisms shared a common dislike of how the self-identified socialist societies were organized and functioned. While the more hostile critics argued that these societies were undesirable because of defects in Marxian theory itself, Western socialist-oriented critics sought to preserve the validity of Marxism itself while distancing themselves from how it had been applied. These societies also had their defenders who argued that those formations were both desirable and reflected valid applications of Marxian theory.

The original conception of socialism, as envisioned by Marx, Engels, and Lenin, was that it would be a transitional form of society between class-based capitalist and classless communist modes of production. The future communist mode of production would be based on common state ownership of means of production, altruistic motivation (the new communist man or woman), full social equality, and highly developed forces of production, which would allow goods to be distributed according to need: "From each according to their ability, to each according to their needs." The future communist mode of production would overcome the major problems that have plagued societies for millennia:

scarcity and class division. Material abundance and human solidarity would make a higher level of social existence possible. That was the promise. But neither Marx nor his followers thought that it would be possible to immediately construct a communist mode of production after the overthrow or collapse of a capitalist society. It would require decades, perhaps centuries, of preparation through the buildup of forces of production (including technological capacities) and transformation of overall social consciousness from individualistic to altruistic motivational bases.

In the socialist transition period between the end of capitalism and the achievement of communism, the state would own and manage society's major means of production according to central planning, but neither full equality nor distribution strictly according to need would yet be possible. "From each according to ability, to each according to what he or she produces—rather than needs" would be the principle of necessity that guided production and distribution in transitional socialist modes of production. At the same time though, it would be possible to progressively narrow gaps in class standards of living and distribute some necessities—such as food, health care, and education—according to need rather than market principles. But, according to Lenin (1918), capitalist interests would never peacefully permit such changes to take place. The revolutionary state would have to force them through by taking the form of a "dictatorship of the proletariat."

Through the end of the 1980s, communist countries were primarily structured according to those economic, social, and political principles. The various communist states owned and managed their societies' major means of production according to central planning. Class differences remained, but in diminishing proportions. Extensive social programs were constructed to allow free access to health care and education. Food prices were subsidized, making food affordable to all citizens. Though supplies of many types of food fell short of demand, resulting in long lines at stores, those supplies were relatively equally distributed. One of the most notable achievements of the communist—compared to capitalist—societies was that they succeeded in effectively eliminating unemployment.

Overall, the communist countries achieved impressive health standards, as Table 5–1, based on World Bank data, indicates. In comparing world health conditions in 1988, the year before the Eastern European countries began to abandon socialism, it was clear that the level of income of a country was related to the health conditions that it could afford. But the type of socioeconomic structure, whether capitalist or socialist, also significantly affected average health conditions. By far, the high-income capitalist countries enjoyed the world's highest average health conditions. But in the low- and middle-income levels where there were communist societies, those societies had significantly better health conditions, as measured by infant mortality rates and life expectancy, than did their capitalist counterparts. **Infant mortality rates**— the number of children who die before their first birthday per thousand live births—and average life expectancy in years are the two central

TABLE 5–1
Health Conditions in Countries of the World in 1988, the Year Before the Eastern European Countries Began to Abandon Socialism

	Population		Average infant mortality rate (per 1,000)	Life expectancy at birth (years)
	(millions)	(percent)		
High Income				
Capitalist	784.2	15.4	9	76
Socialist	0.0	0.0		
Middle Income				
Capitalist	995.9	19.5	54	66
Socialist	434.1	8.5	22	71
Low Income				
Capitalist	1,727.5	33.9	99	54
Socialist	1,158.8	22.7	32	70
World	5,100.2	100.00	57	64

Note: Identified as middle-income socialist countries were the Union of Soviet Socialist Republics, the Democratic People's Republic of Korea, the German Democratic Republic, Czechoslovakia, Cuba, Bulgaria, Albania, Poland, Hungary, and Yugoslavia. Idenfied as low-income socialist countries were China, Vietnam, the Lao People's Democratic Republic, and Mongolia.
Source: Calculated on the basis of data in The World Bank (1990, pp. 178, 232, and 244)

measures of health conditions in comparative development research. Infant mortality rates rise and fall according to public health conditions, such as availability of potable water and sanitation, and access to medical care. The more developed and prosperous the society, the more these are available. The differences were especially significant in low-income countries. Communist low-income countries had average infant mortality rates less than one-third those of low-income capitalist countries (32 compared to 99), and people lived on average 16 years longer. Much of these differences were due to China, which had both a large population and a well-developed public health system, being classified as a low-income country. Thus, communist public health systems impressively outperformed their capitalist counterparts in middle- and low-income countries. At the same time, though, the economies of the communist countries were not as impressive in meeting other, less essential consumer demands.

The Soviet Union and its Eastern European allies ran into deep economic trouble in the 1980s. Communist leaders had originally assumed and promised that the standards of living in those countries would catch up to those of the prosperous West. But by the 1980s, it was clear that this goal was increasingly elusive for a number of perhaps historically unavoidable reasons, causing communism to lose public credibility. In the 1970s, communist countries, such as Hungary, began to take out Western loans to finance projects that would speed up development and increases in standards of living. These projects failed to live up to expectations, resulting in their loan repayments becoming extra burdens in the 1980s on already shaky economies (see Phillips, 1990). In addition, economic growth in the Soviet Union slowed down considerably during this period (Sweezy and Magdoff, 1990), thereby stagnating improvements in public standards of living.

In large part, the 1980s economic downturns in the Soviet Union and Eastern Europe followed a pattern in the world economy: rich economies grew and prospered while poor economies and those of the communist countries suffered sharp reverses. The response of significant proportions of the public in the Soviet Union and Eastern Europe was to blame the economic downturns on the socialist structure of the economy and the governments in power. In low- and middle-income capitalist countries, the response was to blame whatever political party was in power. In the late 1980s and early 1990s, for example, not one incumbent regime other than Mexico was electorally returned to office in Latin America. In the case of Mexico, many domestic and international observers maintained that the governing political party resorted to massive vote-counting fraud to hold on to power.

The pivotal year 1989 saw the unleashing of massive economic and political changes in Eastern Europe and the Soviet Union. Facing perceived stagnation in economic growth and other problems, those countries loosened their states' grip over economic life, hoping that this would lead to economic revival. In some cases, that included significant privatization of state-owned companies; in others, it was restricted to allowing market forces to operate in areas that had formerly been managed by central planning. In some countries, such as Poland, the goal was an all-round restoration of capitalism; in others, it was the establishment of a larger private sector within a mixed economic structure. In 1990, the German Democratic Republic (East Germany), the most prosperous of the Eastern European communist countries, ceased to exist as an independent country after essentially allowing itself to be annexed by West Germany. In 1992, the Soviet Union dissolved itself as an entity and fractured into twelve independent new countries, including Russia, Ukraine, Belarus, and Georgia. Politically, the republics of the old Soviet Union and Eastern Europe abandoned the one-party concept of the state and instituted multiparty parliamentary forms. All of these changes, taken collectively, resulted in a significant restructuring of the postwar world political order and the strengthening of capitalist tendencies within it.

As epochal changes swept through the Soviet Union and Eastern Europe, the other communist countries—China, Vietnam, Cuba, Laos, and North Korea—maintained independent courses of action. All continued as one-party states, though the first four allowed significant private sectors of their economies to develop.

THEORIES AND CLASSIFICATIONS

It became an increasingly capitalist new world order after 1989, but not a homogeneous world order. There remains a steep stratification of the just over two hundred countries in the world today that stretches from comfortable standards of living on average in Europe and the United States to the misery and squalor in the least developed African, Asian, and Latin American countries. The global poles of wealth and poverty intersect within countries as well, for rich countries contain poverty and poor countries contain elites who are rich by anyone's standards. Together, all of these societies make up the contemporary variegated world economy, an overall economy within which the economies of all societies have been increasingly drawn together and subsumed.

Three Worlds

From the 1950s until the 1980s, the divisions in the world economy between capitalist and socialist countries on the one hand, and between rich and poor countries, on the other, led to speaking in terms of distinct **First, Second, and Third World** countries. The tripartite conceptualization of the world economy originally contained five connotations: political alliances in the cold war, type of socioeconomic structure, technological stage of development, geographic location, and standard of living.

First and Second World countries were politically and militarily aligned with the United States and the Soviet Union, respectively; Third World countries were nonaligned. The two superpowers competed for influence within Third World countries and for their votes in international forums such as the United Nations. First World countries had capitalist economies, Second World countries had socialist economies, and Third World countries were largely capitalist.

Technological stage of development, geographic location, and standard of living were thought to largely overlap. Western countries—those in North America and Western Europe—were industrial and enjoyed the world's highest standards of living. Eastern countries—the Soviet Union and its allies in Eastern Europe—were also industrial and had the world's second highest standards of living. Third World countries, which were located in Asia, Africa, and Latin America, were mainly agricultural and poor by international standards.

Three-worlds terminology was evocative of much of the bases of international divisions between countries within the world economy. But it was not without ambiguities and problems. Political alliances, economic systems, technological stages of development, geographic locations, and standards of living ceased to be as clearly correlated as they were in the immediate postwar years. Japan became one of the world's most prosperous countries. Many formerly agricultural Third World countries industrialized rapidly but still remained poor. It was always unclear where to place underdeveloped socialist countries such as Cuba and China. They were politically and economically in the Second World, but technologically and geographically in the Third World, and their standards of living varied greatly. South Africa was both a First and Third World country. Its minority white population enjoyed First World standards of living, while its majority black population had Third World living standards. And since the 1989 and early 1990s, transformations of the Soviet Union and Eastern Europe, there was no longer a separate Second World or socialist camp.

The strength of the three-worlds classification was its evocation of the reality that contemporary societies differed significantly both according to their socioeconomic structures and their standards of living. Those differences could be seen statistically through the 1980s. Of the 163 countries in the world in 1986, 148 with just over two-thirds of the world's people were capitalist, and 15 with nearly one-third of the world's people were socialist. But after 1989 the percentage of the world's population in socialist societies declined dramatically, and with it a large part of the utility of the three-worlds classification. The term Second World is now completely obsolete except for historical use. The terms First and Third World continue to be used, though less so than in the past. A number of sociologists conceptualized international differences in terms of First, Second, and Third Worlds (see, for example, Horowitz, 1966), and today the terms First and Third World continue to be ingrained in international social science. But other sociologists classified international differences in different, more directly sociological, terms.

Modernization

Since its inception, modern sociology has been concerned with the steep stratification of the world's countries. Just as societies are stratified along the lines of upper and lower classes, the world's societies are stratified along the lines of rich and poor countries. But as with many other issues in sociology, there are sharp disagreements and controversies regarding the causes and policy implications of this stratification.

On one side of this debate stands what can be loosely termed the **modernization** approach. According to its proponents—which include the World Bank, the International Monetary Fund, and the U.S. Agency for International Development, as well as a number of sociologists—countries are poor because they remain institutionally mired in premodern, largely agrarian-based structures. If they wish to develop and achieve more prosperity, they must modernize their institutional structures according to the already proven institutional structures of the advanced industrial societies. Among the policy implications of this approach are that poor countries should increase their economic integration with the modern dynamic parts of the world economy through export-oriented trade and hosting foreign investments. Foreign investments facilitate technology transfers from the advanced countries, which will accelerate economic modernization.

World-System

Beginning in the 1960s, some sociologists began to challenge key premises of the modernization school. They questioned whether the motives of rich countries for being involved in the poor countries were as benevolent as modernization theorists assumed, arguing instead that the rich countries had for centuries economically exploited the poor countries and continued to do so. By the 1970s, many of the proponents of this latter perspective developed what came to be known as the **world-system** approach.

Shannon (1989, p. 20) stated that the world-system approach begins from the premise that "an identifiable social system exists that extends beyond the boundaries of individual societies or nations." It is therefore "a mistake to view the world as a set of independent societies that can be analyzed by focusing solely on events internal to them." Sociologists who work within this perspective view the contemporary world-system as having begun to take shape in the sixteenth century; as being stratified between **core**, **semi-peripheral**, and **peripheral** countries; and as having exploitative relations between the core and other countries.

The core countries in the world-system now include the United States, most of the Western European countries, and Japan. As the world's most economically and militarily powerful countries, they are able to dominate the world economy and international politics. This domination has allowed them to economically exploit other countries, the proceeds of which have significantly bolstered their own economic development and prosperity. During the development of the world-system from the sixteenth century to the present, different countries occupied the center of the core: Holland in the seventeenth century, Great Britain in the nineteenth century, the United States in the twentieth and so far in this century.

At the other extreme are the peripheral countries, which include most of the countries of sub-Saharan Africa, China, India, some other Asian countries, and some Latin American countries. They are the world's economically weakest as well as poorest countries. Their main importance for the world economy has been mainly as agricultural and raw material exporters.

Between the two extremes in the world-system are semi-peripheral countries, which include the major Latin American countries, the poorer countries of Western Europe, the formerly socialist Eastern European and Soviet countries, northern African and Middle Eastern countries, and the rapidly industrializing countries of Southeast Asia (Taiwan, South Korea, Hong Kong, Singapore, and Malaysia). These countries contain both core-like and peripheral-like features. A minor but significant part of their economies is industrialized, while other parts remain agricultural or labor intensive.

World-system theorists (such as Amin, 1980; and Wallerstein, 1974, 1984) contend that it is no longer valid to think in terms of entirely separate national economies. Rather, there is now one international capitalist economy—the world-system—which is the basis on which national economies function. Individual countries have progressively lost sovereignty over their own economies. The more powerful the capitalist world-system grows, the more it, rather than national economies, becomes the arena of economic interests and class forces. The core economic powers seek to remove remaining barriers to the complete unification of the market by promoting free trade policies. By lowering tariff walls, they seek complete access to all markets. At the same time, though, political power continues to be based in states. A fragmented political order of different state powers overlays the increasingly unified capitalist world-system.

Development

Uniting all attempts to classify and understand international differences is a concern over **development**. In general terms, a developed society is one that has an economic base that is capable of supporting average standards of living equivalent to those prevailing in the United States, Europe, and other high-income societies. There are thus developed and developing societies. Beneath that broad generalization, though, lie a host of conceptual controversies, such that there is no international consensus on exactly what constitutes development: whether it is a multidimensional phenomenon and, if so, what are its dimensions and the relative importance of each.

Most theories of development emphasize in varying ways the dimensions of technology, income, and health. In the early post-World War II decades of the 1950s and 1960s, the quintessential developed societies of North America and Europe were industrialized, had high gross domestic products per capita by world standards, and enjoyed the highest health standards, as indicated by low infant mortality rates and long life expectancies. Many assumed that of the three dimensions, industrialization was the most important. According to this view, industrialization provided the base for economic growth and health improvements. The United States, European countries, Japan, and other developed societies owed their prosperity to having industrialized their economy. It followed that developing societies would also have to industrialize if they wished to improve their standard of living. Industrialization was thus the key to development.

However, by the 1970s it became apparent that the relationship between industrialization and development was more complex and problematic than originally assumed. Many developing countries accelerated their industrial development by hosting foreign corporate-owned factories. That did not necessarily lead to significant improvements in their standards of living or to any closing of the gap between their living standards and those of the developed countries. Part of the problem was that in the past, the developed countries had had endogenous industrial development based on their own domestic investments, whereas most of the industrial development taking place in the developing countries was being directed by and for foreign interests.

That, in turn, raises the question of the goal of development. Is it to produce a particular standard of living regardless of whether that standard of living has been surpassed by the most developed countries? Access to electricity and indoor plumbing would greatly improve the lives of many people in developing societies. Those improvements alone, however, would not enable them to enjoy typical contemporary developed country standards of living. Or is the goal of development to improve the standards of living to the point that they are equivalent to those of developed societies? The latter is a much more ambitious goal than the former.

There are further issues with the goal of development. The developed countries have high incomes and health conditions. It might be assumed that all developing countries should aspire to both. However, high developed country incomes have led to consumerist societies plagued with waste and the production of ecologically damaging pollution.

The World Bank (2007, Table 1) estimates that the average high-income country produces 12.8 metric tons of environmentally harmful carbon dioxide emissions per capita—sixteen times as high as the 0.8 metric tons per capita of average low-income countries. With the exception of the oil-rich microstate of Kuwait, the United States, with 19.9 metric tons per capita, has the highest rate. Burning of fossil fuels (petroleum, natural gas, and coal for the most part) in cars, for industrial use, to heat homes, and to produce electricity for a variety of uses is the major source of carbon dioxide emissions. These increase greenhouse gases in the atmosphere that are believed to be responsible for global warming. High-income developed societies thus have consumerist lifestyles that depend upon levels of energy consumption that would not be ecologically sustainable for all societies to embrace.

High health standards may well be a more reasonable goal for developing societies than high-income fueled consumerist standards of living. Amytr Sen has written that the goal of development should be to produce societies in which people can live long and live well. The old and seriously sick or injured know that having good health is more important than having money. Attaining the development goal of improved health standards may well be more possible and ecologically sustainable than encouraging the spread of consumerism and its large and ubiquitous shopping malls.

That reallocation of development priorities, in turn, raises the question of whether a world in which health conditions were improved and equalized internationally would require redistribution of income from the developed to developing countries. Less income in the developed countries would, in turn, require cultural shifts to alter styles of living that require high income and wasteful levels of consumption.

Key Terms and Concepts
(in order of presentation)

Capitalism
Commodities
Commodification
Socialism
Communism
Social Democracy

Infant mortality rate
First, Second, and Third World
Modernization
World System
Core, semi-peripheral,
    peripheral

Chapter 6

Global Trends

Global politics and economics in the first decade of the twenty-first century, as in the previous decade continue to be shaped most importantly, by the long-term consequences of the sudden and dramatic collapse of the Second World following 1989. That collapse facilitated acceleration of capitalist development on a global scale. With socialist economic systems no longer existing as an alternative or threat, central governments increasingly adopted free trade and privatization policies to reform and rationalize their economies according to capitalistic principles. **Globalization** became the watchword as transnational corporations, with the threat of socialism having subsided, attempted to draw all societies and regions into an international market in which they are the dominant actors. At the same time, critics such as Petras and Veltmeyer (2001, chapter 1) argue that the concept of globalization masks what is essentially a modern form of imperialism.

There is no question that free trade policies such as the North American Free Trade Agreement (NAFTA) and the General Agreement on Tariffs and Taxes (GATT), by removing governmental attempts to regulate trade and investment, led to a significant rationalization and growth of the world economy, but that growth had significant negative as well as positive social consequences. On the positive side, the prices of many consumer products decreased. On the negative side, the increasingly free circulation of capital was at the expense of worker security in developed countries and the growth of outsourced sweatshops in Third World countries (see Ross, 2004). A further worrisome feature was the effect of economic growth on the environment. Increasing industrial production in a rapidly growing world economy is increasing greenhouse gases and other forms of pollution as well as depleting many of the earth's nonrenewable natural resources.

Replacement of the bipolar Cold War world with a unipolar world-system in which the United States is the dominant military power has generated new antagonisms and conflicts. The United States responded to the 2001 World Trade Center attack in New York City by declaring a "war on terror" (see Chapter Eight) that has, to some extent, reoriented its military priorities. At the same time, the Bush administration pursued an aggressive policy of "regime change" to overthrow governments that did not conform to its foreign policy economic and political goals. It used various means, including supporting opposition parties in the former Yugoslavia, Georgia, Ukraine, and Venezuel,a and military invasions in Afghanistan and Iraq, to topple or attempt to topple existing governments.

In this still unfolding new global environment, the United Nations (2008, p. xxx) currently classifies economies as developed, in transition, and developing. The developed market economies are the traditional First World economies and are the most developed of the formerly communist Central and Eastern societies. The economies in transition are the other, less developed formerly communist societies, including the successor countries of the Soviet Union. The developing countries are the rest, with the UN singling out fifty countries as least developed.

In the discussion that follows, we will follow the UN system of distinguishing developed and developing societies. However, because of their historical importance, former communist and continuing communist countries such as China and Cuba will be discussed separately from other developed and developing countries. We will also discuss continuing socialist and semi-socialist elements of mixed economies and Venezuela's newly adopted "socialism for the twenty-first century."

Table 6–1 offers a quick orienting snapshot of the world's countries. The developed countries contain a little under 14 percent of the world's population and enjoy the world's highest average standards of living in

TABLE 6–1
Countries of the World

	Countries (number)	Population (millions)	Percent of world population	GDP per capita (PPP in US$)	Life expectancy at Birth*	Infant mortality rate
Developed	25	884.6	13.6	33,082	79.2	6
Former Communist	29	407.8	6.3	9,527	68.6	22
Communist	5	1,435.8	22.0	6,408	72.5	22
Developing	135	3,786.6	58.1	5,282	66.1	57
World	194	6,514.8	100.0	9,543	68.1	52

Notes: *years; **deaths in first year per 1,000 live births. PPP is Purchasing Power Parity, which is a statistical measure that adjusts for differences in costs of living. GDP is Gross Domestic Product. Infant mortality rate is the number of infants born live who die within the first year of life per 100,000 live births.

Sources: Calculated from UN (2008, p. xxx); and UNDP (2007, Tables 1, 1a, 5, and 10).

terms of incomes and health conditions; the former communist and communist countries, with 6.3 and 22 percent, respectively of the world's population, have lower average incomes and health conditions; and the developing countries, with the majority of the world's population (58.1 percent), have the lowest average incomes and health conditions.

DEVELOPED SOCIETIES

The developed countries—the United States, Canada, the United Kingdom, the Western European and Scandinavian countries, Japan, Australia, and New Zealand—have the following common characteristics:

- High gross domestic products per capita, average incomes, and capital accumulations, which support the world's highest average standards of living
- In many cases, a history of having held colonial possessions
- Labor forces that are increasingly concentrated in post-industrial service production, as opposed to industry or agriculture
- Labor forces made up of employees, as opposed to small business owners

- Significant exports of finished goods and capital

- Economies that are centers of research in science and technology

- Governments that offer rather than seek assistance from other countries

The economic strength and high average standards of living of the developed societies are products of high levels of capital accumulation built up over several centuries. Domestically, the accumulation process required grueling labor by working classes, in which upwards of sixteen- to eighteen-hour workdays in factories were common, along with high occupational injury rates and low wages. Historically, conquest, colonialism, and slavery played important roles. Profits and resources pumped out of dominated Asian, African, and Latin American countries quickened the rates of capital accumulation. Developed countries continue to significantly augment their capital accumulations through their participation in the world economy. Their international investments and comparative advantages in international trade produce net inflows of capital.

Labor Forces

Labor forces include all of those actively engaged in the production of goods or services. The size of a labor force is smaller than that of the total population of a society, since the latter includes children, retired persons, disabled persons, and others who are not engaged in production, as well as labor force members. (There is controversy over the status of homemakers, overwhelmingly women, who are not currently included. They produce services, but since their labor is not directly paid, they are not currently considered to be labor force members.)

Two great shifts historically have occurred in the distribution of labor forces in developed countries. The first was from agricultural to manufacturing employment. Rising levels of agricultural productivity decreased the need for labor in the countryside and thereby made it available for employment in urban-based factories, a shift that was accompanied by considerable social trauma, including the ruin of many small farmers and their families. Production of virtually all necessities of food, clothing, housing, and even health became industrialized. Tractors, harvesting machines, and food-processing machines made food production a literal industry. Workers operate sewing and sophisticated computer-guided cutting machines to mass-produce clothing. House builders no longer dig ditches and frame houses completely by hand; they have machines that speed and simplify those processes. Hospitals are now loaded with testing and other types of machinery.

The second was the post-industrial shift from manufacturing to service, administrative, and sales employment. Rising levels of industrial productivity decreased the need for factory, mill, and mine labor, making it available for employment in services (entertainment, recreation, restaurants, repair), administration (clerical and managerial), and sales.

The economic significance of post-industrial labor force distributions can be misleadingly overestimated. Regardless of where a labor force is distributed, agriculture and industry are still the essential components of any contemporary economy. No economy, no matter how advanced, can exist without food and other material goods. It is precisely because of the high productivity of agricultural and industrial workers that economies have surplus capital to invest in services, administration, and sales.

Transnational Corporations, Post-Fordism, and Flexible Accumulation

Large corporations, such as Wal-Mart, McDonald's, Microsoft, and General Motors, and the state are the major actors in developed capitalist economies. Up through the nineteenth century, family-owned capitalist firms were the dominant actors. By the early twentieth century, the joint stock corporate form supplanted the family-owned firm in importance. The corporate form arose as a result of fierce competitive struggles among individual capitalist firms in the middle and late nineteenth century for dominance over markets. By combining the capital of many individual capitalists in the form of stocks, corporations could achieve greater size and economic power than family-owned firms.

As these corporations grew, they became more powerful, allowing them to squeeze out competitors and capture increasingly greater market shares. They took over markets that were formerly served by small businesses, resulting in sharp declines in the proportion of farmers, retail store and restaurant owners, and other small business owners in labor forces. Correspondingly, as the proportion of small business owners declined, the proportion of employees grew. Today over 90 percent of the labor forces of the United States and Canada are made up of employees. A century ago in both countries, family farmers, Main Street merchants, and other independent owners predominated.

Corporate owners and managers design and control workplaces according to their interests. In 1914, Henry Ford revolutionized factory production by developing the assembly line, which enabled the mass production of a single standardized product at low cost. He coupled that innovation with paying his workers the then relatively high wage of $5 for an eight-hour workday. Ford challenged the old "Robber Baron" practice in the United States of paying workers as little as possible with the argument that for his company to prosper, his workers had to be able to afford to buy the cars that they built (Harvey, 1989). Ford's argument was similar to that of the economist John Maynard Keynes, who urged central governments during the Great Depression of the 1930s to redistribute some income to the lower classes to allow them to become effective consumers and thereby stimulate the market for factory products.

Ford's assembly-line innovation spread from automobiles to other industries rapidly, with resulting all-around increases in production and overall factory wages for the next several decades. But increases in production and wages were at the expense of workplace satisfaction. Sociologists such as Blauner (1964) interviewed workers and found that assembly-line work caused **alienation**. The restriction of each worker to performing a simple, repetitive motion—once a minute on most automobile assembly lines, day in and day out—produced boredom and precluded any sense of creative satisfaction with the work done. Accounts by workers themselves, such as Boggs (1963) and Hamper (1991), provided further confirmation that assembly-line work was inherently alienating.

Since the 1970s, a number of sociologists and other commentators have used the term **Fordism** for this period of capitalist development that was characterized by mass assembly-line production of standardized products for mass markets. These commentators detected the beginning of a shift in that decade in some industries in the developed countries toward post-Fordist strategies. By that, they meant retooling assembly lines so that they could vary their products to satisfy different consumer demands, with shorter production runs for each. Instead of producing one standardized car, an automobile factory now attempted to develop a number of different models that appealed to different segments of a more diversified market.

Post-Fordism strategies are part of a new stage of **flexible accumulation** in the developed economies. By flexible accumulation is meant that corporations now must increasingly develop ever-changing strategies to remain competitive and profitable as the global economy becomes more competitive. In large part, the shifts from Fordism to post-Fordism and from fixed to flexible accumulation began to occur in the 1970s because Western European and Japanese industry had recovered enough from the damage of World War II to seriously challenge U.S. industry for domination of the world market. U.S. industry had been the undisputed leader of world industrial production for the two decades following World War II, precisely because it had emerged from the war unscathed. With the world economy even more competitive by the 1990s, industrial survival came to depend upon ever more efficient production techniques.

In this context, Japanese industry developed the concept of just-in-time production. Factory production traditionally relied on keeping a warehouse well stocked with raw materials so that they could be used as needed: just-in-case production. But Japanese managers observed that this was a costly practice that drove up overall production costs. They accordingly developed a new system whereby a factory ordered only the quantity of materials that it needed and only when it needed them, thus avoiding the costs of over-ordering and warehousing. With lower production costs, the company could sell at a more competitive lower cost.

On one level, flexible accumulation strategies have produced more efficiency and a greater array of products that are tailored to meet increasingly diversified consumer demands; the great diversity of clothing colors and styles is one example. But it was only a logical next step to adopt a flexible policy toward worker security. If corporations are flexible in how they design products and produce them, they are also increasingly flexible in where they produce, with which workers, and under what conditions of job security. In the fixed-accumulation period, factory production was rooted in particular communities. Once the factory was built, the corporation had to remain there and workers enjoyed a certain stability and job security. There might be layoffs during recessions, but they were only temporary. The factory remained in town and rehired its laid-off workers once the economy improved. But as the global econ-omy became more competitive and the costs of constructing new facto-ries decreased, corporations found that they could lower labor costs by moving from high- to low-wage areas. In the United States this has meant a shift of industrial production from the largely unionized high-wage northeastern and midwestern states to the largely nonunionized low-wage Sunbelt areas of the south and southwest. Internationally, it has meant the shift of labor-intensive industries, such as clothing and electronics, from relatively high-wage developed countries to develop-ing areas, including Mexico and the Caribbean islands.

Even where corporations maintain workplaces in the same communi-ties, they have increasingly used rising proportions of temporary and part-time workers, who are paid low wages, receive few if any benefits, and have little if any job security, in order to lower labor costs. In the United States labor force as a whole, the proportion of temporary and part-time workers has grown. Thus, a decreasing unemployment rate, which has traditionally been taken to be an indicator of economic recovery and increasing prosperity for the labor force, may mask deeper problems, as when a laid-off $17-an-hour worker, who had had a relatively secure job for twenty years with medical, retirement, and other benefits, is only able to find a new job that is part-time at $8 an hour with little security and no bene-fits. The labor force can thus be regarded as having a core of full-time work-ers with relatively secure positions that pay enough to maintain a relatively decent standard of living, and a periphery of low-paid, part-time and tempo-rary workers. Flexible accumulation has been accompanied by the growth of the periphery at the expense of the core.

Growth of the State

By the early part of the twentieth century, governments of the now-developed societies became increasingly involved as accumula-tors of capital through taxation and as employers in their capital-ist-directed economies. State and private economic activities became thoroughly intertwined, with state-collected taxes often being used to fi-nance private corporate activities. State contracts, such as for the pro-duction of military goods, became one of the major sources of business for private corporations. James O'Connor (1973) estimated that in the

United States as much as one-third of the labor force was employed directly or indirectly (through private employers financed by government contracts) by local, state, and federal government. Between 1980 and 2006, as a result of the conservative Reagan and both Bush administrations' attempts to reduce government spending, local, state, and federal government spending as a proportion of gross domestic product shrank from 30.5 to 27.6 percent (U.S. Bureau of the Census, 2003, Tables 440 and 475; U.S. Census Bureau, 2008, Tables 417 and 455). All Western European government spending is higher, ranging from 34.4 (Ireland) to 55.4 (Sweden) percent of gross domestic product (Organization for Economic Cooperation and Development, 2008).

Regardless of whether governments increasingly adopt policies of engaging private contractors to perform functions that they formerly performed directly themselves—for example, engaging a private contractor for garbage collection rather than using city-owned trucks and employees—it is still state revenue that is financing the economic activity.

European Social Capitalism versus American Free-Market Capitalism

Despite sharing similar levels of high national income, the Western European countries and the United States differ significantly in how they economically and socially structure their societies.[1] In particular, they differ in how they deal with capitalism's natural tendency to polarize incomes between the rich and poor. In all capitalist societies, the power to monopolize income opportunities grows with competitive market advantage. Businesses and economic classes rise in the competitive struggle at the expense of their vanquished foes. In time the victors cumulatively become stronger and the vanquished slip further behind. In the completely laissez faire capitalism of Darwinian struggle, the rich would eventually monopolize all income opportunities at the expense of all other classes, producing extreme class polarization, inequality, and potentially political destabilization.

Within a capitalistic framework, the state is the only institution strong enough to counter this natural tendency of market competition to heighten inequality. Governments have the power to use progressive taxation to redistribute income downward through social programs such as free access to health care and child care, which disproportionately benefit disadvantaged classes.

Both European countries and the United States use **progressive taxation**—taxing higher income groups at higher rates—to create social programs that redistribute income. The former countries, however, use progressive taxation more aggressively, which allows them to finance more redistributive social spending. Following World War II, they developed comprehensive welfare states from which middle as well as lower classes significantly benefit. On the other hand, the United States has a minimalist approach to welfare state development, restricting those programs as much as possible to the most destitute.

The European approach, embracing the values of social solidarity and inclusion, uses high taxes and generous welfare programs to ensure that all citizens have equal access to vital social services, such as health care, child care, subsidized housing, and old-age pensions. The American approach, emphasizing the national values of individualism and freedom, has low taxes and few welfare programs. It relies on citizens purchasing their own services according to what they can individually afford. As a result of the different approaches, Western European societies have significantly lower rates of poverty, less inequality, and lower rates of crime (see Table 6–2).

In Europe welfare programs have broad backing, in part because they benefit broad sectors and in part because they conform to continental values of social solidarity and inclusion. In the United States, other than the Social Security program—an American welfare program from which middle classes benefit—welfare programs have been stigmatized because they supposedly drain tax dollars to support an undeserving population of the poor.

At one pole of the developed countries—the most capitalistic, with the United States being the leading example—workers receive most of their income in individual wages, use them to purchase what they need, pay low taxes, and have little in the way of social benefits. They pay individually according to what they can afford for their health care, child care, educational, and other needs. At the other pole—the most social democratic, with most European countries being the leading examples—workers pay higher taxes, receive a smaller part of their income in individual wages, and receive a significant part of their income in what

TABLE 6–2
Europe and the United States

	European Union–15	United States
Population	385,792,000	296,410,000
PPP Income per capita	$34,792	$44,260
Tax revenues as percent of GDP	39.7	25.5
Infant mortality rate	3.9	6.8
Life expectancy	79.1	77.9
Poverty rate (percent)		
absolute	7.4	13.6
relative	9.1	17.0
Income inequality (ratio richest to poorest 10 percent)	9.3:1	15.9:1
Homicide rate per 100,000 population	1.4	5.6
Incarceration rate per 100,000 population	109	738

Notes: Absolute poverty is the percentage of households with less than $11 a day income. Relative poverty is the percentage of households with incomes less than half of the median income of all households. The 15 European Union countries are: Austria, Belgium, Denmark, Finland, France, Germany, Greece, Ireland, Italy, Luxembourg, Netherlands, Portugal, Spain, Sweden, and United Kingdom.
Sources: OECD (2008); World Bank (2007); UNDP (2007).

can be called social wages: that is, free access to government-provided goods and services.

The more incomes are distributed in individual wages, the more unequal is the effect. Each person receives a different amount of wages and consequently can afford a different amount of consumer items. The more consumers receive income in social wages, the more egalitarian is the effect. Each person receives a part of her or his income in items such as health care and education that are shared equally with others. Americans thus consume more individually and unequally; Europeans consume more in common and equally.

The first model maximizes individual choice. If workers receive most of their income in individual wages and are required to give up relatively little of it to taxes, then they are free to use it as they please to consume what they can afford. They can choose to pay a high premium for a health insurance plan that includes coverage for all the possible illnesses or injuries that may befall them, or save some money for other purchases by gambling a bit and paying a lower premium for a plan with less coverage. The market adapts to their freedom of choice by offering a great variety of options. Additionally, the market rewards those who have worked hard to attain higher incomes by allowing them to consume at higher levels than others. Health insurance plans in the United States thus vary greatly in coverage and cost to the consumer.

The second model maximizes egalitarian access to basic goods and services and social solidarity—a felt obligation of the more prosperous to share with the less prosperous. Individuals pay higher taxes but receive more government services, such as free health care and child care. They have less individually disposable income but less expenses. They do not worry about how much health care coverage they can afford because equal access to it, like access to public education, is taken for granted. Even if they are without work or income, they know that should they become injured or sick, they will have as much access to health care as anyone else.

FORMER COMMUNIST SOCIETIES

The United Nations (2008, p.xxx) lists twenty-nine contemporary countries that through the 1980s were countries or parts of preexisting countries, such as the Soviet Union and Yugoslavia, that had combined communist political and socialist economic systems, but since then have developed multiparty political systems with capitalist economies. The UN until recently considered all of them to be "in transition" (between state-planned and market economies). It now considers ten to be developed, and the rest, with the exception of Mongolia, to still be "in transition" (see Table 6–3). The ten were designated as developed when they joined the European Union between 2004 and 2007. The UN does not place Mongolia, which borders Russia, China, and Kazakhstan, in either the developed or in transition categories. Yet Mongolia clearly falls in the general category of a former communist society that has transformed politically with a multiparty system and economically with privatization of industry and market reforms.

In 1989, as these countries abandoned communism and reentered the capitalist world market, the key social question was whether their aver-

TABLE 6–3
Former Communist Societies

	Countries (number)	Population (millions)	GDP per capita (PPP in US$)	Life expectancy at birth*	Infant mortality rate**
Developed	10	102.2	13,868	74.0	8
In Transition	18	3,303.1	8,161	66.8	27
Southeastern Europe	6	24.2	9,171	74.9	10
Commonwealth of Independent States	12	278.9	7,894	66.1	28
Mongolia	1	2.6	2,107	65.9	39
Total	29	407.8	9,466	68.6	22
World	194	6,514.8	9,543	68.1	52

Notes: *years. **death in first year per 1,000 live births. All averages are weighted for population sizes.
Sources: Calculated from UN (2008, p. xxx); UNDP (2007, Tables 1, 1a, 5, and 10).

age standards of living would gradually improve toward those of the First World or sink toward those of the Third World. Or would there be different experiences for different countries, sectors, and classes as new economic and class forces transformed and pulled apart the old orders?

Minimally, the transition from socialism to capitalism in these countries required three fundamental changes: First, a shift from public to private ownership of a significant number of enterprises, resulting in the creation of a new class of entrepreneurial capitalists and the widening of class differences. Second, a shift from centralized state control and administration of prices to letting them be determined by market forces, resulting in immediate increases in prices for basic necessities that had been kept low. Third, in order for privately owned companies to compete in market conditions, they had to have the authority to dismiss unprofitable workers, resulting in these countries' first postwar experience with significant unemployment. Thus, the predictable costs of the transition were increased inequality, higher cost of living, and the introduction of unemployment.

In 1994 the first extensive United Nations study of economies in transition (UNICEF, 1994a) documented the extent to which inequality, cost of living, and unemployment—the negative costs of capitalist development—had indeed increased (see Table 6–4). The study examined the experiences of the nine countries—Russia, the Ukraine, Albania, Bulgaria, the Czech Republic, Slovakia, Hungary, Poland, and Romania—that contained three-quarters of the total population of all countries involved in the transition to market economies. In these countries, average unemployment rates jumped from far less than 1 percent in 1989 to over 10 percent by 1993. Meanwhile, as unemployment was rising, so too was the cost of living, as the average prices of food, rent, clothing, and other necessities rose significantly.

While the upper strata benefited greatly by being able to garner high incomes and amass fortunes that were not possible during the communist era, the majority saw their average living conditions deteriorate dramatically. Per capita real income fell by a quarter. The most severely impacted saw their living conditions slide into poverty. If in 1989 an average of 16.5 percent of people were poor in the nine countries, by 1993 the rate had more than doubled to over 39 percent. If new millionaires were created at the top while average incomes declined and poverty expanded at the bottom, it is not surprising that income inequality grew by an average of 6 percent in the region.

An explosion of criminal activity accompanied the general social deterioration. The crime rate for formerly community countries more than doubled between 1989 and 1993. During the same period the male murder rate increased by 79 percent.

One of the most disturbing impacts of the transition was an increase in death rates. In the same way that the statistical association between rises in unemployment and death rates has been studied (see Chapter One), the association between the transition and rising death rates was examined. Between 1989 and 1993, the average crude death rate (deaths per thousand) for the nine countries jumped from 11.4 to 12.4. Cumulatively in that period, 800,000 more people died than if the nine countries had maintained the same death rates they had in 1989. These avoidable deaths represented the most severe consequences of the transition. Indeed, according to the report, "the mortality and health crisis burdening most Eastern European countries since 1989 is without precedent in the European peacetime history of this century."

Mortality rates, though, did not rise for infants and children. The highest increases in mortality were borne by males between the ages of twenty

TABLE 6–4
Rough Transition; Regional Averages for Former Communist Societies

	1989	1993
Infant mortality rate per 1,000	17.6	17.0
Life expectancy at birth (years)	70.7	70.5
Crude death rate per 1,000 population	11.4	12.4
Unemployment rate (percent)	0.1	10.3
Poverty rate (percent)	16.5	39.2
Index of real income	100.0	74.9
Index of income inequality	100.0	106.0
Index of crime rate	100.0	168.6

Source: Calculated on the basis of UNICEF (1994)

and fifty-nine, according to Giovanni Andrea Cornia (UNICEF, 1994a, p. vi.), for three transition-related reasons: "widespread impoverishment, erosion of preventive health services, sanitary infrastructure and medical services, and social stress." A surge in heart and circulatory diseases, stimulated by the stressfulness of the social adaptation crisis, accounted for about 80 percent of the excess deaths. There was also a significant 25 percent increase in suicide rates. Cornia concluded that:

> Most of the additional mortality due to heart problems, suicide, homicide, alcohol psychosis and cirrhosis of the liver appears to be related to an explosive rise in social stress, a condition which arises when individuals have difficulty responding to new and unexpected situations. Greater poverty, unemployment, migration, divorce, separation, loss of relatives, lack of hope, loss of self-esteem, insecurity about and fear of the future, increase in criminal offenses, conflicts at work and in the family are the main sources of stress. This "social adaptation crisis" has been exacerbated by the collapse of the political, social and economic organizations which framed people's lives for 50 or more years—a collapse entailing loss of national pride, a widespread sensation of meaninglessness and loss of purpose. (UNICEF, 1994, p. vi)

A subsequent study (UNICEF 2001) found that by 1999 the number of excess deaths in the economies in transition had climbed to 3.2 million, most of which were concentrated in the western Commonwealth of Independent States (CIS) states.

It is now clear that while all of the transition countries experienced increases in poverty, inequality, unemployment, and crime and all saw average incomes decline, the negative impacts were more concentrated in some countries than others. The Central European countries of the Czech Republic, Slovakia, Hungary, and Poland and Slovenia from the former Yugoslavia suffered the least; the Western Common-wealth of Independent States countries of Russia, Ukraine, Belarus, and Moldova suffered the most. The former Yugoslavian republics other than Slovenia, Southeast European countries of Albania, Ruma-nia, and Bulgaria, and former Soviet Baltic, Caucasus and Asian re-publics fell in between in negative impacts. The Central European countries hit bottom in 1993, when real wages averaged only 76 per-cent of what they had been in 1989. As of 2002, real wages had recov-ered to 6 percent higher than what they had been in 1989. At the other extreme, real wages in Russia and the Ukraine did not bottom out until 1999, when they hit lows of 36 and 39 percent, respectively, of what they had been in the last year of the Soviet Union. As of 2001, they had recovered to 53 and 59 percent, respectively, of what they had been (UNICEF, 2001, 2004).

The different experiences with inequality provide a partial answer to which of the transition countries are coming closer to First World and which to Third World patterns. All of the countries during their commu-nist periods had less unequal distributions than the developed market so-cieties. In 13 of the 19 for which data were available, inequality had grown by 1999 to surpass the developed society average. In four—Moldova, Armenia, Georgia, and Tajikistan—it had grown to typical Third World levels. The Central European countries and Slovenia con-tinue to have lower than average inequality for developed societies and appear to now fit within the range of Western European average living standards.

COMMUNIST SOCIETIES

The end of socialism after 1989 in Eastern Europe and the Soviet Union reduced by about a quarter the number of people living in commu-nist-governed countries. The net result is that today over one out of ev-ery five of the world's people still live in those types of countries. The Peoples Republic of China is by far the largest and most populous. Its 1.3 billion people make up 91 percent of the total. The other four are the So-cialist Republic of Vietnam (85 million), the Democratic Peoples Re-public of Korea (24 million), Cuba (11 million), and the Lao Peoples Democratic Republic (6 million).

As in 1988 (Table 5–1) middle- and low-income socialist countries continue to have lower infant mortality rates and longer life expectancies than their capitalist counterparts. Nevertheless, there are important concerns over the long-term survival of the socialist model: whether their next stages will result in progress in socialist development or restoration of capitalism.

Three of the five—China, Vietnam, and Laos—adopted one form or another of market socialism in which varying degrees of private business ownership and market development are allowed. North Korea continues to maintain a statist form of socialism, with maximum state ownership of business and central planning. All maintain that they continue to have socialist economic structures, though all are less socialist than in the past, and one may no longer be technically socialist in a strict definition of the term. Cuba made significant changes in its model during the 1990s but stopped short of embracing market socialism.[2]

In the traditional statist form of socialism, sometimes called a command economy, the state developed a central plan for how major economic resources would be collected and allocated, and then set corresponding production goals for state-owned enterprises, which made up the bulk of all major enterprises. Common to market socialist reforms in China, Vietnam, and Laos was to deemphasize the role of central planning so that enterprises could respond autonomously to market conditions. The state continues to influence the general direction of economic development, but without being involved in every decision of production and resource allocation. It shifts from micro- to macro- managing the economy.

State-owned enterprises have been transformed in varying ways. In one reform they remain state-owned but must be self-financing, self-managed, and market oriented. In another they are transformed into cooperatives that their workers own and manage. The most extreme is to partially or completely privatize them; that is, sell stock in them or sell them completely to capitalists. There are limits to how far market socialist reforms can be pushed without the economy becoming substantially capitalist. Up to a certain point, the reforms are simply capitalist solutions to socialist problems, the main problem being that of economic growth. In a parallel sense, developed capitalist societies created welfare states as socialist solutions to capitalist problems.

TABLE 6–5
Communist Societies

	Population (millions)	GDP per capita (PPP in US$)	Life expectancy at Birth*	Infant mortality rate**
China	1,313.0	6,757	72.5	23
Vietnam	85.0	3,071	73.7	16
Laos	2.9	2,039	63.2	62
North Korea	23.6	—	66.8	—
Total	1,435.8	6,408	72.5	22
World	6,514.8	9,543	68.1	52

Notes: *years. **deaths in first year per 1,000 live births. Averages weighted for population sizes.
Sources: Calculated from UNDP (2007, Tables 1, 1a, 5, and 10)

Since 1978 China has engaged in the most extensive market socialist reforms, including privatizing a significant number of state-owned enterprises. As the reforms were implemented, Chinese society took on more of a capitalistic character, with increases in unemployment, job insecurity, and inequality. Its harshest socialist critics maintain that it has become economically and socially capitalist in all but name. It represents the seeming paradox of a nominally communist party guiding capitalist development. Hart-Landsberg and Burkett (2004, p. 109) write that "the Chinese experience reveals that market socialism is an unstable formation whose internal logic tends to marginalize socialism in favor of the market and the full restoration of capitalism."

Vietnam since 1986 has instituted market socialist reforms but not as extensively as those in China. In the 1990s the country restructured rather than privatized state-owned enterprises, so that today they still function as key actors in the national economy while becoming self-financing and market oriented. Vietnam, like China, experienced high GDP growth rates in the 1990s and early part of this century, indicating that restructuring state enterprises can produce as much increase in productivity as can completely privatizing them.

The collapse of the Soviet Union hit Cuba like a bolt from the blue. Loss of its largest trading partner and source of foreign aid sent the economy in a downspin. Gross domestic product fell from 19.6 billion dollars in 1989 to 12.8 billion in 1993, when it bottomed out and recovery began (Brundenius, 2002, Espinosa Martínez, 1999). Cuba then rushed through a series of reforms—including building up a tourist industry, soliciting foreign investment, allowing small private-owned businesses to develop, and creating a dual currency in which the American dollar could circulate[3]—to make its economy more able to compete in the capitalist-dominated international market. Its approach to market socialist reforms is closer to the Vietnamese than Chinese examples, since there have been no privatizations of its own state-owned enterprises (Saney, 2004, p. 184). At the same time, as in Vietnam, the state now enters into joint ventures with foreign capital and, in some cases, allows completely foreign-owned enterprises to operate in the country.

Implementation of market reforms has led to increases in inequality in all of the countries. The share of total national income of the poorest 10 percent of Chinese households has fallen to 1.6 percent, which is similar to the lowest for East and Southeast Asian countries. The shares of the poorest 10 percent in Vietnam and Laos, at 4.2 and 3.4 percent respectively, though, remain significantly higher than the average for those countries. On the other end of the scale, China's new rich of the upper 10 percent have 22 times the income of the poorest 10 percent, a ratio that is higher than that prevailing in the United States (UNDP, 2007, Table 15). In the case of Cuba, Brundenius (2002, p.378) estimates that the share of the lowest 20 percent has fallen to 4.3 percent, while that of the richest 20 percent has increased to 58.1 percent. The rate of inequality is now comparable to that of the United States, though it is still the lowest in Latin America. An important mitigating factor is that Cuba implemented its reforms without altering access to free medical care and education. Social wages in terms of subsidized equal access to state-provided health, educational, and other social services remained the same while individual wage differences increased.

WHITHER SOCIALISM?

There is no question that since 1989 socialism as ideology and practice has declined greatly. To pronounce it dead, though, would be a gross exaggeration. The early decades of the twentieth century, discussed in the previous chapter, saw socialism as a movement divide into the rival wings of social democracy and communism. Both wings in modified forms are active today. Both continue to embrace the goal of one or another form of socialism eventually replacing capitalism.

Although since the 1980s all of the five remaining communist countries have instituted market reforms—China the most and North Korea the least—all maintain that those reforms have been within the context of constructing socialism in the long run. An examination of constitutions and communist party documents from all of the countries finds no evidence that the goal of socialism has been rejected or abandoned, despite the officially permitted growth of capitalist economic activities. The Chinese Communist Party, for example, argues in its constitution that the main objective of the present period, which could last as long as one hundred years, is to build up the economy through multiple means, including expanding private enterprises and market relations. All continue one-party government systems and maintain that these are democratic because the party represents and responds to the interests of the people.

The Socialist International—the major international expression of the social democratic variant of socialism—today has 170 member organizations, including many governing and leading opposition political parties, especially in Europe. It continues to advocate democratic socialism and the creation of public property, albeit within the framework of a mixed economy. The European welfare state, which their social democratic political parties support, arguably incorporates socialist principles.

Virtually all contemporary economic systems in that respect incorporate some socialist principles to the extent that they provide publicly financed services, such as education and mail delivery, to their populations. Virtually all countries have mixed public and private sector economies. It is true that conservative laissez faire ideas have attained great influence in many countries, leading to contractions of public sectors and services. Those contractions, in turn, have led to the exacerbation of old problems, including poverty, deterioration of public servicesa nd increasing costs of deregulated and newly privatized services. To the extent that their public support defending or rebuilding public sectors and services, socialist principles—though not necessarily called such—will rebound.

One of the ironies of the world historical year of 1989 is that, as the Central and Eastern European communist governments were collapsing and social democratic parties were becoming defensive about the concept of socialism, in a Latin American country—Venezuela—"socialism for the twenty-first century" was being born. That year the International Monetary Fund had pressured the Venezuelan government to raise gasoline prices in order to increase revenue to service debts to international lenders. That caused bus prices to go up sharply—the final straw for the poor who rioted in reaction. The army reimposed order at the cost of hundreds to thousands of lives; the full toll is unknown.

The riots and their repression led to a meltdown of Venezuela's traditional governing establishment. In the crisis atmosphere that enveloped the country in the aftermath, Hugo Chávez, a charismatic military officer, captured the imagination of the poor and with their overwhelming support was elected president in 1999.

Chávez saw himself as representing the poor in a revolutionary struggle to transform the deeply unequal country. At first he advocated mild economic and social reforms to increase economic sovereignty and redistribute income to the poor. But as the revolution deepened and he survived an attempted military coup because of support from the poor, his ideas radicalized in a socialist direction. In 2005 he announced that he would be running on a platform of creating "socialism for the twenty-first century" in the 2006 election, which he won handily with 63 percent of the vote.[4]

Venezuela, however, is not a socialist or a communist country. It has nowhere near the development of public ownership and planning as does Cuba. With the notable exception of the publicly owned oil industry, most sectors of the economy are firmly in private hands and will remain so, with the government having no plans to socialize them. In addition, there is no intention to turn Venezuela into a one-party state.

Socialist economic development takes the relatively modest form of the government encouraging and supporting creation of cooperative enterprises, especially among the poor, that operate alongside the traditional capitalistic sectors of the economy (Piñeiro Harnecker, 2005). Politically, the government embraces the concept of participatory democracy by urging the population to become involved in community councils to plan how resources (mainly from oil profits) should be invested in resolving problems. Socially, the government uses oil revenues to sponsor a large number of free educational, health, and other programs for the population.

For the time being, Venezuela's socialism remains a work in progress. They have no firm socialist model in mind. There is no intention to recreate what existed before 1989 in Central and Eastern Europe or to copy Cuba's model. Rather, they are experimenting with policies and programs to create a future model of socialism that they hope will have strong popular support.

Elsewhere in Latin America, leftist and center-left governments have replaced conservative ones. In those most closely allied to Venezuela—Bolivia, Ecuador, and Nicaragua—overt mention of socialist ideas is common. In others, socialist ideas hover in the background as the brakes are being put on the neoliberal capitalistic policies inherited from the 1990s.

DEVELOPING SOCIETIES

Developing (not including communist) societies are concentrated in Asia, Africa, and Latin America and contain 58 percent of the world's population. Between the poorest and relatively most prosperous there are more differences in average living conditions than among developed societies. The ratio between average incomes in Portugal, the relatively poorest of the developed countries, and the United States, the richest, is about one to two. In contrast, the ratio between average incomes in the low-income and upper-middle-income developing countries is about one to four. The difference in the Western Hemisphere, for example, between average living conditions in low-income Haiti and upper-middle-income Argentina is much greater than between those of the United States and Canada (World Bank, 2007, Table 1). Caution must therefore be exercised in drawing generalizations about developing countries. Nevertheless, it can be concluded that developing societies tend to have:

- Lower gross domestic products per capita, average incomes, and accumulations of capital than those prevailing in the developed countries
- Extensive poverty

- In many cases, a history of having been a colony
- Relatively high proportions of their labor force still in agriculture
- Significant imports of finished goods and capital in the form of loans and investments; reliance on the export of a limited number of raw materials and/or goods assembled in foreign-owned factories.

The typical developing country has a foreign-dominated economy, with its economic functioning being dependent on continual infusions of foreign investments, loans, and aid from developed countries, for which it pays a high price in profit repatriations (profits sent to the investor country), interest payments, and economic sovereignty. Their economies thus function at, and are integrated into, a lower level of the world economy and division of labor.

There is considerable dispute among social scientists regarding the historical origins of Third World inequality. Dependency theorists, such as Baran (1957), Frank (1969), Wallerstein (1974), and Amin (1980), hold that as the capitalist world economy developed, European countries seized control through conquest, colonialism, and other forms of

TABLE 6–6
Developing Societies

	Population (millions)	GDP per capita (PPP in US$)	Life expectancy at birth*	Infant mortality rate**
Arab States	313.9	6,716	67.5	46
East Asian and Pacific	559.7	6,805	69.6	34
Latin American and Carribean	545.3	8,467	72.7	26
South Asia	1,587.4	3,416	63.8	60
Sub-Saharan	722.7	1,998	49.6	102
Other	57.6	—	—	—
Least developed	765.7	1,499	54.5	97
Total	3,786.6	5,282	72.5	57
World	6,514.8	9,543	68.1	52

Notes: *years. **deaths in first year per 1,000 live births. All averages weighted for population sizes. Excludes communist societies.
Sources: Calculated from UNDP (2007, Tables 1, 1a, 5, and 10)

domination of large parts of the economies of Asia, Africa, and Latin America. They forced Third World economies into molds that served their own development interests. The agriculture of Caribbean island countries, for example, was oriented toward production of sugar for export to the international market rather than all-around production for domestic needs. Modernization theorists, such as Rostow (1960), Hagan (1962), and Eisenstadt (1966), hold that the causes of Third World poverty and misery are primarily domestic, lying in precapitalist and pre-industrial institutional structures that are antithetical to development needs. Still other social scientists blame rising population growth rates for continuing poverty in the developing countries (an argument that will be treated in detail in Chapter Twelve).

Overall, since 1965 there have been improvements in average living conditions in developing countries, despite the existence of extreme poverty and starvation in some areas. Infant mortality rates for the first year of life, for example, fell between 1970 and 2005 from an average of 109 to 57 per thousand live births, indicating significant average improvements in nutritional and public health standards (UNDP, 2007, Table 10). However, at the same time, the gap between average living conditions in the developed and developing countries has been growing rather than declining. In 1980 the 18 percent of the world's people who lived in upper- income countries consumed 77 percent of total world income; in 2006 the proportion of the world's people living in the upper-income countries had declined to 15.8 percent, but they consumed the same percent of total world income (World Bank, 1988, 2007). Hence, while absolute living conditions are improving on average in developing countries, the gap between them and those of the developed countries continues to widen.

Virtually all development theorists agree that agricultural efficiency is the primordial first step of development. The more technologically efficient the agriculture of a country, the more agricultural workers can be shifted to industrial and service production. The more developed a country, the relatively lower the number of agricultural workers in its labor force and the lower the proportion that their product represents in the total economic product. The World Bank (2007, Table 4) reports that in 2006 agricultural production accounted for only 2 percent of the total gross domestic products of all high-income economies, compared to 20 percent for low-income economies, ten times as high. Agricultural workers take up an even larger proportion of the labor forces of low-income countries, since agricultural products generally have lower market values than other products.

The more agricultural the technological level of a country, the more it must rely on agricultural exports to finance its imports and development projects. This is a problem, since the prices of agricultural commodities have tended to decline over time relative to those of other goods on the world market. Hence, countries dependent on agricultural exports are in a precarious position in the world market.

While the prices that food exports fetch on the world market have tended to decline relative to those of other commodities, those are often prices that are higher than what could be gained from domestic sales. For that reason, many, especially large, landowners in developing countries have reoriented their production from domestic to more lucrative First World markets. In a number of cases this practice has caused shortages and corresponding price rises for food staples of the poor. In Brazil, large landowners shifted production from black beans, a diet staple of the poor, to soy beans, which fetched a higher price on the international market. As the production and therefore the supply of black beans decreased, their domestic price went up and out of the reach of many poor people. In Central America, landowners turned cropland into pastureland on which to graze cattle ultimately destined to feed the voracious appetite in the United States for fast-food hamburgers. Export-oriented agricultural practices since the 1960s have forced Mexico to import corn and beans, the traditional diet staples of the poor (see Barkin, 1990 and Philip L. Russell, 1994).

The problem of food exports is linked to the larger problem of reliance on raw materials versus finished product exports. In 1970, 72 percent of all exports from developing countries were in the form of agricultural, fuel, mineral, and other raw materials, whereas 73 percent of all exports from developed countries were in the form of finished industrial goods. As with food exports, over time the value of most other raw materials, with oil being a notable exception, has declined on the world market, while that of many finished goods has increased. Many developing countries thus found the value of their exports decreasing at the same time that the costs of their imports were increasing. As a result, a number have adopted development strategies of shifting away from reliance on raw material exports. By 1992, only 47 percent of developing country exports were in the form of raw materials, a sharp decline from the 72 percent recorded in 1970 (World Bank, 1994, p. 190). However, it still remains true that a large number of especially low-income developing countries remain reliant on a small number of raw material exports for the bulk of their export incomes.

As development strategies have inevitably led toward industrialization and away from reliance on raw material exports, many developing countries, such as India, Mexico, Brazil, and Argentina, have in recent years substantially industrialized large parts of their economies. But this industrialization has not automatically resulted in closing the gap between First and Third World living standards. As developing countries have increased their rates of industrialization, the developed countries have increased their competitive advantages in the world market by controlling the production of high-technology goods.

The effects, whether beneficial or harmful, of First World investments and loans to the developing countries have been the subject of considerable debate. First World multinational corporations own and control large parts of the industrialized sectors that do exist in developing countries. While the multinational corporation provided the initial capital and technological expertise to set up the employment-providing activity, much of the profits are repatriated to the source country, precluding their use for the development benefit of the host country.

Foreign investment in industry has taken different forms in the developing countries. In some cases it involves setting up a factory in the host country to avoid having to pay tariffs. Volkswagen, for example, set up a factory in Brazil in order to be able to sell its cars there at a competitive tariff-free price, just as it and Japanese auto makers do in the United States. In other cases, it involves setting up a factory solely to take advantage of low-priced labor, with the resulting goods being sold primarily on the world, as opposed to the developing country's, market.

In this latter respect, since the 1960s multinational corporations from the United States, Japan, and other developed countries have set up large numbers of assembly plants in Taiwan, South Korea, Mexico, Singapore, Haiti, and other developing countries. In a typical arrangement, components of blue jeans are designed and produced in the developed country. They are then shipped to the Third World factory for assembly, and the final product is then exported back to the developed country for sale. The Mexican border cities as well as large parts of the Caribbean Basin and Southeast Asia are now major locations for these types of assembly plants.

Foreign investors, along with host Third World government officials and developers, maintain that these factories bring needed technology transfers, industrial development, and employment opportunities. Critics counter that they are only a new form of exploitation in a more highly developed international division of labor. They argue that these working classes are now producing products as well as profits that will be exported, rather than serve national development needs.

In Mexican border cities, such as Mexicali, Ciudad Juárez, and Matamoros, these assembly plants are called *maquiladoras*, and they have displaced the tourism industry as the major source of employment. Up until recently, over 80 percent of the maquiladora work force was young women in their teens and twenties. As the maquiladoras expanded in the 1990s, they added more male workers, but most still rely primarily on the labor of young women, who now make up about 60 percent of the work forces. Maquiladora managers believe that young women are more dexterous than men and therefore more suited to quick-paced assembly work. They also believe that they are more docile and thus less likely to cause labor problems.

Maquiladora industrialization has had social consequences. On the positive side, it has produced economic growth in the border cities that has contributed to improvements in standards of living. But with employment opportunities more available for young women than men in the Mexican border cities, family roles have been severely disrupted. Women who had not been part of the paid labor force are now in it, while many men have had to remain at home unemployed. Tensions have grown within families, and the rate of male family desertion is high. Considerable numbers of children are now being brought up only by mothers who work full days in the maquiladoras. Adequate child-care facilities are in chronically short supply. It is thus clear that maquiladora industrialization has been experienced as a mixed blessing in the border cities.

Since the 1970s, payments of interest on loans held by foreign banks, governments, and multilateral agencies (primarily the International Monetary Fund and the World Bank) have surpassed repatriation of profits from investments as the largest source of the foreign drain of potential Third World capital. For the most indebted of the developing countries, foreign debt service (principal and interest) payments represent a serious hemorrhaging of potential development capital. Mexico and Brazil, for example, made payments in 2005 on their foreign debts equal to 17.2 and 44.8 percent, respectively, of their total export earnings. That would be comparable to an individual having to make credit card payments of almost a fifth to almost a half of her or his income. Overall for the developing countries, foreign debt service was 13 percent of export earnings (UNDP, 2007, Table 18).

From the point of view of First World financial interests, the danger that lurks in the Third World debt crisis is that there will not be the wherewithal to keep up with payments, thereby causing interruptions in cash flow. From the point of view of developing countries, the heart of the crisis is that debt servicing payments are increasingly made at the expense of providing necessities for domestic populations, as well as having funds available for investment in development.

In a number of cases, severely indebted countries have reached the point where they did not have sufficient export earnings to maintain payments, resulting in crises. News of Third World debt crises is in and out of the newspapers, like a sore on the world economy that festered and receded but never fully healed. The International Monetary Fund (IMF), an organization to which most countries belong but which is controlled by the developed countries, manages the debt crisis on a country-by-country basis. The customary IMF resolution of a country's debt crisis is to require that it adopt an austerity plan that includes lowering government spending and wages. The intended effect of each IMF-prescribed austerity plan is to lower costs of production of the country's exports and make them cheaper on the world market, thereby increasing demand for them and overall export earnings. Part of the increased earnings can then be used to resume payments on the country's debt. In return for adopting an austerity plan, the IMF gives the green light to other international lenders to resume short- and long-term loans. In the short run, cash flows resume the circulation. But in the long run, new loans only add to the accumulating mountains of debt, as well as mortgaging the future financial sovereignty of the country.

By 1988, it was clear that the mounting debt of many Third World countries was unpayable, and that attempts to force payment through imposition of IMF austerity programs were provoking civil disorder. In February 1989, riots against the IMF austerity program for Venezuela resulted in hundreds of deaths. The exact toll has never been determined. U.S. Treasury Secretary Nicholas Brady then announced a new policy, known as the Brady Plan. First World lenders and multilateral agencies, including the IMF and the World Bank, would forgive part of the principal of loans in return for the country's adopting a more favorable climate for foreign investment and free trade. Specific agreements would be worked out on a country-by-country basis. In 1996 the World Bank and IMF developed the Heavily Indebted Poor Countries Initiative. As a result of it and other plans, there has been significant debt reduction. According to the United Nations (UNDP, 2007, Table 18), foreign debt service as a percentage of export earnings for the least developed countries declined from 16.9 in 1990 to 7.0 in 2005. Debt relief, however, has come at a high price: it has been conditioned on acceptance of privatization, free trade, and other IMF and World Bank dictated policies that severely compromise economic sovereignty and, in many cases, have worsened living conditions for the poor (see Jubilee USA, 2003).

An additional problem facing most developing countries is the tendency for their upper classes to claim unusually high proportions of national income for their own consumption. The standards of living of the Third World rich rival and sometimes surpass those of their First World counterparts. To maintain those styles and standards of living, they corner as much of the national income as they can, precluding the distribution of many necessities to the majority poor; and much of that income is spent out of the country on shopping trips to Europe and the United States, vacations, luxury imports, and foreign schooling for their children. The Third World rich hence attempt and largely succeed in living a lifestyle that is equivalent to that of their First World counterparts. But the cost of that lifestyle, especially the part that is spent outside the country, weighs heavily on the country.

We can summarize the relationships between technological development, foreign economic domination, and living standards in the developing countries as follows. First, while Third World stages of technological development are low compared to those of First World countries, it is no longer accurate to simply state that Third World countries are agricultural and First World countries are industrial. That simple dichotomy leads to the false conclusion that industrialization automatically increases living standards. Second, foreign First World interests through investments and loans significantly dominate much of developing economies and thereby siphon off profits and interest payments. Instead of contributing to domestic capital formation and growth, these profits and interest payments rebound to the benefit of the already stronger First World investor economies. Largely as a result of these two conditions, the living standards of developing countries remain low compared to those of developed countries.

Key Terms and Concepts
(in order of presentation)

Globalization	Flexible accumulation
Development	Free market capitalism
Labor force	Social capitalism
Alienation	Progressive taxation
Fordism	Foreign debt

ENDNOTES

[1] I have discussed this topic comprehensively in *Double Standard: Social Policy in Europe and the United States* (Lanham, MD: Rowman & Littlefield, 2006).

[2] Cf. "Cuba does not give a name to its socialism. I personally have used the term 'socialism of the possible' because the conditions that Cuba finds itself in now have limited our dreams. We have given a greater role to the market. There are forms of agreements and alliances with fractions of transnational capitalism that result in mixed enterprises and other forms of association. But we have not given up on forming new men and women. Politics and ideology continue to be in first place with a permanent campaign that we call the battle of ideas." (Communication to the author from José Bell Lara, sociology faculty, University of Havana, January 18, 2005)

³Cuba stopped circulation of the dollar in 2004 in response to U.S. efforts to enforce its economic blockade of the island by punishing European banks that accepting Cuban-origin dollars.

⁴For historical background, see Gott (2005). For a revealing account of the relationship between Venezuelan poverty and the rise of Hugo Chávez, see Hardy (2006). For an analysis of the elements of Venezuela's "socialism for the twenty-first century," see Lebowitz (2006).

Chapter 7

Classical Sociological Theory

Three nineteenth- and early twentieth-century theorists—Karl Marx (1818–1883), Emile Durkheim (1858–1917), and Max Weber (1864–1920)—established the most important parameters and controversies of classical sociological theory. They had different philosophical premises, methods for studying societies, and research interests. They had different perspectives regarding the character and future of **capitalism** as a way of structuring societies and ways of life. And they had different perspectives regarding **socialism** and the active socialist movements of their day that advocated it.

Marx concluded that conflicts of interest lay at the roots of capitalist societies, which he considered to be history's most sophisticated embodiments of class exploitation and alienation. He sought, in theory as well as practice, the complete revolutionary overthrow of capitalism and its institutions. Durkheim was more inclined to stress the extent to which the institutions of contemporary societies functioned to produce relative social harmony. As a reformer, he believed in the continued existence of capitalist and class societies, but with modifications to make them function better. Weber was a pessimistic realist who viewed societies as being dominated by powerful elites. He granted that capitalist societies were alienating and exploitative but could see no better alternative.

In one way of viewing classical theory, Marx, Durkheim, and Weber arrived at different intellectual conclusions, founding respectively what are called today the conflict, functional, and elite approaches to social theory and sociology in general. But from another point of view, the foundations of divisions in social theory simply reflected the ideological struggle between capitalism and socialism and the consequent division of the technologically advanced countries into First and Second World societies. In one camp belonged the works of Durkheim and Weber; in the other those of Marx.

All of the classical theorists viewed the modern era as being qualitatively different from the past. But how they conceptualized the differences between past and present, as well as future implications, differed. Each identified the onset of the present era with different though overlapping developments: commodity production for Marx, complex divisions of labor for Durkheim, and formal rational modes of thought for Weber. Each emphasized a different variable as an important determinant of the character of societies: Marx, the importance of economic institutions; Durkheim, the growing complexity of social relations; and Weber, the importance of cultural conditions, including religions and other belief systems. Both Weber and Durkheim found in their analyses of Protestantism important keys to understanding Western societies. Weber found a relationship between the culture of Protestantism and the cultural conditions necessary for capitalist development, while Durkheim found a relationship between Protestant individualism and the propensity to commit suicide.

MARXIAN THEORY

Socialist ideas and movements spread in Europe in reaction to the early nineteenth-century industrial factory system. Grimy factory districts, grueling sixteen-hour workdays, low pay, high industrial accident rates, and employment of child labor produced widespread revulsion. Capitalism as a system came under close moral scrutiny. Some urged reforms, such as limiting the length of the workday, increasing rates of pay, and abolishing the use of child labor. Others went further, concluding that the capitalist system as a whole needed to be replaced by a socialist one of equality and common ownership of factories, mines, banks, and other workplaces. Marx and his collaborator, Frederick Engels, were the greatest exponents of the latter course of action. Through their relentless and meticulous critique of the capitalist present, they constructed the theoretical basis for a socialist future. They saw their role as revolutionaries whose theoretical and scholarly work had practical revolutionary ends. They did not see themselves as academics producing scholarship for scholarship's sake.

The Dialectics of History

Materialism and **dialectics** were the key premises of Marx's and Engels' approach to social understanding. As materialists, they believed that human, not providential, actions were responsible for determining the fates of societies and courses of history. This fundamental premise immediately put the founders of modern socialist theory at odds with religious thinkers, who correctly accused them of being atheists. For generations, there was a consequent clash between Marxian and religious ideas. In the 1960s, though, the seemingly unbridgeable gap between Marxian and religious social beliefs began to close somewhat with the development of the Catholic theology of liberation movement. Catholic activists, especially in Latin America, found common ground with Marxist revolutionaries. They shared a commitment to social justice for the poor. Even on the basic philosophical and religious question of belief in God, Marxist revolutionaries and theologians of liberation concluded that their differences did not keep them from being on the same side in social struggles. For that reason, the period since the 1960s witnessed the formerly unthinkable phenomenon of a guerrilla priest fighting alongside Marxist-inspired revolutionaries. Camilo Torres, a sociologist and a priest, fought and died as a guerrilla in Colombia in 1965. His example inspired the activism of many in the Catholic theology of liberation movement. The character of the Nicaraguan Sandinista Revolution was also importantly influenced by the alliance of Catholic adherents to the theology of liberation and Marxist-inspired revolutionaries.

As dialectical thinkers, Marx and Engels believed that reality was always in a process of change. They sought through their materialist and dialectical approach to uncover the human causes of social and historical change.

According to dialectical logic, which Marx and Engels inherited from G.W.F. Hegel (1770–1831), all processes of change have three abstract component parts or stages: **thesis, antithesis, and synthesis**. The thesis is the beginning stage of development. Since nothing remains permanently the same, antithetical conditions arise that make the continued existence of the original thesis stage impossible. The antithetical conditions force a change in the thesis, resulting in the synthesis stage of development. But dialectical change does not happen once and for all. It keeps on going as chains of development, each link of which has its own separate thesis, antithesis, and synthesis "moments." Each synthesis is simultaneously the thesis of a new round of dialectical development.

Put differently, dialectical logic assumes that change develops as a result of resolving **contradictions**. Contradictions are problems. What causes change is the existence of contradictions that need to be resolved. Humans continually resolve the contradictions or problems of their existences. The task of social science is to identify those contradictions and work on their resolution.

Marx and Engels believed that social and historical development followed this kind of general dialectical pattern. Communal societies with primitive technologies were the thesis of world history, class societies the antithesis, and a future high-technology-based communism would be its synthesis. The task of Marxist social scientists was to accurately portray and actively participate in the changes that resulted in the progress of history toward its communist-egalitarian future and synthesis. For the capitalist present, the task was to reveal how the capitalist system worked. In particular, it was to uncover the economic, class, and political dynamics of capitalist societies so that the working class—the agent of socialist change—would be conscious of both its historical mission and the obstacles it faced.

While Marx and Engels as dialectical thinkers saw all of their work as occurring within the broad context of the unfolding of world history, which they sought to understand, they concentrated their energies most on analyzing the capitalist present. Future socialism would come about, in their view, not by utopian designs and wishful thinking, but rather because unresolvable contradictions would develop within the capitalist system that could only be resolved by a complete socialist transformation. Their task was to analyze how the capitalist system functioned and to identify those unresolvable contradictions.

To give the devil his due, Marx and Engels clearly noted that capitalistic societies had been history's most technologically innovative and materially productive, but at great human cost. Capitalist societies produced great wealth through exploiting labor under alienating conditions.

Value Theory and Exploitation

Marx powerfully argued that exploitation was the lever of capitalist accumulation. According to his **labor theory of value**—the key premise of Marxian economic theory—all economic value in capitalist societies results from the labor of those who work directly on products. Economic value as used here is what Marx called **exchange value**, which he distinguished from **use value**. The first type of value refers to the value of a commodity in the marketplace, such as the price of the pencil is eighty-nine cents. The second type refers to the value that a commodity has for a consumer, such as the value of a pencil to a person is that it enables her or him to write or draw.

According to the theory, stock owners, speculators, financiers, and other members of the capitalist class control but do not produce exchange value. Workers produce more exchange value each workday than the amount of value that capitalists invest in their wages and other costs of production. Marx (1867) called this extra sum produced by workers **surplus value**. Hence, workers produce but do not receive surplus value. Rather, capitalists exploit workers by expropriating the surplus value that workers have produced.

Out of surplus value comes profit. Part of profit is distributed as income to capitalists and their families. The other part is set aside to form new capital. The origin of capital, then, is surplus value produced by workers. Capitalists pump surplus value out of workers, which is turned into profits and new capital and is used to continually control workers.[1]

Alienation and Labor

Marx (1844) saw **alienation** as the necessary complement of exploitation. By alienation he meant that the worker was objectively removed from control over the capitalist-owned means of production and resulting products. Ownership of the **means of production** gives capitalists the power to set the conditions of labor. Workers work on someone else's product, under conditions designed by others, and in the interests of others. As a result, their job is performed under objectively alienating conditions.

Marx viewed labor in the abstract positively. Labor was the synthesis of specifically human activity. Laborers creatively think out resolutions to contradictions of existence and then effect them through work. Creative labor is a specifically human activity in a double sense. First, humans are the only animals to have the capacity for creative thought. They can labor consciously. Second, through exercise of their creative capacities in their labor, they develop themselves. But wherever the conditions of labor are objectively alienated, as they are for large parts of the labor forces in capitalist societies, they lose this potential for their work to be a humanly fulfilling experience.

Marx's theory of labor alienation under capitalist conditions was part of his more general theory of alienation, which he saw as occurring in all class societies. According to him, both creative labor and human solidarity are necessary conditions for human fulfillment, either one of which could be alienated. Creative labor is precluded for large parts of the labor force when they do not own the means of production. Human solidarity is precluded in all societies based upon divisions of class interests; that is, all types of class-based societies, not just capitalism.

Class Conflict and Revolution

Capitalists and **workers**, in the Marxist understanding, are the fundamental classes in capitalist societies, and their interests are antagonistic. Marx (1865, p. 64) noted that "if wages fall, profits will rise; and if wages rise, profits will fall." But more importantly, according to him, capitalists have an interest in maintaining the system that has profited them so much, but workers have a historic interest in ending their exploitation and alienation. In his and Engels's view, capitalist governments, like all governments, exist ultimately to maintain the prevailing economic system and protect the interests of its dominant class, despite whatever democratic pretensions they may exhibit. Marx and Engels (1848, p. 110) concluded in a famous formulation that "the executive of the modern State is but a committee for managing the common affairs of the whole bourgeoisie."

They considered ideology to be an important underpinning of the capitalist system. In an early writing, they maintained that the ideas of the ruling classes tended to be ruling ideas:

> The ideas of the ruling class are in every epoch the ruling ideas: i.e., the class which is the ruling material force of society is at the same time its ruling intellectual force. The class which has the means of material production at its disposal, consequently also controls the means of mental production, so that the ideas of those who lack the means of mental production are on the whole subject to it. The ruling ideas are nothing more than the ideal expression of the dominant material relations, the dominant material relations grasped as ideas; hence of the relations which make the one class the ruling one, therefore, the ideas of its dominance. (Marx and Engels, 1846, p. 67)

Put simply, according to the Marxian view, the economically dominant class is able to make its own ideas and perspectives "ruling ideas" through its ownership or control of "means of mental production" such as newspapers, television stations, publishing houses, and educational institutions. In that sense, the economically dominant class has the most power to make its ideas ruling ideas. But its power is not absolute. Nonruling classes have different experiences and social perspectives. They can develop ideas of their own, especially concerning social questions. Logically, the different experiences of each class foster different consciousnesses.

Marx and Engels were especially concerned with the development of working-class or proletarian **class consciousness**, which they saw as a revolutionary force. They optimistically assumed that eventually the working class would gain a class consciousness of its historical interests and struggle to end capitalist domination. In its place, they would establish a socialist society through common public ownership of at least the major productive, financial, and commercial institutions. The goals of socialism would be to progressively end class exploitation and institute egalitarian solidarity.

Marx and Modern Sociology

Marxian theory and ideology have had a large impact on sociology, the social sciences in general, and the development of subsequent history. Marx, Engels, and other socialist theorists fundamentally challenged the bases and legitimacy of capitalist societies and their dominant classes. They threw down the gauntlet, setting off raging controversies, which will continue into the future, over the fundamental question of whether humanity would be better served by continuing the capitalist form of organization or by replacing it with socialistically organized societies. From Marx and Engels came the overall materialist and dialectical theories of historical development, which posit the eventual supplanting of the capitalist stage of history by higher socialist and communist formations in which equality and social justice would reign, and the theories regarding the economic, class, and political characteristics of capitalist societies.

Marx and Engels's social theories have influenced contemporary sociology in particular in a number of ways, two of which stand out. First, their radical critique of capitalism with its revolutionary implications set off a furious ideological struggle that continues to rage across all of the social sciences. Their social theories remain the standard from which all socialist alternatives proceed. At the same time, they are the target of all ideological defenses of capitalism. Neither side of this debate, which has continued with rivers of ink as well as blood for over a century and a half, has been able to definitively prove its case. Each has proved its case to its own satisfaction, but not to that of the other side. History may well be the ultimate and only possible judge of whether Marx and Engels were fundamentally right or wrong. In any event, they achieved world historical importance for formulating the debate over the origins, character, and future of capitalist societies.

Second, their class theories and hypotheses have had a special influence within sociology. Their class definitions continue to be adhered to by their followers. As capitalist societies develop, Marxian-influenced sociologists attempt to chart the internal development and changes in the working class (for example, the growing proportion of white-collar workers), study the internal development of the capitalist class, chart the decline of small businesses, and interpret the meaning of the growing importance of employed professionals and managers (often referred to as a new middle class), and portray the overall dimensions of the class system as it develops. Marx and Engels's hypothesis that eventually the working class would develop a class consciousness of their historical class interests continues to intrigue social theorists and be a question for social research.

Leninist Theory

If Marx and Engels were the towering figures of nineteenth-century Marxism, V.I. Lenin (1870–1924) was the comparable figure for the twentieth century. As architect of the 1917 Bolshevik Revolution in Russia, he more than any other single individual was responsible for setting the century's subsequent course. The Bolshevik Revolution originated the cleavage between First and Second World countries. If it had not occurred, the course of twentieth-century history, including the character of the present period, would have been substantially different.

In addition to his world historical importance as the practical leader of an epochal revolution, Lenin was a theorist in his own right. Like Marx and Engels, his writings were wide-ranging, producing social theories in a number of areas. The centerpieces were theories of imperialism, revolution, and the state. All three are components of what today is known as **Marxism-Leninism**, which for decades was the dominant school of social science as well as ideology in Second World countries and influenced such Third World revolutionaries as Mao Zedong, Ho Chi Minh, and Fidel Castro. It continues to be the ideological paradigm of the ruling communist parties in communist countries.

Lenin's (1916) theory of **imperialism** represented an updating of Marx's and Engels's analyses of capitalism. Marx had constructed a theory of the inner logic of the capitalist mode of production. Lenin, building upon that analysis, noted that by the early twentieth century, two developments—monopolization of ownership and internationalization of investments—within the leading capitalist countries had added new dimensions to the system. Marx and Engels had noted them as incipient tendencies in the nineteenth century. By the early twentieth century, the time of Lenin, those tendencies had matured into prominent characteristics of the capitalist system whose full analysis was unavoidable. Lenin defined imperialism as:

> capitalism at that stage of development at which the dominance of monopolies and finance capital is established; in which the export of capital has acquired pronounced importance; in which the division of the world among the international trusts has begun, in which the division of all territories of the globe among the biggest capitalist powers has been completed. (Lenin, 1916, p. 737).

Within the leading capitalist countries—Great Britain, the United States, Germany, France, and Japan—fierce competition between corporations for shares of markets had resulted in winners who enlarged their shares and losers who were driven out of business. Smaller numbers of corporations now controlled larger shares of their respective markets, giving them near-monopoly powers, allowing those corporations to realize superprofits. But not all of the excess capital that they thereby accumulated could be reinvested profitably in their own countries. They had to find outlets for it in colonial and semi-colonial areas controlled by their countries. Following the development of the monopoly stage of capitalism in the last quarter of the nineteenth century, there was a mad scramble by the great powers to increase colonial possessions and semi-colonial spheres of influence.

By 1900, all five of the great powers had substantially increased their colonial possessions and enlarged their economic influence in formally independent Third World countries. Lenin (1916, p. 726) cited Supan, who calculated that between 1876 and 1900 the proportion of African territory colonized by the European powers jumped from 10.8 to an astounding 90 percent. In language that strikingly foretold contemporary issues of Third World development, Lenin (1916, p. 734) characterized as semi-colonial "the diverse forms of dependent countries which, politically, are formally independent, but in fact, are enmeshed in the net of financial and diplomatic dependence."

Monopoly corporations expanded their foreign investments, gaining control over mines, plantations, and factories within colonial territories and semi-colonial spheres of influence. These favored investments turned out to be even more profitable than investments within their own countries, stimulating further investments and economic domination of Third World countries by the great powers.

All of the great powers scrambled to expand their colonial possessions during the transition from competitive capitalism to **monopoly capitalism** and imperialism. In Asia, Great Britain had India, the world's second most populated country. France had Indochina; the origins of the Vietnam War go back to this French colonial period. The United States defeated Spain in the 1898 Spanish-American War and took Puerto Rico and the Philippines as colonies. According to Lenin's

(1916, p. 730) figures, by 1914, over one-third of the world's people were living in colonies.

Lenin predicted that two types of wars would characterize the twentieth century. The great powers would fight among themselves as each attempted to expand, at each others' expense, colonial possessions and semi-colonial spheres of influence. At the same time, colonized Third World countries would seek independence through wars of national liberation. Lenin characterized World War I as a war of the first type, in which the great powers were fighting over the redivision of economic control of world territories. Wars of the second type, that is, of national liberation, broke out especially following World War II in Algeria, Indochina, Mozambique, Angola, and other Third World colonies.

Lenin advocated that workers in First World countries oppose militarist policies that led to wars of the first type. His clear advocacy of colonized countries having the right to self-determination (political independence) won a following for himself and his party among such revolutionaries in the colonized countries as Vietnam's Ho Chi Minh.

Lenin believed that part of the relative prosperity of First World countries resulted from repatriation of superprofits derived from foreign investments in the colonial and dependent countries. Part of those superprofits underwrote the incomes of the best-paid sectors of the working class, producing political conservatism and acquiescence to imperialist policies among them. Lenin's solution to this dilemma was for First World revolutionary parties to organize sectors deeper within the working class who did not have a material stake in the continuation of the imperialist system.

Lenin's theory of revolution in Russia was earlier developed in such pragmatically titled writings as "Where to Begin" and *What Is to Be Done* (1902). Capitalism had developed relatively late in Russian history. Even at the beginning of the twentieth century, precapitalist economic and social conditions prevailed in large parts of the country. Urban workers—the base of what Marx and Engels had assumed would be a revolutionary proletariat—were a small minority. The economy was still mostly rural, with semi-feudal landlord and peasant classes. Unlike in the Western European countries, there was little hint of democratic development within the state. The state retained the autocratic character of centuries-old czarism.

In one way of thinking, Russia was an unlikely candidate for the type of socialist revolution envisioned by Marx and Engels. It was economically and politically backward. In one of Marx's (1859) original conceptions, socialist revolutions would take place after all of the developing potential of capitalism had been exhausted. That was hardly the case in turn-of-the-century Russia. But in another way of thinking, the Russian situation was potentially revolutionary. It was a part of the capitalist world. It was clearly ripe for change. The slowly dying body of czarism was surrounded by many would-be successors. In the struggle for post-czarist power, Marxists had as much chance as anyone.

Lenin, as did many, foresaw the eventual disintegration of czarism, and he created a strategy of preparation for that event. The revolutionary vanguard party was the key instrument of that strategy. In an early debate and resultant split with less radical social democratic socialists, Lenin (1902) argued the need for a vanguard rather than a mass party as the vehicle of socialist strategy. A mass party is open, above ground, loosely organized, and seeks to gain as many members as possible from the public. Lenin argued that such a party could not succeed in actually carrying out a revolution against czarism or the socialist transformation of Russian society. Rather, he argued, a tightly organized and disciplined party of professional revolutionaries with highly developed Marxist principles of ideological unity was needed.

Lenin's theory of the **vanguard party** proceeded from the observation that most revolutions did not fully command the support of more than a minority of the population. The American Revolution, for example, was fully supported by only about one-third of the population. One-third was against it, favoring continued colonial status, and the remaining third did not take a position. The same had been true of the French Revolution. Lenin believed as a kind of historical truism that as periods of potential revolution approached—in Marxian language, as dialectical contradictions began to ripen—populations stratified into vanguard sections that desired revolutionary change, reactionary and backward sectors that wanted to maintain the status quo, and middle sectors that vacillated or did not take positions. The concept of the vanguard political party, which would be made up of self-conscious revolutionaries recruited from the vanguard sections of the population, flowed from that observation.

Such a political party would be made up of full-time, tightly organized revolutionaries. While not appealing for mass membership, it did appeal for mass support among those oppressed classes of the population—workers and peasants—that it believed had an objective interest in revolutionary change. Party members would be drawn from two sources: the oppressed classes—in whose interest the revolution would be carried out—and supporters from other classes. Workers and peasants stood to gain the most from a revolution. Capitalists and landlords had the most to lose. Small-business owners—the petty bourgeoisie—would be in the middle, gaining some advantages from a radical change and losing others. Clipping the wings of the strong competition from big businesses would be to their advantage. But a socialist state would also follow policies that would curtail their freedom to market goods to their best advantage.

The overall revolutionary potential of the different classes thus became stratified according to their economic interests. Also, within each class there would be class-conscious individuals, whose class stand would be directly based on their class's objective interests, and others, who would either be neutral toward a revolution or take the position of a class other than their own.

In many ways the strategy was based on merging the radical intelligentsia from middle- and upper-class origins, who saw the necessity of a revolutionary transformation, with the working and other oppressed classes—especially the peasantry—who would be the vehicles for that transformation. Lenin's strategy for merging radical intellectuals with the working and other oppressed classes was consistent with an important observation made earlier by Marx and Engels:

> In times when the class struggle nears the decisive hour, the process of dissolution going on within the ruling class, in fact within the whole range of old society, assumes such a violent, glaring character, that a small section of the ruling class cuts itself adrift, and joins the revolutionary class. (Marx and Engels, 1848, p. 117)

Lenin envisioned revolutions as occurring in two stages. In the first, the old regime would be defeated. During this stage, broad unity could be achieved around the single goal and perceived necessity of ending the old form of government. The defects of old regimes—such as oppressiveness, corruption, and foreign domination—were usually glaring. Once the old regime was defeated, the revolutionary process would enter its second stage, that of defining and constructing a new type of government. During this stage, there would be inevitable differences among the forces that had brought down the old regime. The ensuing struggle for power would narrow the basis of unity.

A revolutionary party, in Lenin's reasoning, had to be conscious of the different conditions prevailing in the two stages. Its tactic in the first stage was to detonate the revolutionary process by appealing to broad unity around such goals as independence for a colony, ending dictatorship or military rule, and getting rid of corruption. (The famous slogan of the first stage of the Russian Revolution was "land, peace, and bread," which responded to peasant landlessness, the war weariness of the Russian people as World War I dragged on, and famine conditions resulting from the war.) The goals would be based on the prevailing conditions. The party would not prominently agitate for socialism. Once the old regime had been defeated, the party would then move to a higher level of struggle in which its goal would be the construction of socialism.

Lenin's theory of the **two-stage revolution** dovetailed with his analysis of class positions and stands cited above. In the first stage, elements from all classes, not just workers and peasants, would unite around broad goals of ending the discredited regime. The core of unity would narrow in the second stage to those who had revolutionary socialist working- and peasant-class stands.

Lenin advocated organizing the revolutionary party according to **democratic centralist** principles. The party was to be democratic in the sense that all the incumbents of leading committees and offices were to be elected by members. It was centralist in the sense that it was organized as a strict hierarchy with the decisions of higher bodies binding for lower ones. Base members would vote for leaders, who would represent them in higher decision-making bodies, but there would be no direct election of the highest leaders by all of the members. The highest leaders would be elected by members of high-level bodies who had been elected to represent lower-level members. In the interest of effectiveness, decisions once made would have to be carried out and publicly supported by all members, even those who were in disagreement.

Lenin (1917, 1918) maintained, as had Marx (1875) before him, that the new socialist state had to take the form of a revolutionary **dictatorship of the proletariat**. By that he meant that it had to represent exclusively the class interests of the working class and its allies. The class interests of capitalists and landlords would not be represented. Furthermore, the working class, through its vanguard party, had to have a firm hold on state power in order to survive. Counterrevolutions, led by ruling classes driven out of power and supported by foreign powers, were virtually inevitable after every radical revolution.

Societal unity, in Lenin's reasoning, would be a necessary condition for constructing the new socialist order. As factional fighting within a revolutionary party would divert energy away from the revolutionary tasks at hand, competing political parties within a new socialist society would bottle up the energy needed for carrying out radical economic and social transformations.

The Leninist model of democratic centralist party organization was carried through to the construction of the Soviet state after the triumph of the Bolshevik Revolution and the successful defense of its power during the 1918–1920 civil war and attempt at counterrevolution. It became the political model of the one-party centralized Bolshevik state. Leninists argued that by promoting unity rather than political divisiveness, one-party systems advanced the socialist goal of social solidarity. They also justified one-party systems with the argument that workers and other oppressed classes had one overall class interest—attaining social justice through ending exploitation—which could be most efficiently advanced by a single unified revolutionary political party. However, creation of highly centralized control through one-party states has long been viewed by critics as inherently undemocratic.

Leninist social theories have had relatively little influence in Western social science, where they were either ignored or treated simply as part of the cause of fundamental defects in communist-organized countries. Their influence continues, of course, in the remaining communist countries of China, Vietnam, Cuba, North Korea, and Laos. In Third World countries, Lenin's theories of imperialism and revolution continue to circulate widely.

EMILE DURKHEIM

When Emile Durkheim was thirteen years old, the citizens of Paris, dissatisfied with how their government was conducting a war with Germany, rose up and seized control of the city. They declared it an independent commune—what came to be known historically as the Paris Commune. French troops with tacit German cooperation then retook the city in fierce street fighting that left twenty thousand people dead.

Marx (1871) condemned the brutal repression of the communards and judged their struggle as having been a progressive response to class conflict that pointed the way toward socialism. Indeed, the Paris Commune is often cited as the world's first socialist revolution. Durkheim, when he came of age a few years later, would see it differently: as a breakdown in social order to be avoided at all cost in the future. His social theory would become an alternative to Marx's analysis of capitalism by providing social policies to shore up the social order. If Marx was a revolutionary who advocated transforming the basic structure of the social order, Durkheim was a reformer who sought changes that would make the existing social order function better. In contemporary ideological terms, if Marx laid the theoretical bases for socialism and communism, Durkheim contributed to the development of early twentieth-century liberalism. He is to social liberalism what John Maynard Keynes was to economic liberalism.

Positivism and Functionalism

Durkheim's approach to sociology embodied strong elements of **positivism** and **functionalism**. He inherited the positivism from August Comte, the mid-nineteenth-century founder of sociology, and shared with early anthropological theorists of his day an organic and functionalist approach to the study of societies.

Positivists believe that sociology can and should adopt natural science methods to study societies objectively. In their view, social scientists should follow the basic natural science procedures and techniques: classification and measurement of matter, determination of cause and effect relations among variables, and experimentation to test hypotheses. Contemporary neopositivism also emphasizes that sociology should deliver nonpolitical and value-free analyses. Positivism and neopositivism have had considerable influence in the development of sociology, but not without controversy.

There is also a strong strain of antipositivistic thought in sociology that believes that the emphases of positivism and neopositivism are misplaced and misleading. Antipositivists argue that the objects of natural science and social science are fundamentally different. Natural scientists study the essences and interactions of nonthinking or noncreatively thinking entities that are of a different order than themselves. Social scientists study the meanings and interactions of creatively thinking beings who belong to their own species. Because of the fundamental difference in the objects of study, antipositivists believe that different methods of study are needed in the natural and social sciences.

Antipositivism has two branches. The first stems from the belief that the object of the human sciences should be to uncover the subjective meanings of human interactions. This approach is represented in some parts of the work of Max Weber, George Herbert Mead, hermeneutics, and phenomenological sociology. The second branch stems from the belief that it is both impossible and undesirable for sociology to be value-free. They believe that there is no contradiction between the need of objective understanding and the need to actively engage in reforming or radically changing a society. This current of antipositivism runs through the works of Marxist and other activist-oriented sociologists.

Functionalism is an approach to the study of societies that is rooted in the **organic analogy** that there are a large number of parallels between the functioning of a human organism, with its brain, central nervous system, cells, muscles, and heart, and that of a society, with its ideas, classes, division of labor, and culture. Functionalists believe that the relations between the parts of society are thought to be similar to those between the organs of a human body. As the human body is an organism in which the whole is greater than the sum of its parts, societies can be viewed as social organisms in which their wholes are greater than the sums of their parts. Neither one are simply collections of their constituent parts, since the parts when combined create new higher level entities—life in the first case and social existence in the second. If societies, like human bodies, are viewed as functioning organically, then each subpart must have a function—that is, a role—in contributing to the survival of the entire organism. The task of the social theorist is to determine what those functions are.

Durkheim's functionalism greatly influenced anthropological theory and studies. Anthropologists such as A.R. Radcliffe-Brown (1881–1955) and Bronislaw Malinowski (1884–1942) approached non-European and usually preliterate societies as social organisms to be understood unto themselves. Instead of applying ethnocentric European ideas of how a society ought to be constituted, they attempted to freshly determine in each case how it actually functioned by analyzing the role that each of its social parts—its culture, belief systems, religion, and kinship institutions—played in establishing and maintaining overall social order.

The Division of Labor in Society

Durkheim's functionalism is evident in his early work, *The Division of Labor in Society* (1893, p. 45). In it he announced that his purpose was to "determine the function of the division of labor" for modern societies. By that he meant that he was not just investigating how modern labor forces were divided into occupational specializations and class positions, the components of the **division of labor**. Rather, his more important purpose was to find out what modern divisions of labor contributed to how different modern social systems operated.

To do that, he had to first examine how premodern societies with their divisions of labor operated. The divisions of labor of past societies were, according to his analysis, simple because economic specialization was as yet undeveloped. Most peasant households performed similar subsistence-oriented tasks. They produced most of what they consumed. They gained very few, if any, consumer necessities from trade with others. There was thus little division of labor between households and villages, with each being an autonomous economy unto itself. Yet these households and villages were linked together as similar segments to form larger, more geographically encompassing societies. What held these larger societies together were commonly held deep religious and other ideas. Despite each household or segment being an economic isolate in the sense that it produced alone nearly all of what it consumed, it shared deeply held worldviews with other households.

This ideological conformity was the product of what Durkeim called a **collective conscience**, by which he (1893, p. 79) meant "the totality of beliefs and sentiments common to average citizens of the same society." These commonly held beliefs formed systems of thinking or belief systems that were powerful frames of reference through which individuals interpreted their experiences. As "determinate systems," they followed semi-autonomous logics of their own.

The monopolistic religious and ideological power of Catholicism over the mental life of medieval European feudalism would be a clear example; so too would be the deeply held religious beliefs of the Aztecs in Mesoamerica. In both cases, the function of the powerful common conscience was to provide cohesion and social order to a society that was otherwise scattered or segmented into largely self-sufficient autonomous estates, villages, and rural households.

There was little room for ideological or other types of nonconformity in traditional segmental societies. Since ideological conformity was a critical pillar of societal structure and stability, it had to be maintained and reinforced. Ideological and normative nonconformity threatened the very existence of the society. For that reason, according to Durkheim, law tended to be highly repressive. The state meted out excessively cruel punishments to those who stepped outside of legal and normative boundaries, as if to recapture the social balance that depended so heavily on complete conformity. Often punishments were carried out publicly, with hangings in the plaza or other forms of execution preceded by lengthy torture and bodily mutilation to reaffirm the conformism of the majority and warn would-be nonconformists.

Modern societies are, according to Durkheim's theory, structured very differently. There is an extensive economic division of labor, such that very few people or households remain that are wholly self-sufficient. Objective economic interdependence provides the most important basis of the cohesion of modern social orders. In answer to his original research question, Durkheim concluded that the function of the division of labor in modern societies was to provide the basis for social order by making each person dependent on all others. Interdependence within the modern division of labor replaced ideological conformity as the foundation of social cohesion and order.

In modern societies, the role of collective consciousnesses has been greatly reduced. There is no longer as great a need for powerful ideological or religious institutions to provide social cohesion because people are now more objectively interdependent owing to the growth of complex divisions of labor. Each household and unit of production is tied to others through nets of interdependency that provide the basis for social cohesion and order. With the decline of both the power of and the need for a collective conscience, individualism and nonconformity correspondingly increased. Put differently, societies vary according to whether they contain a single unitary dominating belief system or a number of competing ones; whether, as in medieval Europe, one institutionalized belief system, Catholicism, almost completely embraces and engulfs the terrain, or whether, as in contemporary Western countries, a number of belief systems run as different thought currents through social life.

Durkheim's general theory thus interpreted history as moving from societies with simple divisions of labor and strong collective consciences to modern societies with complex divisions of labor and weak collective consciences. Objective interdependence replaced ideological conformity as the basis of social order. What he called **organic solidarity** based upon interdependence replaced **mechanical solidarity** based upon ideological sameness.

Anomie

Modern societies with complex divisions of labor were not without problems. They faced serious structural problems in that two of their critical functions were either not being fulfilled or were only being fulfilled partially. First, the division of labor was objectively interdependent, but it was not self-regulating. It needed to be managed rationally if it were to function smoothly. Second, the decline of religion had left an ideological vacuum that needed to be filled.

One of Durkheim's great social insights was that as a result of these and other structural problems, modern societies suffered from a condition that he called **anomie**. Human beings, according to the premises of his theory, needed reasonably well-defined structures within which to function. They needed to know what to expect from their routine interactions with others, whether in family, work, or other environments. When predictable social intercourse was not present, or when that to which the person had been accustomed collapsed, stress-inducing social destructuralization and disorientation—the anomic condition—resulted. The tradition-bound social life of premodern societies had been, in that respect, superior to that of modern societies. It had been less anomic than that of modern societies, which were constantly undergoing technological and social changes. Anomie was like, in his words, a constant wind that blew across modern societies causing uneasiness and, in extremes, suicide-inducing anxiety.

The Liberal State

The modern state was, according to Durkheim's analysis, the appropriate agency to redress these structural problems. The state would plan and regulate—through taxation, credit, and other policies—the economic division of labor. To replace the ideological vacuum left by the fragmentation and decline of religious institutions, it would socialize young people through public education into dominant social, political, and economic norms and values. As a result, anomie would be minimized, for a well-regulated society would be a less anomic society.

Durkheim's advocacy of an enlarged economic and ideological role for the state was in line with turn-of-the-century liberal thinking. Capitalist economies, in the modern liberal view, required governmental investment and regulation if they were to function properly. The ideal capitalist economy would be one in which the state fine tuned the relationships between market-oriented production and consumer demands through laws, taxes, regulatory agencies, and control of the credit system.

Education and the Division of Labor

One of the problems of modern societies, which Durkheim sought to remedy through state action, was the chaotic and inefficient ways in which labor forces were trained and rewarded. Inept progeny of rich tycoons took over companies, while intelligent children of workers went uneducated. Modern societies allocated their collective labor forces inefficiently, wasting talented but poor people in humble positions and suffering from the inept sons of the privileged in powerful positions. To remedy this problem, Durkheim advocated using public schooling to sift and winnow children according to their native abilities, educationally prepare them according to their potential—what later became known as tracking—and see that they ended up in jobs that paid accordingly.

Durkheim's assumption that there is a single scale of vertical differences in intelligence can and should be questioned. Although there are clear intelligence differences between the extremes of genius and intellectual disability, the intelligence capacities of the vast majority of people lie between the extremes. The most important differences in their capacities may well be more horizontal than vertical, in the sense that there are different types of intelligence. A person may be good in one type of mental activity, such as musical ability, and poor in another, such as mathematics. A person may be a good parent and a poor speller. If the most important differences in intelligence are more horizontal than vertical, then the critical pillar of Durkheim's justification for social inequality in modern societies collapses.

Attempts to vertically measure intelligence in France and elsewhere began in the 1890s shortly after the publication of *The Division of Labor in Society,* in which Durkheim laid the theoretical groundwork for structuring education and societies according to intelligence differences. The results of those tests—now known as IQ tests—have been used to justify tracking in schools—stratifying children in different classes according to supposed intellectual ability, with gifted and talented, college-bound, vocational, and other types of tracks—but their validity has always been mired in controversy. Working-class and minority children usually score lower on such tests than their middle-class and majority-culture counterparts. This has led to the charge, which has been borne out in a number of studies, that the tests are class and culturally biased (Ballantine, 1993). The results of intelligence testing thus may be distorting the horizontal differences of capabilities among a population into a vertical scale to justify social inequality.

Nevertheless and ideally, according to Durkheim, it would be possible through state planning to coordinate four hierarchies: ability, education, occupational position, and income. People would be educated according to their abilities and then receive appropriate jobs and income. Low-ability students would be educated only up to a minimally necessary point and then receive unskilled jobs with low incomes. High-ability students would receive higher educations appropriate to professional and managerial positions that would pay accordingly.

Contemporary sociologists have long noted that these hierarchies are, in fact, often not coordinated, leading to problems of morale and inefficiency. Highly educated teachers, for example, are often paid less than less-educated managers. Today sociologists use the concept of **status inconsistency** to refer to situations where people have inconsistent positions in the hierarchies of educational achievement, occupational position, and income.

Durkheim's model modern society was one in which the state oversaw an organically integrated and smoothly functioning capitalist economy with a class division of labor. Society should be constituted, according to Durkheim's (1893, p. 377) bluntly worded formula, "in such a way that social inequalities exactly express natural inequalities." Durkheim thus advocated a kind of meritocracy in which one's position and rewards in life would be determined by one's abilities. He did not advocate social equality, since he assumed that people should receive greater or lesser incomes according to their abilities and contributions to society.

Ultimately, in Durkheim's view, capitalist and class societies could incorporate social justice so long as their reward systems reflected actual differences in ability and function in contributing to the general welfare. As they stood, they were for the most part just, though in need of some reform to eliminate the effects of inherited privileges and disadvantages on filling upper-class and working-class positions, respectively. Exploitation, by the logic of this explanation, only existed in the extremes of capitalist societies. By the logic of his analysis, he would have interpreted as exploited those workers paid below the minimum wage or high-intelligence workers who did not have the opportunity to prepare educationally for higher-level positions. But for the most part, people were paid according to their abilities and consequent contributions to society, and therefore not exploited.

Durkheim's theoretical justification for maintaining social inequality was in many ways symptomatic of both liberal and middle-class thinking. It was liberal in the sense that it advocated aggressive use of the state to reform problems in the functioning of capitalist societies. It was middle class in the sense that it advocated a meritocracy in which the middle-class educated professional classes would gain more power and income at the expense of both uneducated workers and undeserving upper-class inheritors.

Suicide

Durkheim's theory of suicide, briefly described in Chapter One, remains a classic in sociology. He published the shockingly titled *Suicide* (1897) four years after *The Division of Labor in Society*, and there is a clear theoretical continuity between the two works. As in the former work, Durkheim identified individualism and anomie as endemic features of modern societies that, if unchecked, would aggravate a number of social problems, including suicide.

He offered a sociological explanation for the causes of suicide, when most considered a psychological explanation to be more appropriate. His was thus a theory of the specifically social factors involved in the causation of that most seemingly individual of acts: the taking of one's own life.

Durkheim identified four types of suicide—egoistic, altruistic, anomic, and fatalistic—according to their social causes, although the last remained undeveloped in the theory. Under **egoistic suicide** he included suicides that resulted from an excess of individualism, which he had earlier discussed in *The Division of Labor in Society* as a problematic feature of modern societies. Excesses of individualism could be considered to exist when persons were insufficiently integrated morally into surrounding communities, including religions, groups, and families. (The meaning of moral, as used by Durkheim, is close to the concept of norms or rules for social behavior; it is loosely related to notions of right or wrong, as the concept coveys today.) Moral integration means that group members internalize the norms of the group. When moral integration is not strong, the group has little moral influence over the private and personal actions of its members, including suicidal decisions. Even if the community has a strong moral opposition to suicide, the member will feel free to act independently. This was his explanation for why Protestants had higher rates of suicide than did Catholics. While both religions equally condemned suicide as an option, the moral prohibition had a less binding effect on Protestants, since their churches encouraged free inquiry—resulting in a kind of intellectual individualism—while Catholicism was predicated on the member's acceptance and internalization of the church's strict moral authority.

Durkheim also used the concept of egoistic suicide to explain why people with different family and educational backgrounds had different suicide rates. A single person is more likely than a married person to commit suicide because he or she lives alone rather than as an integrated member of a family. Married persons with children are less likely to commit suicide than those without because the larger the family group, the greater its moral influence over individual members. The higher the formal education of a person, the greater the propensity for suicide, because education encourages free intellectual and moral inquiry. In the same respect, men committed suicide more often than women because they were more educated at the time Durkheim was writing.

If egoistic suicide resulted from social ties being too loose, **altruistic suicide** was the opposite, resulting from the ties being overly strong. In egoistic suicide, the person places her or his own desires above those of the community. In altruistic suicide, the person places the community's needs above her or his own. Examples of such suicides include Japan's Kamikaze pilots during World War II, who intentionally crashed their planes into enemy ships, elderly Eskimos who took their lives when they could no longer produce so as not to endanger the survival of the community, and military heroes who take actions for the greater good, but which will most certainly result in their destruction. Suicide bombers, as they are called in the Western press, in contemporary Middle Eastern conflicts would also be examples. In the eyes of their proponents, though, they are viewed not as suicides but rather military martyrs, confirming that the line between military heroism and suicidal behavior is not always clear.

One could interpret the mass suicides at Masada in Roman times, and Jonestown, Guyana in 1979, as related to, but not exactly the same, as altruistic suicide. At Masada in 66 A.D., Roman forces were about to overtake the mountain fortress of Jewish rebels numbering just under one thousand. Rather than submit, the rebels committed mass suicide. At Jonestown, a Protestant congregation in self-imposed exile from the United States was facing increasing scrutiny from outside authorities.

Believing that the authorities were about to destroy their community, over nine hundred people then committed suicide together, most by drinking poison. In both cases, the suicides demonstrated the primacy of community identity over individualism and are thus related to Durkheim's category of altruistic suicides. But in altruistic suicide proper, the suicide occurs in order to ensure the survival of other members of the community, whereas in the examples of mass suicides cited, whole communities marched together in solidarity across the divide separating life and death.

The anomic conditions of modern societies that breed insecurity and instability are a further cause influencing suicide rates, what he called **anomic suicide**. Durkheim viewed rapid economic changes, whether for better or worse, as destabilizing the social situation to which people have adapted and become accustomed. These destabilizations result in anomic conditions that provoke stress, anxiety, and, in the extreme, suicidal behavior.

Durkheim and Modern Sociology

Durkheim's theories, or at least thinking that is similar, continue to be highly influential in contemporary Western sociology and social thought in general. The state's economic and social role in guiding and attempting to stabilize the development of Western societies, as advocated by him, has grown enormously. Contemporary public schooling in Western countries functions largely as an agency of ideological socialization. Through tracking of students according to supposed abilities, it begins the process of social ranking; or more often, and contrary to what Durkheim would have hoped for, it simply mirrors the previously existing social ranking of students' family backgrounds. Education is viewed as the means for students from lower-class backgrounds who have ability to get ahead. His notion that people ought to be socially ranked according to merit, as opposed to family background, has general liberal appeal. Durkheim can be properly interpreted as a thinker who both foretold and influenced these developments in Western societies and their social ideologies.

Durkheim's dichotomy of simple and complex societies, in addition to referring to past and present societies, can also be interpreted as referring to the dichotomy between the European societies of his day and their colonies in Asia, Africa, and Latin America. As such, it represented a late nineteenth-century theory of the differences between First and Third World societies. European societies had complex organic divisions of labor: traditional Asian, African, and Latin American societies had simple mechanical divisions. This interpretation has made the theory relevant to modern attempts to understand Third World underdevelopment. Many contemporary theorists now associate the development of complex divisions of labor with development and modernization.

Unfortunately, though, the theory as originally espoused by Durkheim contained racist assumptions about the inhabitants of colonized societies. Durkheim not only believed that European societies were structurally more complex than colonial and other non-European societies, but also that the minds of Europeans were anatomically more developed and complex than those of the peoples in less developed societies. In astonishingly characteristic racist prose, he maintained that:

> The more primitive societies are, the more resemblances there are among the individuals who compose them. One who has seen an aboriginal American has seen all aboriginal Americans. On the other hand, among civilized peoples, two individuals are distinguishable from each other at a glance, and no preparation is needed for such an observation. There is no doubt that the organic likenesses correspond to psychic likenesses (Durkheim, 1893, p. 133f).

As unacceptable as Durkheim's slips into racist-based arguments were, it would be an error to completely dismiss his theory of grand historical change and modern society on that basis alone. His racism was not essential to the overall theory. It could be safely discarded without the theory collapsing.

Durkheim's concept of anomie continues to be especially influential in contemporary analyses of alienation and social stress. It has been applied in a variety of settings, including studies of the stressfulness of divorce on children and former partners, unemployment on workers, and uncertain employment prospects on graduating students.

His theory of suicide remains the starting point for all contemporary theoretical discussions of the topic. Modern researchers continue to subject Durkheim's statistical and theoretical reasoning regarding the social causes of suicide to intense scrutiny. A number, such as Pope (1976) and Stark and Bainbridge (1982), have argued that the differences between Protestant and Catholic suicide rates that Durkheim found reflected more the socioeconomic differences between the two groups than the nature of their respective communities. Much of the difference between Protestant and Catholic suicide rates vanished when the two groups were compared within the same class levels—that is, upper-class Protestants with upper-class Catholics, middle-class Protestants with middle-class Catholics—on the basis of a study of suicide rates in 49 countries (Girard 1993) that questions Durkheim's more general explanation that the strength of a person's social ties protects against suicide.

On the other hand, Simpson and Conklin (1989) found, on the basis of a cross-national study, that Islamic rates of suicide were low, even when socioeconomic factors were considered, suggesting that in this case Durkheim's original thesis that a traditional religion that strongly bound individuals to a collective belief system had an independent effect on reducing the propensity to commit suicide. None of these modern researchers, however, regardless of their evaluation of Durkheim's particular conclusions, have questioned his general conclusion that there are social causes of suicide, and thus that psychological explanations alone are insufficient.

MAX WEBER

Max Weber viewed capitalism critically as a system of domination in which human and cultural values were often victims of expediency, but defending it as preferable to socialism. The critical theoretical analyses and insights of Weber into the character of capitalism often overlapped those of Marx, despite the two having very different political values. It is not without justice that Weber has often been called the bourgeois Marx. Regarding his relationship to Durkheim, even though the two were contemporaries in neighboring countries, there is a puzzling lack of references to each other's work.

Comparative Research

Weber studied and worried about the meaning of life in the Western capitalist countries as they drifted inexorably toward increasingly efficient bureaucratic control. As more and more aspects of everyday life became rationally organized in the interest of remote elites or just for the sake of abstract principles of efficiency and progress, more substantive questions of freedom, spiritual meaning, and purpose receded into the background, producing a generalized cultural alienation.

Unlike Marxists, who found hope in revolutionary socialism, or romanticists, who found solace in mental flights into the past, or later existentialists, who created meaning out of the individual stance in the face of adversity, Weber judged the human condition to be hopelessly bound for even more difficult times. There was no light at the end of the tunnel. His life ended as elements of European fascism were beginning to emerge from the rubble of World War I.

What made life in the West all the more puzzling was that it was both very rational in one sense and deeply irrational in another. Madness, as in nuclear war and death squads, can be rationally organized. In many ways, Weber's interpretations paralleled those of his contemporary, Franz Kafka (1883–1924), whose novels portrayed men trapped in bureaucratic nightmares. What for Kafka was a theme worked out in literary form and content, for Weber became the structure for a complete philosophical stance and research method.

To fully comprehend Western society, Weber attempted to locate its origins in a confluence of historical events, of which the Protestant Reformation was of unique importance, to define the logic of its institutions and to predict its fate. His studies ranged over continents as well as back into the far reaches of history. He studied the histories, religions, economies, and other institutions of China, the Middle East, and India, as well as those of the Western countries, producing volumes of work that continue to intrigue specialists. All of this was done to shed light by way of contrast on what the unique factors were that made for the development of what he (1905) called "this sober bourgeois capitalism" in the West. He employed a comparative method on a truly global and grand historical scale. Because of the way he thought and the encyclopedic nature of what he knew, his mind constantly jumped cross-culturally and historically as he compared his materials.

Max Weber is often described as the last of the great universal theorists of sociology. World history was the backdrop for his portrayal of a large variety of Eastern and Western social formations. Religion, law, economics, music, princes, and armies contend and interrelate across pages of detailed attempts to portray how various societies formed and held together.

Weber's quest, however, was not systematic. His interests sent him in one direction—the study of commerce, for example—and then another—ancient society—and only later did he attempt to put them together in an overall framework. Reading Weber chronologically is to read successively seemingly unrelated lines of inquiry: commerce, law, rural areas, ancient societies, methods, the origins of Western capitalism, economy and society, religions of the East, and politics. Although general themes run through the work, there is no overall systematization that Weber was able to accomplish. Unlike a Durkheim or Marx, who found clear albeit different logics to history, Weber shied away from finding any such key. Rather, history and societies were a grand variety of different puzzles or constellations, each of which had to be interpreted in its own right, and only then related to general trends.

The Protestant Ethic and the Spirit of Capitalism

In *The Protestant Ethic and the Spirit of Capitalism* (1905), Weber concluded that it was no accident that Protestantism and capitalism developed during roughly the same period in Europe. His general thesis was that the mentality promoted by early Protestantism was more in tune with the necessities of capitalist development than that which had been associated with medieval Catholicism. The rise of Protestantism had broken the ideological monopoly of Catholicism, which had had many doctrines and practices antithetical to the needs of capitalist development.

Medieval Catholicism had, for example, prohibited charging interest for loans—which it called usury—as immoral. Money, in the medieval Catholic view, was like a tool. If a person had a tool that was not being used, and a neighbor wanted to borrow it, then morality dictated that it simply be loaned without thought of requiring payment. In the same way, if a person had extra money that another needed to borrow, he or she should simply loan it without expectation of being repaid a sum higher than the original. The Catholic prohibition on charging interest precluded development of capitalist banking. Early Protestantism took a different view, finding no moral difficulty with the charging of interest.

Medieval Catholicism viewed worldly pursuits of wealth and success as being at the expense of religious devotion. The church demanded that surplus time and funds be invested in noneconomic religious pursuits. To be fully devout, a man withdrew from the economic world and entered a monastery. The best investment of village surplus funds and time was in the construction of elaborate cathedrals. The village might well be poor, but their church would be grand. The retreat from economic activity to pursue religious devotion was also reflected in the large number of holy days that were celebrated in medieval Europe, as many as one hundred days a year. The Catholic attitude toward worldly economic pursuits thus slowed capitalist development because the church absorbed time, and economic surpluses could not contribute to the accumulation of economic capital.

Protestantism took a different view of the relationship between religious devotion and economic pursuits. It considered hard work at economic success as not subtracting from devotion to God. Luther viewed economic work as a vocation. A person glorified God through hard work and success at his worldly vocation—the origin of the **Protestant work ethic**. One did not have to retreat from the economic world into a monastery in order to serve God directly. He could instead work hard at his business. Economic success, in Calvinist doctrine, was a sign of religious grace (that one was predestined to go to Heaven). Protestantism did not demand that communities invest all of their surplus time and funds in building enormous and finely crafted churches. Its churches were models of simplicity. If the grand cathedral had been the architectural symbol of Catholic-influenced feudalism, the no-nonsense factory would become that of Protestant-influenced capitalism. And as Protestantism gained in a region, the number of holy days celebrated declined. Business (from "busy-ness") days crowded out holidays (from "holy days"). Generations of Protestant overworkers and underconsumers resulted in accumulations of capital that accelerated capitalist development.

Weber saw the effects of Protestantism on capitalist development within a larger cultural and historical context. Protestantism did not spring anew. It manifested a current of Western culture that, while submerged during Catholicism's feudal reign, had existed since at least the time of the Romans. The key characteristic of this thought current was a particular concept of **rationality**, in which life activities were viewed in terms of goals that had rationally calculable means to their attainment. The key goal of a capitalist business, for example, is profit. All aspects of the business, including labor, can be rationally analyzed and measured in terms of how they contribute to the central goal of making the profit. Double-entry bookkeeping was invented in the West as a way of keeping track of business expenses and revenues in order to calculate profit rates exactly.

The great irony and unintended consequence of Protestantism was that its leaders and followers had no idea that the effects of their efforts to glorify God would be to free up the ideological terrain for capitalist development, which, once institutionally established, would relegate religion to distinctly secondary importance in daily life. Weber saw Protestantism as simply a temporary carrier of the Western concept of rationality. Later thinkers, such as Benjamin Franklin (who penned such capitalistic aphorisms as "a penny saved is a penny earned" and "time is money") inherited and carried on the rational ethic, but one that was shorn of religious trappings. For Franklin, the Protestant work ethic became simply the work ethic, a seemingly self-evident virtue as it is for many today.

Much of Weber's later studies were devoted to examinations of non-Western cultures and religions in order to understand why capitalism had not developed as early in those areas as it had in Europe. In general, he believed that a set number of material and ideological conditions had to be in place for capitalism to develop. Many non-European regions had had all of the material prerequisites for capitalist development, but their religions and cultures were antithetical to its development. Without the ideological prerequisite—a general type of rationalist mentality that could function in a capitalistic context—there were not sufficient conditions for capitalist development to flourish.

Rationalization

The concept of rationality is often identified with the concepts of truth and validity. But one of the great insights of Weber was that what is perceived to be rational is culturally variable. What is rational within one cultural context is not necessarily so within another. In the West, a particular type of rationality increasingly took hold that was both different from those of other cultures and compatible with capitalist development.

Weber (1922) noted that all cultures implicitly or explicitly incorporated notions of **substantive rationality**; that is, they defined life activities in terms of how consistent they were with the attainment of their cultural values. They judged an activity to be substantively rational if they believed that its pursuit or accomplishment would bring about the realization of a collectively held goal or value. Christian prayer was substantively rational, since it facilitated religious devotion, a Christian value. So too was Aztec human sacrifice, since within its cultural context, it was believed to facilitate the physical survival of Aztec society. What determined whether something was rational, in this sense, was not whether it actually would lead to the accomplishment of what it was supposed to—there is no evidence that human sacrifice actually prolonged the physical survival of Aztec society—but rather, whether it was culturally believed to be consistent with that accomplishment.

In addition to incorporating a strong cultural dimension, Weber's concept of substantive rationality was also essentially qualitative. Basing himself in the classical philosophical distinction and contradiction of quality and quantity, he saw activities as being consistent with goals and values as long as they were oriented toward their achievement, regardless of whether progress toward that achievement could be quantitatively calculated. A person could fast in hopes of attaining spiritual enlightenment without knowing exactly how long the fast would have to last or whether the enlightenment would necessarily come.

Where the West culturally turned the corner on rationality, in Weber's judgment, was in its increasing definition of it in terms of quantitative and calculable criteria, producing what he called **formal rationality**. If substantive rationality represented defining life activities in terms of goals whose attainment could not necessarily be exactly and quantitatively calculated, then the originally Western concept of formal rationality represented defining life activities in terms of goals whose attainment could be exactly and quantitatively calculated.

Some life activities are easily thought of in formally rational terms. The attainment of a business's central goal, profit, is eminently measurable, as are the means to its attainment. But other goals are not, and here Weber's comparing substantive and formal rationality leads to critical as well as cultural insights. None of such central life goals as well-being, significance, and happiness can be exactly measured, nor can means to their attainment be fully calculated. Yet they are goals that are no less important than those which are calculable. People can live longer quantitatively without having qualitatively better lives. Education can be thought of in substantively rational terms as enlightenment and development of the mind. There is no way to exactly measure how educated a person is, though it can be thought of in narrow, formally rational terms as the number of educational courses a person takes, but at much expense to its substantive meaning. As nearly everyone knows, hours spent in a classroom do not directly or even necessarily add up to proportionately more enlightenment and development of the mind. An even more absurd example would be to think of religious goals in terms of numbers of hours spent praying.

Substantive considerations are always more profound than formal ones in judging overall rationality. The more that rationality of life activities is seen in purely formal terms, the shallower and less complete the resulting mentality. The more capitalism and Western culture in general developed, according to Weber, the more formal and less substantive their notions of rationality became. The increasing sway of formal conceptions of rationality and consequent **rationalization** of life activities was, hence, in Weber's estimation, the motor force of Western development.

Bureaucracies

Bureaucracies, in Weber's view, were the organizational manifestations of the concept of formal rationality. They were impersonal large-scale organizations within which component parts were rationally organized as a means for attaining central goals. Increasingly, according to Weber (1922), working relationships in the West took place within bureaucratic contexts. As such, the bureaucratic form had become the dominant organizational context of economic life. Weber viewed it as both highly efficient and alienating. It was an efficient form for organizing and coordinating labor, but it was alienating in the sense that its elevation of organizational goals was often at the expense of the goals and needs of the people who worked within it.

Bureaucracies were also highly effective forms of domination in two senses. In the first, they were like organizational machines that elites controlled and used to control the rest of society. In the second, managers dominated workers within them. Beyond being a form of personal domination, bureaucracies were also a type of impersonal domination. Because of their internal dynamics, bureaucracies took on lives of their own, which were often beyond the control or intentions of their creators. Weber believed that bureaucratic domination was inescapable in the future of the West, whether capitalist or socialist.

Unlike Marx or Durkheim, Weber did not view the future optimistically. He saw increasing bureaucratic domination and the crushing of humane cultural values. He was writing on the eve of Germany's plunge into fascism, when his worst fears came true. Bureaucratically organized death camps became the horrifying symbol of new realities. The Allied defeat of Germany and the other fascist powers in World War II ended the worst manifestations of the developments that Weber feared, but it did not end the long-term development in itself. He undoubtedly would have seen bureaucratic domination, impersonality, and alienation continuing in the postwar institutions and drift of Western culture.

Though not optimistic about what the future held for the subjective life of the West, Weber was a great believer in the scientific outlook and pursuit as an antidote, if not a resolution, for the increasing stifling of human creativity in bureaucratized societies. Science could not produce happiness, well-being, or even existential meaning for life, but Weber clung to the belief that it at least helped one in uncertain times. The pursuit of science—knowledge for its own sake—did not proceed for Weber with the positivistic self-assurance of a Comte or Durkheim that it would bring us that much closer to full knowledge about society. Weber's goals and claims were much humbler: science helped one to keep his or her bearings in a journey whose outcome was perhaps condemned from the beginning.

Weber, Modern Sociology, and Postmodernism

Max Weber exercised enormous influence over the development of twentieth-century sociology. His influence continues to be felt, especially in the sociology of religion, studies of large-scale organizations, and studies of politics and the state (see Chapter Eight). In addition, Weber's general orientation to social thought continues to find resonance in contemporary times. His advocacy of a detached and objective sociology, as opposed to one engaged in social reform or revolution, appeals to many. His conclusion that the march of rationalization and modernization would be at the expense of human and cultural values foresaw contemporary concerns.

Marx and Durkheim can be considered to have been modernist theorists in the sense that they equated historical development with human progress. They were also modernist thinkers in the sense that their theories implied that societies needed to be revolutionized or at least reformed by removing anachronistic institutional features. Max Weber, on the other hand, saw historical societies as simply different cultural constellations to be understood in their own terms, rather than ranked according to progress toward an ideal. Since Weber was completely agnostic about what the goals, if any, of history might be, he could not view history in terms of progress, much less unequivocally endorse wholesale modernization of institutional features. In this sense, Weber was among those thinkers who doubted whether the quality of life of modern societies was any better than that of past societies. If anything, Weber would have identified modernization with the formal rationalization of institutions about which he had deep misgivings.[2]

A half-century after Weber's death, in the early 1970s, **postmodernism** began as a thought movement in the First World countries and similarly challenged the identification of human progress with historical development and modernization. Since the 1970s its proponents in such diverse areas as social theory, architecture, city planning, music, and painting, have critically challenged much of what has been done in the name of modernizing societies.

According to postmodernist theorists, both capitalist- and socialist-guided notions of development had resulted in the wholesale destruction of the humanly valuable parts of societies and their replacement by alienating structures. When urban planners, for example, redesigned metropolitan areas so that traffic would flow more freely, they often ran expressways through the heart of what had been vibrant neighborhoods. What appeared to be a rationalization and modernization of the metropolitan area was at the expense of existing human communities within it. Postmodernists in general stressed the concepts of relativism, diversity, quality, and pluralism over what they identified to be the modernist concepts of progress, standardization, rationalization, and universal truths.

As such, and like Max Weber before them, postmodernist theorists critically questioned both what constitutes human progress and whether it can or should be planned by societies acting collectively.

Key Terms and Concepts
(in order of presentation)

Capitalism	Dictatorship of the proletariat
Socialism	Positivism
Materialism	Functionalism
Dialectics	Organic analogy
Thesis-antithesis-synthesis	Division of labor
Contradiction	Collective conscience
Labor theory of value	Organic solidarity
Exchange value	Mechanical solidarity
Use value	Anomie
Surplus value	Status inconsistency
Alienation	Egoistic suicide
Means of production	Altruistic suicide
Capitalist class (bourgeoisie)	Anomic suicide
Working class (proletariat)	Protestant work ethic
Class consciousness	Rationality
Marxism-Leninism	Substantive rationality
Imperialism	Formal rationality
Monopoly capitalism	Rationalization
Vanguard party	Bureaucracies
Two-stage revolution	Postmodernism
Democratic centralism	

ENDNOTES

[1]Marx's theory of capitalist production was most developed in his magnum opus, *Capital*, Vol. I (1867). A shorter and very clear presentation of the theory is contained in his "Wages, Price and Profit" (1865), beginning with Section 5.

[2]For a different discussion of the relationship between postmodernism and the classical sociological theories of Marx, Durkheim, and Weber, see Lembcke (1993).

Chapter 8

Power, Politics, and the State

In all contemporary societies, individuals have unequal control over the decisions that govern their lives, whether in the setting of families, workplaces, communities, or whole societies. Power structures exist in most social settings. Parents, supervisors, and state officials exercise power over children, employees, and citizens. However, while most adults are able to exercise some power as parents within families, their power does not extend beyond the walls of their houses. A much smaller minority of adults have sufficient power to dominate workplaces, communities, and societies. These latter minorities are the focus of what in political sociology is called **power structure research**.

Possession of power in and of itself has its privileges and pleasures. For some, its attainment surpasses that of wealth as a goal. Similarly, for some, exercise of power is more rewarding than consumption of riches. Since possession of power is a goal that both rivals and often facilitates the possession of wealth, it is not surprising that power struggles are an omnipresent part of social life.

Power can be private or public. It is private when it is attached to a position within a family or privately owned workplace. It is public when it is attached to a position within a state or government. For the most part and in its most commonly accepted meaning, **politics** is about the struggle for decision-making control within private and public settings. When individuals engage in public politics, they do so within the arena of the state or government, and they espouse, or at least adhere to, whether consciously or not, different theories or ideologies over how governance should proceed.

POWER STRUCTURES

There are three major competing approaches to the understanding of power in contemporary sociology: the pluralist, the elitist, and the class. The **pluralist** approach, which has roots in the theories of Emile Durkheim and functionalism, assumes that power in modern democratic societies neither is, nor should be, monopolized by any one individual, organization, or class. Rather, depending on the decision being made, different interest groups mobilize and exercise influence. Public decision making continually shifts between different interest groups and individuals in relatively modern and democratic societies.

To the question "Who rules?" pluralists respond, "It depends upon the issue. No one individual or group monopolizes all decision making because a plurality of interest groups have access, at least temporarily, to the exercise of power if they prevail in the competitive struggle." In one administration, lobbyists for business interests will have relatively great influence; in another, lobbyists for labor interests will have more influence.

Elitist theory, which has roots in a broad spectrum of theories, including rightist and pre-fascist, nineteenth- and early twentieth-century theory associated with Vilfredo Pareto (1848–1923) and Gaetano Mosca (1858–1941), the work of Max Weber, and critical sociologists on the left, such as C. Wright Mills (1916–1962). It assumes that all societies have elites and masses, with the former ruling over the latter. For classical rightist elitist theorists, the existence of such elites is not so much a problem as a simple reality underlying all types of societies.

History records the cyclical replacement of one elite by another. An elite can be overthrown by a revolutionary counter-elite, but both are elites nonetheless, regardless of the ideologies that they espouse. From an elitist theoretical perspective, the Bolshevik Revolution represented the czarist elite being overthrown by a Leninist one, a rightist elite being replaced by a leftist one.

Classical elitist theorists found it revealing to distinguish between those elites that allow the entry of fresh blood into their ranks from the masses below and those that are closed to new members. The former, by co-opting talented members of the masses, are more successful at pre-cluding the formation of counter-elites that will threaten their existence.

Critical theorists, following from Mills (1956) in the United States, adopted the elite-mass analytical model, but used it as a basis for left-wing rather than conservative political conclusions. For them, according to Egan and Chorbajian (2004, p. xvi), "elite rule constitutes a disturbing and antidemocratic force in American society because it promotes a narrow band of interests at odds with the best interests of the citizens."

Class-based theories of power, which follow mostly, but not exclusively, from the work of Karl Marx and Frederick Engels, assume that ultimate power in a society resides in control over its means of production: land, factories, raw materials, etc. For capitalist societies, that means that the class that owns the factories, banks, major stores, and other means of production ultimately, either directly or indirectly, exercises control over the state.

While the pluralist, elitist, and class-based approaches represent distinct conclusions about how power functions, many sociologists combine insights from more than one for their own understanding and orientation. It is not uncommon, for example, to view power in terms of both classes and elites or to acknowledge the existence of pluralistic struggles within levels of what is viewed in overall terms to be an essentially class-dominated power structure.

Power Structure Research

Contemporary studies of power structures have proceeded at both local and national levels. On the local level, some individuals are able to put into motion or approve decisions that will greatly affect the subsequent life of the town or city. They can mobilize capital to finance an urban renewal project or rearrange how public schooling will be carried out. On the national level, there are individuals who are in a position to decide such important questions as whether the country will go to war or whether interest rates will rise. In both cases, local or national, most ordinary citizens are not involved in the decision making, despite being deeply affected by its results.

Both types of power structures—community and national—are subjects of research for a double purpose: to determine who the often-hidden wielders of power are and to refine the understanding of how power functions in communities and societies.

There have been three traditional approaches to determining who exercises power in a community. The first—the **decision-making approach**—which is most closely associated with pluralist assumptions, studies how and by whom significant decisions are made. Decisions in which competing interests clash are studied to determine the balance of power. For example, the decision to undergo urban renewal in a city brings out into the open a large number of competing interests. Depending on how urban renewal programs are planned, landowning interests stand to gain or lose significant amounts of money. A convention center will raise land values around it, but at the same time, businesses and residents may be forced out to make way for the new building, causing them significant losses. In such projects, it is rare for there not to be both gainers and losers. It is a question of the relative power of the competing interests as to which fate besets which.

Decision-making studies, however, have several important drawbacks. They may only give partial glimpses of how power is wielded in communities or societies if the real holders of power delegate decision-making power to loyal managers and agents. Those who make the decisions—for example, on city councils—thus may not be the ultimate holders of power. Also, there are types of questions that may never come up for decision-making if they are not in the interest of the powerful.

A second approach to determining community power structures—the **positional approach**—relies on identifying the occupants of powerful positions. This is done by first identifying the economic, political, and social organizations through which power is wielded within the community. Then the actual individual occupants of those positions are identified and studied. Once individuals and positions are identified, it then becomes possible to determine how powerful organizations are interrelated. Powerful individuals tend to exercise power in more than one organizational context. Corporate leaders sit on several boards of directors. Top managers serve in voluntary organizations such as the United Way. Top bankers are members of university boards of trustees.

The positional approach has the empirical advantage of clearly identifying the actual occupants of powerful positions, who can then be sociologically studied as a group. However, it shares the same disadvantage as the decision-making approach in that the occupants of formal positions of power may be subordinates of still more powerful individuals behind the scenes.

A third approach—the **reputational approach**—attempts to identify individuals who hold both formal and informal power. In this approach, researchers survey individuals presumed to be knowledgeable about power in a community. They ask each to identify a set number of individuals who they think are the most powerful in the community. They then compare and tabulate the lists, with those individuals named on the most lists being considered the most powerful. After identifying those with reputations for being powerful, researchers can then study them sociologically as a group. Most community power structure studies that have followed this approach have usually turned up lists of individual financial and corporate leaders whose names were mostly unrecognizable by the general public.

C. Wright Mills and *The Power Elite*

By far, the most discussed and influential study of national power structures in modern sociology has been C. Wright Mills's *The Power Elite* (1956), which portrayed the United States. Following from a model of the institutional structures of modern societies developed earlier with Hans H. Gerth (Gerth and Mills, 1953), Mills concluded that power in the United States resided in the commanding positions of three institutional hierarchies: the economic, military, and political. Those who controlled these institutional orders coalesced into a power elite that controlled the country as a whole.

Mills examined the occupants of these positions—who included corporate owners and executives, the joint chiefs of staff of the military, and such key political figures as the president, vice president, members of the cabinet, key senators and members of congress, and governors and mayors of major states and cities—and concluded that most of them came from elite social backgrounds. Most often they were educated at private prep schools and colleges. Most of the members of the power elite thus came from social backgrounds and socialization experiences that were distinctly different from those of the mass of ordinary citizens. He further found that the occupants of the commanding positions within each of the institutional orders where power resided—the corporate, military, and political—tended to move back and forth. A corporate executive would receive a cabinet appointment, or a retired top military official would join a corporate board of executives.

Mills's portrayal of power in the United States as being monopolized by a small group was immediately questioned by pluralists, who contended that there was much more competition and circulation of different interest groups in the corridors of power. Marxian theorists (see Sweezey, 1956) questioned the seeming parity between corporate, military, and political bases of power that Mills's model assumed. They viewed corporate power as being paramount, with military and political power being derivatives. Nonetheless, Mills's work continues to be the modern classic in the area of national power studies, influencing subsequent work in the United States (see Domhoff, 1967, 1983) and other countries (see, for example, Porter, 1965).

THE STATE

The classic theorists of sociology—Durkheim, Marx, and Weber—all recognized the special importance of the **state**—that is, the governing power within societies—but their emphases were different. Durkheim, as described in the previous chapter, viewed the state positively as the institution ideally suited to regulate the functioning of modern societies and resolve many of their problems. Marx and Weber emphasized more the state as an instrument of domination.

Class Domination

Marx and Engels (see Engels, 1884) categorized state forms according to the class interests that they protected. The slave state protected the class interests of slave owners. The feudal state protected the class interests of landlords. The capitalist state protected the class interests of capitalists.

When the state does not function in the interests of the economically dominant class, there is a contradiction because economy and state are not integrated. In "The Communist Manifesto," Marx and Engels (1848) emphasized that the bourgeoisie had achieved economic dominance long before it gained political power. They believed that the contradiction between the bourgeoisie's growing economic power and relative political powerlessness was the underlying cause of seventeenth-, eighteenth-, and nineteenth-century revolutions and civil wars in England and continental Europe. It took centuries for the bourgeoisie to break the grip the economically declining feudal nobility continued to hold on state power. Only then could the bourgeoisie consolidate its economic dominance with political power. Only then could it complete its historical destiny and become a politically ruling as well as economically dominant class. In a famous formulation, Marx and Engels (1848) concluded that as a result of this development "the executive of the modern state is but a committee for managing the common affairs of the whole bourgeoisie." In other words, the capitalist class became a politically ruling as well as an economically dominant class. In a modern capitalist society, according to the Marxian understanding, the owners and managers of the major private industrial, financial, and commercial enterprises, through a variety of means—including campaign contributions, which are seen as investments, lobbying, and organization of public policy think tanks—control the general course of state decision making.

Military Domination

The theme of domination was also present in Weber's theory of the state, which has had enormous influence in contemporary political sociology and political science. He (1918) defined the state as "a human community that (successfully) claims the monopoly of the legitimate use of physical force within a given territory." While dominant classes dominate economically by virtue of control over the means of production, states dominate politically by virtue of control over the means of violence—weapons—and the men and women who wield them as soldiers and police. That is the heart of state power.

No state can survive for long if it does not have ultimate control of the weapons and military forces within its territory. The popularly elected

Aristide government of Haiti (1990–1991) was vulnerable to overthrow precisely because it did not have control over its own military and it was overthrown. Aristide controlled the state administrative apparatus, but he did not have control over the most essential ingredient of state power: the military. It was an elected government without real state power. He would later return to power tenuously because of an American military intervention, only to be removed again from power in 2004 by former members of the Haitian military with the tacit approval of the United States. He was vulnerable to overthrow each time because he did not have military control.

For more militarily secure states, military force is their final trump card when in danger, and it has been played innumerable times in past and present crises. In 1968, the French government maneuvered tanks on the outskirts of Paris as a warning to striking students and workers. In 1989, the Chinese government used troops to violently suppress student demonstrators. The appearance of tanks and troops indicates that a political crisis has reached the boiling point.

Weber's definition both differed from and overlapped that of the Marxists. Its most important difference was that it did not categorize states according to the class interests that they served. Its most important similarity was its emphasis on military force being at the center of state power. Weber (1918) approvingly noted Leon Trotsky's statement that "every state is founded on force" and undoubtedly would have agreed with Mao Zedong that "political power grows out of the barrel of a gun."

Legitimacy and Hegemony

In Weber's conception, weapons and armies, while crucial to any state's existence, are not sufficient to guarantee its long-term stability. Governments also need to be perceived as legitimate by their citizens. To govern effectively, they need to have the consent of the governed, or at least a substantial portion of them. No government can exist for long if it is viewed as illegitimate by a substantial segment of its population. Its command over guns will keep it in power for the short run, but it will have to change to accommodate the wishes of its population or it will be overthrown.

The concern with **legitimacy** is also evident in the prison writings of the early Italian Communist Party leader Antonio Gramsci (1891–

1937). After being arrested by Mussolini's fascist authorities in 1926, he spent the last eleven years of his life in jail, where he wrote some 3,000 pages of analysis that are important to Marxist theories of the state. According to him (1985 edition), a rising class, such as the bourgeoisie or the proletariat, becomes a ruling class not solely through seizing the state apparatus and coercively imposing its will over civil society. In addition, it has to establish its moral, political, and cultural leadership—what he termed **hegemony**—over allied strata.

Much like Lenin's theory of the two-stage revolution discussed in the previous chapter, Gramsci saw a great range of forces allied against an old order. Many classes and strata could unite over the goal of deposing an old corrupt or simply reactionary ruling class. But there would be far less unity over how the new order should be constructed. It is here that Gramsci argued that if the working class were to become a ruling class, it had to first convince its potential allies that its vision of the new order was in their interest and attractive. This, Gramsci implied, was a process that occurred historically as the working class developed into a hegemonic class. It was not to be confused with temporary alliances, as in electoral campaigns. The beginning of the first stage would long predate the outbreak of a revolutionary crisis or imminent collapse of the old order. Hence, in contrast to some interpretations of Lenin's theory of the two-stage revolution and concept of the dictatorship of the proletariat, Gramsci saw the working class coming to power less through coercion than through democratically establishing its ideological, moral, and cultural leadership—in Weber's term, legitimacy—and uniting the majority of society.

All states attempt to produce and maintain legitimacy. They face legitimacy crises and weaken when substantial numbers of their citizens perceive them as corrupt, incompetent, oppressive, or dominated by foreign interests. It is not so much the legitimacy of particular government officials that is at issue. They can always be replaced. Legitimacy crises of these types can be handled within the governing system, as when Richard Nixon was obliged to resign the presidency of the United States after the Watergate scandal. Rather, the more serious type of legitimacy crisis is one of confidence in the governing system itself. Legitimacy crises of this type require radical institutional changes to be resolved. The 1989 crisis in Venezuela led to an entirely new constitution ten years later.

State and Nation

For purposes of legitimacy, ideally **nation**, state, and territory coincide to form one integrated nation-state. In order to be perceived as legitimate, the state must be closely identified with the nation over which it rules. There are always underlying legitimacy problems when nations are ruled over by alien or foreign-identified state apparatuses. Contradictions between nation and state have indeed been the largest cause of wars in this century. Unresolved national issues continue to underlie armed conflicts in many parts of the world, including Northern Ireland, Israel, Iraq, and Ethiopia.

Weber (1921) defined the nation as a "community of sentiment." People who share the same national origin feel a common bond, which they do not share with people from other national backgrounds. Weber added as an almost defining characteristic that nations normally tend to produce their own states. If they are frustrated in that quest and must endure being dominated by a state with which they do not identify, instability results.

Colonialism was the clearest example of the contradiction between nation and state. In all colonial situations there are actual or potential legitimacy problems due to the contradiction between the different national identities of state rulers and the ruled, since colonizing powers form their own state apparatuses to administer their territories. France appointed French citizens to administer the governments of Algeria and Indochina in the nineteenth and twentieth centuries. For hundreds of years Great Britain used British citizens to govern India and a number of African colonies. Until 1952, the United States directly formed the government that administered Puerto Rico.

The same contradiction can emerge in **neocolonial** situations, where foreign powers indirectly dominate countries. If state officials are too closely identified with those interests, they can lose the confidence of their compatriots by being open to the charge of betraying the nation to foreigners. In a different manner, contradictions between state and nation can besiege **postcolonial** countries. Most of the present boundaries separating African countries were established during the colonial period by France, Britain, Germany, and Portugal according to their interests and relative powers, rather than according to the logic of prenational

tribal identities. Tribal areas and peoples were split by colonial boundaries, sowing the seeds of future problems.

LEGITIMATIONS OF POWER

Beyond the question of national identification, Weber concluded that
there were different reasons why people accepted the authority of states
to rule over them. Different states rest on different types of legitimacy.
In his view, three different types of legitimacy—**traditional**, **legal-
rational**, and **charismatic**—had played roles in history as foundations
facilitating state governance. A fourth type, **democratic**, has since become especially evident.

Traditional

In states underpinned by traditional legitimacy, people obey out of
long-standing habit. They take for granted their governing system and
authorities because they have been institutionally entrenched for so
long. Alternatives to status quo arrangements are unknown or incon-
ceivable. In Weber's view, traditionalism accounted for the widespread
public acceptance—either active or resigned—of most precapitalist
state structures. The slow pace of social change in feudal and other
precapitalist societies encouraged a conservative traditional worldview.
Rulers could change through death or replacement, but the essential traditional structure of governance and obedience would remain unchanged. Traditionalism was also a strong force in the twentieth century.
It underpinned state structures in China before the communist revolution, Japan until the end of World War II, and Ethiopia until the death of
Emperor Haile Selassie. It continues to be an active force underpinning
contemporary Middle Eastern monarchies.

Legal-Rational

Weber's description of legal-rational legitimacy was a logical extension
of his theory of the growing dominance of formal rational modes of
thought in modern societies, as discussed in the previous chapter. He
contrasted legal-rational to traditional legitimacy as the form most

suited to modern state structures. In this type of legitimacy, people obey because they believe that state rulers and rules have been chosen on the basis of reasonably devised constitutional procedures with which they agree. They presumably obey, not out of habit or ignorance of alternatives as in traditionalism, but rather out of reasoned acceptance of the rules of the game. Formal-rational systems vary according to whether state rulers are chosen democratically, with the democratic variety having developed as the most important contemporary form of legitimation of state power.

Charismatic

This is an historical wild card that often augers a period of significant change, for better or for worse. At various times and in various situations, truly exceptional leaders emerge. What makes them exceptional is that they are perceived by their followers as being uniquely gifted to lead. Charismatic leaders have auras about them that magnetically draw committed followers. The charismatic situation is characterized by a sense of immediacy and communion between leader and followers. Unlike traditional situations, where people obey out of long-standing unreflected habit, or the legal-rational situation, where they obey out of reasoned agreement with how the system works, people follow and obey the charismatic leader out of attraction to her or his magnetic personal qualities.

The leader's perceived charisma may be a function of extraordinary public speaking skills or simply a mode or style of being. It may as much be created by the wishes of followers as emanate from leadership qualities. Charismatic situations are often associated with periods of significant social change, often upsetting traditionally or legal-rationally constituted state structures. Charismatic leaders can dispense with traditionally accepted or constitutionally based norms and directly appeal to their followers: "It is written, but I say to you." Charismatic leaders—such as V.I. Lenin, Adolf Hitler, Mao Zedong, Ho Chi Minh, Ayatollah Khomeini, and Fidel Castro—played instrumental roles in the shaping of the political history of the twentieth century. There is a strong component in charismatic appeal, especially to the poor, that explains Hugo Chavez's electoral success in Venezuela.

DEMOCRACY

Democratic legitimation became a near-universal norm in world politics by the middle of the twentieth century, with most of today's world leaders claiming the right to rule on the basis that they were constitutionally selected through formally democratic means. All of the leaders of the world's developed societies claim that they have been selected through democratic processes. So too did the leaders of the post-World War II socialist countries, though that was widely disputed. The same claim is made by the majority of Third World leaders. If democratic rule is met with near-universal approval, dictatorial rule—whether carried out by an individual, family, or group—is met with near-universal disapproval.

The road to democratic legitimation in world politics has been long. Before the twentieth century, very few societies had instituted formal processes for democratically selecting leaders. The dominant classes of most societies saw little need or felt little pressure to involve ordinary citizens in any way in governance. Once democratic selection processes began to be instituted, they often contained significant restrictions, such as restricting voting rights to property owners, males, or those who were literate. It was only in the twentieth century that voting rights were extended to all adults in the First World countries.

While democratic legitimation has become nearly universal, it would be, however, a mistake to assume that the claim of democracy is the same as democracy itself, or that formal democracy necessarily constitutes substantive democracy in a given society. Democracy (from the Greek *demos* or "people," and *kratos* or "rule of") generically means "rule of the people." As such, the concept is contrasted to other types of rule, including monarchy (rule of the one), aristocracy (rule of the best), and oligarchy (rule of the few). But if democracy means rule of the people, to what extent do the people actually rule in any modern society?

The answer to that question depends upon how the notion of rule is defined. If rule means participation in the actual making of all decisions, then the people rule nowhere. If rule means participation in the selection of the people who make decisions, then the people rule, at least indirectly or formally, in many societies. However, the extent to which the wishes of the people are represented in the decisions that are actually made varies greatly.

Although the world contains a large number of societies that have formally democratic constitutions, there is no one universally approved form of formal democracy. Rather, the world's nominally democratic societies differ according to how they institute democratic participation, with the different systems having different consequences for the character of politics. In some systems, such as that of the United States, there is direct voter selection of the top leader. Systems vary according to whether there must be a run-off election if no candidate receives over 50 percent of the vote. The Brazilian constitution requires that there be a run-off election in such conditions, while the U.S. Constitution does not. Bill Clinton could take the office of the presidency in the United States in 1993 despite having received only 41 percent of the vote in a three- way race. In other systems, which are in place in the majority of European countries, there is indirect selection, with voters selecting the members of a national parliament, which in turn selects the top leader.

The nature of national parliaments varies. They can be made up of representatives of single geographically defined districts, where the top vote-getter represents the district. They can be made up of representatives of political parties, with each party being awarded representatives according to its proportion of the total vote. In some systems, representatives to the parliament vote strictly according to party guidelines; in other systems, they vote more independently.

Systems of formal democracy vary according to the number of political parties that substantively participate. The postwar Eastern and Central European socialist countries, which claimed to be formally democratic (the formal name of East Germany, for example, was the German Democratic Republic) invariably took the form of one-party states, as in the continuing communist countries of China, Vietnam, North Korea, Cuba, and Laos today. Their ruling communist parties were constitutionally guaranteed a monopoly over the exercise of political power. Such other parties as there were led entirely token existences. Article 6 of the Soviet Constitution stated:

> The leading and guiding force of Soviet society and the nucleus of its political system, of all state organizations and public organizations, is the Communist Party of the Soviet Union. The C.P.S.U. exists for the people and serves the people.

The Communist Party, armed with Marxism-Leninism, determines the general perspectives of the development of society and the course of the domestic and foreign policy of the U.S.S.R., directs the great constructive work of the Soviet people, and imparts a planned, systematic and theoretically substantiated character to their struggle for the victory of Communism.

Communists justified their monopoly over political power with the claim that they democratically represented the interests of the proletariat, that is, the working class. This, according to their justification, represented substantive socialist democracy, since the working class was the majority.

A number of developing countries have also had single dominating political parties and claimed to be formally democratic. Single-party Third World states have often emerged from revolutions, with revolutionary leadership either transforming its organization into a ruling party or reconstituting itself as such a party. Those developments have been especially apparent in countries where the ruling party claimed revolutionary nationalist legitimation in a revolutionary struggle against a colonial, foreign-dominated, or corrupt regime. Examples in the twentieth century could be found in the histories of Mexico after the 1910–1917 revolution, Algeria after the 1962 defeat of French colonialism, and Iran after the 1979 overthrow of the Shah.

Developed countries vary according to whether they have two or multiple parties. In general, two-party systems are favored in countries where parliaments are made up of representatives from single districts. Multiple-party systems emerge in those countries where parliaments are made up proportionally of representatives of the parties that contend according to votes received. It is difficult for third parties to emerge in systems where there is single-member representation of districts because voters are reluctant to give their votes to candidates who are not perceived to have a chance of winning. In **proportional representation** systems, on the other hand, voters are more willing to give votes to minority parties, because those parties, so long as they pass a minimum vote threshold, are represented in the parliament even if they do not receive a majority of the votes. Proportional representation tends to favor more ideological pluralism in politics. The two-party system, according to its advocates, favors the center of the political spectrum and more efficient decision making.

POLITICAL STABILITY

Political stability varies greatly among the world's societies. At any given time there are crises or potential crises, including civil wars, revolutions, and coup d'états, that threaten the existence of state apparatuses somewhere in the world. State power and political stability rest, if we follow Max Weber's conceptualization, on the material and ideological foundations of control over the means of violence and command of legitimacy or consent. Few contemporary world political leaders or theorists would disagree.

Weber's conceptualization of state power lends itself to a useful typology (Figure 8–1) constructed from its two constituent variables of military control and legitimacy. A given state can be in control of both, one or the other, or neither of the variables. The typology yields four types of state situations that affect political stability: (1) military control with legitimacy (the most stable), (2) military control without legitimacy, (3) legitimacy without military control, and (4) neither military control nor legitimacy (the most unstable). For convenience, we will call them, respectively, secure states, military-backed states, endangered civilian states, and crisis-prone situations.

Secure states (type 1) rest on military control with legitimacy. For obvious reasons, they have the most stable political situations. The govern-

LEGITIMACY

MILITARY CONTROL		Strong	Weak
	Strong	1 Secure state	2 Military rule
	Weak	3 Endangered civilian government	4 Crisis

Figure 8–1   Typology of Political Stability

ment has firm control over its military forces, and they are clearly superior to any other armed groups that might exist within its boundaries. Citizens view the state as governing with their consent. They may elect new officials to replace old ones whom they no longer support, but there is no perceived need to replace the whole political system. At the present time all developed and a number of other societies fall into this category.

Military-backed states (type 2) have firm military control, but govern without sufficient consent from the governed. State systems of this type may be able to last for long periods of time, as the Pinochet military government of Chile and the apartheid state system of South Africa demonstrated, but they face continuing obstacles to governing effectively. General Pinochet, who headed an outright military dictatorship since overthrowing the civilian socialist government of Salvador Allende in 1973, was obliged to hold an election for the presidency in 1990, which he lost to Patricio Alwin, a civilian. The white government of South Africa, which did not allow its majority black population to vote, lost power in 1994 when internal and external pressure obliged it to institute universal suffrage.

Endangered civilian states (type 3) enjoy sufficient popular support, but either do not control their own militaries or their militaries are weaker than competing forces within their territories. The Aristide governments in Haiti, mentioned above, were in that situation and therefore vulnerable to being overthrown, as they were in 1991 and 2004. The military forces of the elected Spanish Republic proved to be weaker than those of the insurgent fascist general Francisco Franco during the 1936–1939 Spanish Civil War.

Crisis-prone situations (type 4) exist when states have neither military control nor legitimacy. They are states in name alone. Lebanon in the 1970s and 1980 was a well-known example. Its military had very little territorial control, with most of the country having been divided into fluid zones fought over by rival nongovernment militias. The same situations frustrate American attempts to create stable states in Afghanistan and Iraq. As of 2008, neither state militarily had complete control its territories nor had popular backing. Neither state had enough stability to survive a complete withdrawal of American military forces. The United States attempted to create legitimacy for the states by organizing elections. But foreign-sponsored elections rarely are perceived to be fully legitimate. Here it is important to distinguish the formal claim of legitimacy from its substantive actuality. A population can go through the formal exercise of voting without considering the results to be representative of its will.

TERRORISM

The concept of **terrorism** moved to center stage in the United States with the September 11, 2001 attack on the World Trade Center in New York City and the Bush administration's subsequent declaration of a "war on terror." In a number of ways, this has replaced the Cold War as the focus of the country's military strategy.

Terrorism itself, however, is not a new issue. Since the nineteenth century, governments facing domestic insurgencies have used the word to tarnish their opponents. In recent decades, the word had been used to describe opposing sides of conflicts in the Middle East, Central America, Europe, and elsewhere.

Terrorism as an analytical concept is problematic because it is politically charged. If democracy connotes a nearly universal positive value that almost all governments claim to practice, terrorism connotes a universal negative, with nearly all political actors denying that they practice it. Everyone seems to agree that terrorism exists and that it is to be abhorred, but there is no universally accepted definition of exactly what it is, much less which actors practice it.

It is often stated cynically but with a certain amount of truth that one person's terrorist is another's freedom fighter. In the 1980s the United States supported muhajadeen guerrillas fighting the Soviet occupation of Afghanistan and contra rebels fighting the Sandinista government in Nicaragua. President Reagan referred to both forces as the "moral equivalents of our founding fathers." The United States government did not complain when the muhajadeen fighters carried out beheadings of Soviet troops and their Afghan supporters. It did not complain when the contra rebels killed civilians in schools and health clinics. Now, though, it denounces as terrorism those same tactics when they are directed against its own occupations of Afghanistan and Iraq.

If terrorism is to be a useful analytical concept, its reality must be separated from the politically motivated rhetorical uses to which it has been employed. However, because of its widespread rhetorical usage as a pejorative to brand enemies, there is no universally agreed-upon definition of the term.

The United States government, while purportedly being engaged in a war on terrorism, does not employ consistent definitions of what terrorism is. The Federal Bureau of Investigation and Central Intelligence Agency employ two different but overlapping definitions. Following the definition contained in the Code of Federal Regulations (28 C.F.R. Section 0.85), the FBI considers terrorism to be "the unlawful use of force and violence against persons or property to intimidate or coerce a government, the civilian population, or any segment thereof, in furtherance of political or social objectives." By that broad definition, all revolutionaries, including the members of the Boston Tea Party, would be terrorists. It conflates terrorism with all forms of violence. It also includes acts against property carried out by revolutionary groups. Thus, in 2004 the FBI categorized a 1981 robbery committed by a Puerto Rican independence organization as an act of terrorism.

The CIA (2005) has a less broad and more precise definition of terrorism as "premeditated, politically motivated violence perpetrated against noncombatant targets by subnational groups or clandestine agents, usually intended to influence an audience." Its definition, though, seems to imply that terrorism can only be used against—not by—a state. While that interpretation spares the government of having to judge whether it has ever engaged in terrorism itself, it rules out of the question a very significant form of terrorism: state terrorism.

We can construct a more satisfactory definition, or at least the elements of a definition, by starting with what nearly all commentators agree upon about terrorism: that it involves violence directed at civilians for political goals. That distinguishes it from the violence that militaries direct against each other during warfare and from the violence associated with common crime.

Identifying terrorism with violence against civilian targets, though, is not as unambiguous as it may seem. A uniformed military target is clear enough. More ambiguous is whether targeting out-of-uniform soldiers or nonmilitary enemies such as collaborators constitutes terrorism.

Nearly all commentators agree that a primary purpose of terrorism is to sow terror among civilians. Therefore, targeting civilians in or-

der to spread fear among them for political ends constitutes terrorism. Blowing up an electrical tower as sabotage or robbing a bank to
obtain funds to finance the organization does not, contrary to the FBI
definition.

Terrorism, it would seem, is a tactic, not an ideology or type of organization. No organization practices it for its own sake. Rather, organizations and individuals practice terrorism to achieve particular political
goals. For that reason, it makes little sense to brand an organization as
terrorist. That is a rhetorical use of the term, used as a slur against one's
enemies. Rather, the more accurate use of the term is to identify organizations that employ terrorism among their range of tactics to achieve
their political goals.

Oppositional movements in a wide range of countries have employed
terrorist tactics, in part because as national armies have become better
armed, they have become more invulnerable to frontal attacks. That has
increased the likelihood of insurgents choosing so-called "soft" civilian
targets. The very building up of armaments by national armies thus
makes terrorist targeting of civilians more likely.

The goal of oppositional terrorism in the long run is to attain power. In
short and medium runs, it is often to destabilize political situations or developments that are deemed to be unfavorable. If, for example, an
oppositional movement contains differing factions, a minority faction
might commit a terrorist bombing of civilian targets to derail an agreement that the major faction is about to enter into with the commonly opposed government.

If terrorism is a tactic of using violence to spread fear in civilian populations for political goals, it follows that both states as well as their opponents can employ it. Repressive states employ terrorist tactics to instill
fear in subject populations so that they will not join or cooperate with
oppositional movements. Other states employ terrorist tactics against
enemy populations in times of war, in some cases to shake their confidence in their own government's ability to provide protection.

When death squads connected to the Salvadoran government tar-
geted civilian supporters of their guerrilla opposition, a weak argument could be made that that did not constitute terrorism since the
supporters were involved in the struggle. But when the death squads
left the mutilated corpses in public places, that was a calculated terror-

ist tactic to spread fear in the civilian population to decrease potential support for a revolution.

The Nazi Party rose to power in Germany in part by selectively using violence to frighten would-be opponents into quiescence. The Nazi government would later use selective violence to frighten whole populations in the countries its troops occupied into obedience. A motive for the United States in dropping atomic bombs on Japanese civilian populations at the end of World War II was to terrorize them into surrender.

A key question for the future is whether it will be possible, on the basis of international agreements, to expand the Geneva Conventions of 1949, which established definitions of war crimes in conventional wars, to proscribe the varied forms of terrorism.

POLITICS AND IDEOLOGY

A left-right ideological spectrum underlies politics in the Western countries. The distinction between right- and left-wing politics originated in nineteenth-century European parliaments, where supporters of the government sat on the right side and those of the opposition on the left. **Right wing** became associated with conservatism and defense of the status quo, while **left wing** became associated with opposition politics and advocacy of social change. Those vague political meanings carried over into twentieth-century usage. But more importantly, current usage of the concepts of rightism and leftism is more directly concerned with economic policies and class interests. Rightist parties are associated with capitalist-style reforms and upper-class interests, and leftist parties with socialist-style reforms and working- and lower-class interests.

The five most significant political ideologies for most of the last century, ranging from right to left, have been fascism, conservatism, liberalism, socialism, and communism. They have constituted the spectrum of secular politics. Other political ideologies, such as anarchism, have existed but not with the same impact.

Fascism

Fascism is an extreme right-wing authoritarian ideology that embraces using highly repressive means to maintain order, especially during deteriorating economic or political conditions. Fascists have often come to power with the support of dominant capitalist classes to protect their interests in such conditions.

Fascists believe that the masses are incapable of democratically governing themselves. Rather, they must be governed firmly if order is to prevail (Mannheim, 1936). Fascist governments have used state terrorism—assassination, torture, paramilitary death squads, concentration camps—to repress lower-class movements and left-wing opponents. Fascists envision a hierarchically structured organic society in which elites govern willing masses cleansed of subversive elements. Pre-World War II German and Italian fascism was characterized by both charismatic leaders and mass support. Fascism, however, need not have a mass base. The military government of General Augusto Pinochet, which overthrew the socialist government of Salvador Allende in Chile in 1973, was often described as fascistic despite lacking a mass base of support. The fascist ARENA party, which became the governing political party of El Salvador in 1989, is an in-between example. It was able to attract significant votes despite its leaders being linked to death squads that were used to repress labor, peasant, and student organizations.

Conservatism

The basic thrust of contemporary economic **conservativism**—also referred to in Latin America and parts of Europe as neoliberalism after a nineteenth-century laissez-faire variant of liberalism—is advocacy of free-market rather than state-regulated capitalism. Private enterprise, according to conservatives, should have full reign, with state economic regulation and interference kept to a minimum. Except for defense spending, state budgets should be trimmed back. Social spending on education, health, and housing should be cut back.

The market should be the ultimate economic regulator. If companies cannot survive market competition, they should go bankrupt. If individuals cannot earn enough income to avoid poverty, they should be poor. The market, according to conservative beliefs, is thus the best judge of economic quality and the dispenser of social rewards and punishments.

In the 1980s, conservative economic ideology was embraced by the Reagan and Thatcher administrations in the United States and United Kingdom, inaugurating a significant rightward policy shift that had international influence and consequences. Both Bush administrations continued to embrace it and make it the center of Washington's approach to international as well as domestic economic policy.

If economic conservatives have a laissez-faire approach to economic issues—namely, that governments should not interfere with the private market–social conservatives in the United States have had an opposite approach to a number of social and moral issues. Instead of leaving the decision to have an abortion up to women, they advocate government laws to prohibit it. Instead of leaving religious beliefs and practices as private affairs, they advocate state encouragement of them through school prayer and religious references in national symbols.

Liberalism

Liberals advocate state-regulated capitalism. They share with conservatives a general belief in the viability and desirability of private enterprise in market-based economies, but they believe that if capitalist tendencies are not regulated, economic and social crises will occur. Since the world depression of the 1930s, liberals have successfully advocated that states use controls over credit systems to regulate business cycles so that recessions do not slide into depressions. In the social sphere, liberals advocate that the state use its taxing power to redistribute some income from the top to the bottom. Liberals believe that if the gap between class living conditions widens too far, social crises will break out, which will threaten the stability of the whole system. In the United States, the dominant part of the Democratic Party advocates liberal economic and social policies.

Socialism

Nineteenth-century **socialists** originally advocated revolutionary change to produce economies with complete public ownership of the means of production. But by the early decades of the twentieth century, socialists or social democrats, as they are also called, increasingly endorsed evolutionary rather than revolutionary change. They believed that socialism would come about through elections of socialist governments that would gradually increase the state sector at the expense of the private. Socialists and social democrats today firmly endorse the notion of mixed economies with public and private sectors. Like liberals, they advocate use of the state to regulate the market and social relations. Unlike liberals, they are in favor of state ownership of a number of key enterprises, which can include banks, mines, and manufacturing concerns. Socialists more aggressively advocate than do liberals state financing of extensive social programs, including free national health systems. Socialist and social democratic parties have been governing parties in England, France, West Germany, Italy, the Scandinavian countries, Greece, Spain, and Portugal, among other countries. The United States, however, has never had a socialist party with national power.

Communism

Communist parties share a core belief in the basic validity of Marxism and its consequent commitment to working-class interests and socialist goals. They believe that the working class is the basic agency for socialist change and are in favor of a much more rapid construction of socialism than are socialist parties. Consequently, they advocate a greater extent of public ownership and state control over the economy than do socialists.

The Bolsheviks were the first major communist party in the twentieth century. Following the success of the 1917 revolution in Russia, communist parties rapidly organized in most other countries during the 1920s. They remained aligned with the Soviet Union through the 1940s. The strength of that alignment began to weaken after World War II, with a number of Western and Third World communist parties distancing themselves from the Soviets. The Sino-Soviet split, which surfaced in the early 1960s, was the final indication that world communism was no longer unified. From the late 1950s until the downfall of the Soviet and European socialist countries beginning in 1989, there were considerable ideological and strategic differences in points of view between communist parties.

Today's ruling communist parties in China, Vietnam, Laos, and Cuba have made major concessions to market economic policies and have retreated from earlier socialist development goals. North Korea continues to embrace the earlier model of socialist development. Nonruling com-

munist parties and organizations continue in most countries, with varying degrees of significance and modified economic positions.

The Future of Political Ideology

The world historical year of 1989 symbolized a new era in world politics. The beginning of the collapse of most of the socialist countries that
year capstoned a decade-old rightward shift in world politics, signaled
most clearly by the conservative economic policies of the Reagan administration in the United States and the Thatcher government in the
United Kingdom.

In the developed countries, the rightward shift pulled Western liberals
and socialists away from their original moorings. Socialist parties, such
as those of Spain and France, embraced privatization of state-owned enterprises for which they themselves had advocated public ownership in
previous decades. With the pendulum of state economic policy having
swung so far to the right, statist solutions to capitalist problems, not to
mention socialism itself, were increasingly edged out of political dis-
course in the Western countries.

In the Eastern countries, a number of former communists recast themselves as democratic socialists, while many others abruptly turned into
their opposites and became capitalists. As reality inverted itself in the former socialist countries, a confusing inversion of the meanings of left and
right emerged. Journalists increasingly described those advocating market reforms and privatization of state-owned industry as liberals, and
those defending public ownership as conservatives. And as tight communist ideological control over the old order crumbled, suppressed
nationalisms violently erupted into warfare in regions of what had been
Yugoslavia and the Soviet Union. If the soldiers of the old Warsaw Pact
countries—the Soviet Union and its East European allies—were permanently poised to go to war over the ideological dispute that generated the
Cold War—a war that never came—those same soldiers after 1989 were
more likely to be actually at war over one or another domestic eth-
nic-based conflicts.

The 1980s also saw the ascendance of religious-based politics. The
1979 Iranian revolution brought to power Islamic fundamentalists who
sought to infuse politics with their religious principles. Islamic funda-

mentalism now represents a serious force in nearly every Middle Eastern country. In the United States, evangelical Protestantism—the Christian Right—became a political force, similarly seeking to reverse the secular separation of religion and the state.

These rapid shifts in world politics—the rightward move, the resurgence of nationalism, and the attack on secularism—produced a kind of political anomie. The old structures governing ideological politics—especially the Cold War conflict between the superpowers—dissolved, while new structures and their ideological reduxes had yet to fully take their places.

Despite the continuing anomic nature of world politics, what can be predicted with confidence is that there will continue to be lefts and rights in politics. What will remain as the basic, but not exclusive, question of politics for this century, as it was in the previous one, is what the relationship should be between the state and civil society, between public and private interests, with leftists opting for the primacy of the former and rightists for that of the latter.

Key Terms and Concepts
(in order of presentation)

Power structure research
Politics
Pluralist
Elitist theory
Class-based theorists
Decision-making approach
Positional approach
Reputational approach
State
Legitimacy
Hegemony
Nation
Colonialism, neocolonial, and
  postcolonial

Traditional legitimacy
Legall-rational legitimacy
Charismatic legitimacy
Democractic legitimacy
Proportional representation
Terrorism
Left wing
Right wing
Fascism
Conservatism
Liberalism
Socialism
Communism

Chapter 9

Class, Race, and Gender

When the *Titanic* sank, the mortality rate for women and children with third-class tickets was much higher than that for first-class ticket holders. Investigations after the tragedy revealed that the luxury liner's captain had ordered the crew to block third-class passengers from access to the lifeboats until the first-class passengers had been seated. Since there were not enough lifeboats, proportionately more third-class passengers drowned (Lord, 1955; Davie, 1987). During the Vietnam War, U.S. soldiers from poor families were much more likely to serve and be killed than were those from more affluent families (Zeitlin, Lutterman, and Russell, 1973). In the United States, black babies are 2.4 times as likely to die during their first year of life as are white babies (U.S. Census Bureau, 2007, Table 108). In 1980 the highest income group in the United States lived on average 2.8 years longer than the lowest income group. Since then, the gap has grown to more than 4.5 years (Sing and Siahpush, 2006). These are all examples of the consequences of social stratification. They indicate in a very literal sense that groups within a society enjoy different access to what Max Weber (1922) called life chances.

The sociological concept of **stratification** is based on a geological analogy. Like rocks, which are formed by vertical layers or strata of

TABLE 9–1
Titanic Percent Survival Rate by Class of Ticket Held

	Men	Women	Children
First Class	34.0	97.2	100.0
Second Class	8.0	83.9	91.7
Third Class	12.0	54.7	30.3

Source: Lord (1955) and Davie (1987)

TABLE 9–2
Poverty and the Risks of War. Family Backgrounds of Wisconin Soldiers Killed in Vietnam Compared to All Families*

	Families of Killed Soldiers	All Families
Poor	27.2	14.9
Nonpoor	72.8	85.1
	100.0	100.0

*Percent poor among the parents of Wisconsin servicement killed in Vietnam through December 31, 1967, compared with the parents of male seniors in the Wisconsin high school class of 1957.
Source: Zeitlin, Lutterman, and Russell (1973).

physical substances, societies have vertical layers (strata) of people. The purpose of stratification research is to describe and analyze layered interaction within societies. Put differently, the purpose of stratification research is to determine how different stratification systems operate and what their consequences are for other societal features.

There are three overlapping angles from which to analyze much of contemporary social stratification and inequality: class, race and ethnicity, and gender. As a structural principle, class inequality runs through all contemporary societies, with people occupying unequal positions of power and pay at work, living in unequal housing, wearing clothing of unequal quality, and having unequal educational opportunities, among other inequities. Class inequalities are most fundamentally based on economic structures, but they often are related to historically created racial and ethnic divisions as well. Blacks in the United States, for example, disproportionately occupy lower-class positions because of the history of racial discrimination that originated with slavery. Similarly,

Southern and Eastern European immigrants to the United States disproportionately occupied lower-class positions because of ethnic discrimination. Crosscutting the inequalities wrought by class, race, and
ethnicity are the social inequalities attached to the biologically given position of being males or females within societies.

Investigating and determining how class, race and ethnicity, and gender inequalities—socially created inequalities that are associated with
economic structures, historical developments, and biological differences—interrelate and often reinforce each other within societies is one
of the principal challenges facing contemporary stratification research.
Beneath this now commonplace trilogy of class, race, and gender are
considerable theoretical issues, controversies, and debates.

Marxian, nationalist, and feminist theorists place priority on, respectively, class, racial or ethnic, and gender issues. In extremes, these
amount to ignoring the importance of the nonprioritized inequalities:
the Marxist who sees only class struggle, the narrow nationalist who
refuses to recognize class conflict or gender issues within the oppressed racial or ethnic group, the ultra-feminist who sees men as the
enemy. But, more commonly, they represent different sensitivities and
advocacies in contemporary critical attempts to grapple with social inequality.

ECONOMIC AND SOCIAL CLASSES

The concept of class (from classify) has a long and controversial history
in sociological research. We can distinguish two broad traditions within
this research: one that concentrates on analyzing different **economic
classes**—such as employers, workers, and small business owners—that
make up the labor forces of societies, and another that concentrates on
analyzing different **social classes**—such as upper, middle, and lower
classes—that live within communities and societies. What differenti-
ates the two traditions are the settings—labor forces or communities—within which people are classified into classes. It follows that the
two traditions offer complementary portraits of inequality at work and
inequality in communities.

The first tradition, which has roots that go back to Max Weber and Karl
Marx, relies on what can be called a relational concept of class, with eco-

nomic classes being defined according to the different relationships that people have to the means of producing wealth in a society. Each type of economic system in world history beyond the earliest communal societies has contained a central means of producing wealth, the control of which has been monopolized by the most powerful economic class. In state societies, royal families and high officials controlled the state apparatus, which allowed them to collect taxes from peasants. In slave societies, owners controlled slave labor, which was the most important generator of economic surpluses and wealth. In feudal societies, landlords controlled the land, which allowed them to collect rent from peasants. In capitalist societies, capitalists owned the means of production (capital) and employed workers from whose labor they garnered profits. In postwar communist societies, managers and political officials controlled state-owned businesses that employed most of the labor forces.

Outside of these primary class locations, there have been other secondary class positions within economic divisions of labor. In slave societies, merchants existed alongside of masters and slaves, as they did in most feudal societies alongside of landlords and peasants. In capitalist societies, middle classes exist alongside of and between capitalists and workers.

The second tradition of class research, which has theoretical roots that go back most directly to the work of W. Lloyd Warner and Joseph Schumpeter, concentrates on how people experience and perceive social inequality in their communities. Social classes, in this tradition, tend to be defined according to the different levels of income and standards of living within which individuals and families live. Social classes thus are made up of people who share a common standard of living—rich, poor, or some position in between—within a society. There is also a tendency for people within the same social class to see themselves as social equals and as different from people in higher or lower classes.

Social class position is related to, but not wholly deducible from, economic class position. In general, incomes derived from economically dominant class positions support upper-class lifestyles, while incomes from economically dominated class positions support less prosperous social class lifestyles. But a particular economic class position can be associated with more than one possible level or class of social standard of living. A Main Street clothing merchant, who is economically a small-business owner, can enjoy a proper middle-class standard of living. Down the street, a shoeshine operator, who is economically also a small-business owner, will be much more likely to have to endure only a lower social class standard of living.

In sum, then, to this point, economic class position is determined by location within the economic division of labor. The level of income or relative standard of living within the society determines social class position. Economic-class terms have to do with relationships of work or production (masters, slaves, capitalists, workers), while social-class terms generally have to do with consumption possibilities (rich, poor, upper, middle, lower).

The first step in developing a class profile for a particular society is to determine what economic and social classes exist and calculate their relative sizes. The next step is to determine how class stratification is influenced by and interrelated with other forms of stratification, such as racial, ethnic, and gender inequalities. Put differently, it is important to determine the correlates of economic and social classes; that is, to what extent racial, ethnic, gender, and other groupings are proportionately or disproportionately represented within each of the economic and social class categories. This profile can then serve as a basis for documenting causes and results of institutional forms of class, racial, ethnic, and gender discrimination.

In examining the recent and contemporary world, it is apparent that the class structures of developed societies differ from those of developing societies.

Developed Societies

The labor forces of developed capitalist societies generally have four economic classes: capitalists, the new middle class (employed professionals and managers), small-business owners, and workers. These reflect the economic division of labor of advanced industrial market societies. Capitalists (the bourgeoisie in classical language) own businesses that are large enough to have employees or workers. Capitalists thus function economically both as owners and employers. The **capitalist class** includes all individuals whose income is derived from the profits of large businesses. Such profits can be derived directly from ownership of a particular business or indirectly from investments spread over different stocks. Some members of the capitalist class directly work where their capital is invested. Others are *rentiers*, people who do not work but instead live off dividends, interest payments, and capital gains. At most, capitalists account for 2 percent of the labor forces of developed societies.

The **new middle class** developed in the twentieth century with the growth of state and corporate bureaucracies, which created positions for employed professionals and middle-level managers. In the past, most professionals, such as doctors, lawyers, and architects, were owners of their own small businesses. Likewise, the vast majority of positions that required managerial skills were in small businesses. With the development of corporate and state bureaucracies and the parallel decline of small businesses, the location for exercise of professional and managerial skills shifted from self-employed to employed locations. Sociologists (see Mills, 1953, for example) refer to this as the shift from the old middle class of small-business owners to a new middle class of middle-level employees in large corporate and state bureaucracies. Employed middle-level professionals and managers now make up as much as 20 percent of the labor forces of developed societies.

The classical **small-business owning class** was composed of farmers (the largest sector), professionals, merchants, and artisans (self-employed skilled workers, such as carpenters and electricians). Like capitalists, small-business owners derive their income from business profits. But unlike capitalists, they are not fundamentally employers. At most, they employ a few auxiliary helpers, often family members. Small-business owners' most important employees are themselves. Small businesses continue on the margins of the corporate economy, employing now not more than 10 percent of the labor force in the United States, down from a high of 70 percent or more in the nineteenth century.

The **working class** is made up of all those below middle-level managers and professionals in the employed labor force. During the industrialization phase of capitalism, most workers were employed in factories, but with the rising productivity of the industrial sector of the economy, it has been possible for increasing numbers of workers to be shifted away from factory employment and into offices, sales, and services. Workers of all types make up as much as 65 percent of developed capitalist labor forces, by far the largest share of any economic class.

Many people have income derived from both capital profits and the sale of their labor. It is the relative proportion of each that identify their substantive class position. A capitalist may work at a profession and have a public identity as such. But that may mask her or his real class identity. According to newspaper reports, the late Jacqueline Kennedy, widow of both a former president and a shipping magnate, earned a salary of $45,000 as an editor in 1990. She also had a fortune of $200 million that generated in that year at least $15 million of additional income. Put differently, at least 99.7 percent of her income was generated by the capital that she owned.

In the 2008 presidential election in the United States, of Republican Party candidate John McCain's income of $405,409 for tax year 2007, 72.6 percent came from his salary as a senator. Most of the rest came from capital profits. That ratio of wage and salary to investment or capital income is deceptive, though. Senator McCain filed his income tax separately from that of his wife, Cindy Hensley McCain, the heiress of an Arizona beer distributorship fortune. Capital income makes up the vast majority of their combined income, though the exact proportion is unknown, because her income tax return has not been made public. Democratic candidate Barack Obama and his wife, Michelle, had an income of $3,972,821 of which only 6.6 percent came from wages and salaries (http://www.taxhistory.org/). The 2008 candidates thus were both members of the capitalist class, Senator McCain by virtue of marrying into it and Senator Obama by virtue of being able to capitalize on public fame to generate enough speaking and book-writing income to amass a capitalist fortune. The vice presidential candidates, Senator Joe Biden and Governor Sarah Palin, on the other hand, had more modest incomes.

For the previous 2004 election the bulk of the income for all of the presidential and vice presidential candidates came from capital. In 2003 President George W. Bush and his wife, Laura, had a combined income of $822,126. Forty-eight percent of their income came from his presidential salary, the 52 percent balance from returns on the ownership of capital. Vice President Dick Cheney and his wife, Lynn, had a combined income of $1,267,915—64 percent from returns on capital. In 2004, Democratic presidential challenger John Kerry had an income of

$395,338—63 percent from returns on capital. His wife, heiress Teresa Heinz Kerry's income of $2,291,137 was all from capital returns. Democratic vice presidential challenger John Edwards and his wife, Elizabeth, had a combined income of $305,836—54 percent from returns on capital (http://www.taxhistory.org/).

Two facts stand out: First, since the source of both of the 2004 candidates was capital returns, both were technically members of the capitalist class. Second, both came from the upper ranges of the richest 1 percent of Americans. In 2006 the richest 1 percent of tax returns began at over $500,000 (http://www.irs.gov/taxstats/).

On the other side of the ledger, workers, middle-class professionals, or small-business owners may divert a part of their savings into stock investments. Income from these investments, though, only accounts for a small fraction of their total income. Just as Jacqueline Kennedy's having a job did not make her a member of the working or new middle class, a worker's minuscule stock holdings do not make her or him a capitalist.

Economic class categories reflect the structure of a society's economic division of labor. But, as mentioned, the way in which people perceive their class existence does not necessarily directly reflect economic class categories. College students from middle-class families may take summer jobs as workers. Economically, they function as workers for that period of time, but socially they more likely continue to identify with a middle-class social existence. Even where adults have settled into life-long economic class roles, they may not perceive their class existence in those terms. Especially in developed societies, where consumerism has become an important way of life, what may be paramount in the minds of many is the standard of living or lifestyle that their incomes afford.

There are a number of ways of getting at how people perceive their social class existence. W. Lloyd Warner pioneered much of social class research by simply asking samples of people within communities to name what they thought the town's classes were. From these interviews (Warner, Meeker, and Eels, 1949), he was able to derive a six-class model: upper upper class (old wealth), lower upper class (nouveau riche), upper middle class (professionals, business owners), lower middle class (sales clerks, office workers), upper lower class (regularly employed workers), and lower lower class (the unemployed and poor).

For a number of years in the United States, researchers polled people, asking them with which of three broad social classes—upper, middle, or lower—they identified. Eighty percent or more usually answered "middle class," which led to various conclusions that the United States was a middle-class country or that class divisions had nearly disappeared. Then Richard Centers (1949) modified the design of the questions, giving respondents four, rather than three, choices. They were now asked which of four social classes—upper, middle, working, or lower—they identified with. The results were that 51 percent identified with the working class, 43 percent as middle class, and as in the original research, very small percentages with either the upper (3 percent) or lower class (1 percent) extremes, percentages of social class identification that have continued to hold in the United States. In a 2000 national survey, 45.4 percent of respondents identified themselves as working class, 45.2 percent as middle class, 3.8 percent as upper class, and 5 percent as lower class (Gilbert, 2008, p.183).

Although there are many different views today regarding the identity and number of social classes in developed countries, Centers's original conclusion that there were four—the **upper class**, the **middle class**, the **working class**, and the **lower class**—continues to resonate with the greatest acceptance among the general population and a large number of social scientists.

Joseph Schumpeter (1927), Paul Sweezy (1953), and others have importantly identified the characteristics of social class existence by noting that social classes are like communities in which one moves freely and comfortably among equals. Moving in social classes above or below one's own presents difficulties and is uncomfortable. Sweezy characterized a social class as a network of "freely intermarrying families." The patterns of social class existence are also evident in where people eat. Max Weber used the term "commensality," which refers to whom one feels comfortable eating with. Quite clearly, restaurants have social class characters. Their prices act to restrict access to particular income levels. The prices reflect not only the quality of the food and its preparation, but also the exclusivity of the clientele and atmosphere. One is reminded in this context of C. Wright Mills's (1956) observation that rich people never have to read the right-hand columns of menus. Bars follow the same pattern. People like to drink with social equals, resulting in

lower-, working-, middle-, and upper-class bars. Finally, most cities res-
identially reflect social class patterns, with observable upper-, middle-,
working-, and lower-class neighborhoods and districts.

In addition to developing economic and social class profiles, stratification researchers quantitatively measure a number of related issues. There
is considerable research into the degree of relationships between positions
within stratification hierarchies and such varied characteristics as voting
behavior, health, educational achievement, and entertainment habits. As
alluded to in the beginning of the chapter, social class position affects survival. Spruit (1982) extensively reviewed studies of the relationships between social class and mortality and morbidity (sickness) and found
invariably that the lower the social class the higher the rates of both.

The issue of social mobility commands much research attention. To
what extent is class position inherited and passed on intergenerationally
within family lines, and to what extent is there opportunity for people to
rise above their class origins? The concerns of this research follow from
the original circulation of elites proposition (see Chapter Seven) that
closed class systems are vulnerable in the long run to stagnation and the
rise of revolutionary challenges from below if they continue to frustrate
the aspirations of talent from humble origins.

Developing Societies

Since virtually all developing societies now have capitalist market economies, their economic class divisions of labor resemble to a degree those
of developed societies, with roles for capitalists, workers, small-business owners, and a new middle class of employed professionals and
managers, but the relative sizes of these classes differ, and there may be
sizeable peasant classes in the countrysides.

The relative distribution of the labor force between the two economic
middle classes—small-business owners and the new middle class of employed managers and professionals—resembles that which existed in developed societies a number of decades ago before corporate and state
bureaucracies developed as major employing entities. There are more
small-business owners than employed managers and professionals. Third
World cities, and even the countryside, abound with commodity enterprises. Vendors push carts hawking everything from food to apparel.

Other merchants compete for buyers in open-air markets. Craft workers' shops line whole streets and districts. While some of these small-business owners are indeed socially as well as economically middle class, most live socially at working- or lower-class levels. They form a kind of **lumpen** (from the German "rag") **bourgeoisie**. If developing societies follow the general stages of development that have already occurred in developed societies, it can be expected that in time their large businesses will squeeze most of these microbusinesses out of the market.

Peasants, in the economic meaning of the term, are small farmers who, along with household members, consume most of what they produce. They are fundamentally outside of the market economy. They may create surpluses and sell them on market days, and they may purchase some commodities, but most of what they produce they consume themselves, and most of what they consume comes from their own products. In a number of developing societies, there are still substantial classes of people who live in this manner.

Use of the term "peasant" in a Third World context can be confusing because it is employed in both an economic and a social sense, which are different. In its Third World social connotation, the term simply means the rural poor, who include the types of noncommodity-producing farmers just cited, commodity-producing farmers (who, economically, are a rural small-business class), and landless rural laborers (who, economically, form the rural working class). In most cases, the three rural economic classes of peasants, small-business farmers, and workers merge socially in the sense that they share similar standards of living and consider themselves to be social equals. They form a single peasant social class despite being drawn from three different economic class positions.

Social scientists often use the haunting concept of *marginalized* to refer to people on the peripheries of Third World labor forces. These include landless peasants in the countryside, for whom there are no regular sources of employment, and urban dwellers who have recently migrated from the countryside and similarly are unable to find steady employment. Together, they make up the poverty-stricken social lower class.

The source of their misery lies in the economic transformation of agriculture. Large landowners have increasingly monopolized ownership of land and, along with competition from low-price imported grains and other foodstuffs, squeezed small producers out of local markets. As food production in general has become more efficient economically, in the sense that fewer laborers are needed to produce the same amounts, increasing numbers of rural workers have been released from that type of employment. The result of these and other trends is that Third World countrysides support proportionately less people than they did in past eras. As misery increases, people leave for the cities, but the urban economies are not so developed as to be able to absorb them productively. These marginalized people crowd into shanty towns that ring the larger cities, eking out existences as best they can.

Social scientists have also increasingly used the concept of the popular classes to refer to all of those who, in an absolute sense, share the fate of being poor. These include workers, small-business owners, and the marginalized. Together, they make up absolute majorities in most developing societies.

What is striking about Third World social class structures, in comparison with those of developed countries, is their greater rigidity and inequality. Perhaps because many developing societies retain significant feudal vestiges, at least in the area of their consciousness and ideology, the notion of significant class mobility is not seen, especially by the upper classes, as either a realistic possibility or necessarily desirable.

Postwar Communist Societies

The postwar communist countries developed class structures that were uniquely different from those of the developed capitalist countries, but as they began in the 1980s to move away from strict state ownership and toward mixed economies, their class structures correspondingly shifted and began to approach those of capitalist countries. Nevertheless, their class structures remain worthy of examination as important alternative experiences.

Given the different nature of their economic systems, the postwar communist countries had different structures of economic classes than did developed capitalist countries. There were no capitalist classes of any significance, since the state, rather than private individuals, owned the major means of production. Direction or management of the state-owned means of production rested in the hands of a class of managers and political officials from the governing communist parties. Together, these functioned economically as a class, in the sense that they performed a particular role in the division of labor of the production systems. Below them were middle-level managers and professionals, who were comparable to their counterparts in the Western countries. At the base of communist societies were the majority working classes. On the margins of the economies, small-business owners—farmers and shopkeepers, mainly—continued to exist.

There were thus clear economic role differences within communist production systems, which were qualitative enough to be considered economic class differences. Indeed, it would be difficult at this point in history to conceive of any large-scale production system that could function without class differences between managers, workers, and intermediate ranks. Such class systems were a natural concomitant of the size and complexity of socialist production systems, within which large-scale bureaucratic organizations were the most typical locations for working relationships. The existence of such economic class differences, though, did not mean that the postwar communist countries were unable to make progress toward their implied goal of abolishing class distinctions.

The ruling working-class ideology dignified in an almost ennobling sense the status of being a worker. Unlike in the developed capitalist countries where class mobility into middle- and upper-class positions was the mark of success, in the communist countries one was encouraged to feel proud of being a worker. However much there were functional differences between working- and middle-class occupations, these did not produce as much pronounced social class and status differences as they did in Western countries.

In short, while economic class differences necessarily remained, social class differences narrowed considerably. The introduction of market reforms and privatization in Central and Eastern Europe and the countries that once belonged to the old Soviet Union has had the inevitable effect of widening income differences and thereby social class differences. Market reforms have had similar effects of widening social class differences in China, Vietnam, Laos, and Cuba (see Chapter Six).

DISTRIBUTIONS OF WEALTH AND INCOME

Distributions of wealth and income are important indicators of class equality and inequality within societies. There are two types of wealth:

Personal wealth includes properties, such as homes, cars, and boats, that owners consume as private citizens. **Capital wealth** includes all properties, such as land, businesses, and stocks, from which owners derive income. Income includes everything that individuals receive from all sources: from wages, salaries, invested capital wealth, or indirectly from benefits available to all citizens (the social wage), such as state-subsidized free or reduced-cost public education.

Two individuals can have equal amounts of income, but if the source of one's income is interest and dividend payments from invested capital wealth and the source of the other's is wages or salaries, the first has distinct advantages in terms of living conditions over the second. The first can devote time to pursuits such as politics, culture, or leisure without having to worry about whether they pay an adequate income. The second must always keep a paying job. The first can always easily get a job if more income is desired. The second does not have the option of easily acquiring capital property to supplement the paycheck.

As we have seen above, in capitalist societies the richest individuals and families get the bulk of their income from the ownership of capital wealth (stocks, bonds, and real estate for the most part). Middle- and working-class people get the bulk of their income from wages or salaries. Put in more classic political economic terms, capitalist income comes from profits derived from the ownership of capital wealth, while the income of most other people comes from the sale of their labor. **Distribution of wealth** is invariably more unequal than is distribution of overall income because only small minorities of the population own significant amounts of capital wealth.

Figures on distribution of overall income are publicly accessible for many countries. They indicate that **distribution of income** is highly unequal in all countries. It tends to be significantly more unequal in developing than developed countries. On average, the richest 10 percent in developing countries receive 37.2 percent of all personal income, which greatly exceeds the 25.3 percent received by their developed countries' counterparts. The richest 10 percent in the United States, the most unequal of the developed countries, take 29.9 percent, which is not greatly higher than the developed country average. On the other hand, in Namibia, the most unequal of the developing countries, the rich take 64.5 percent, which greatly exceeds the developing country average (United Nations Development Programme, 2008, Table 15). Part of the reason for this pattern is that because of television and increased international travel, global standards have developed for upper- and middle- class lifestyles whose maintenance requires larger proportions of national incomes in poorer than in developed countries.

There are exceptions to the pattern. Several developing countries—Algeria, Yemen, Korea, Pakistan, Ethiopia—have distributions of income that are within the range of those of developed countries. Latin American and Caribbean countries on average have the most unequal distributions of income of the developing countries.

Before 1989, the least unequal income differences were in the communist countries. In Poland and Hungary, for example, the top 10 percent received about 21 percent of the national income, compared to 25 percent for their First World and 39 percent for their Third World counterparts, respectively (World Bank, 1994, p. 220). Thus, in most cases, there was a greater difference in the pattern of the distribution of income between developed and Third World capitalist countries than there was between developed capitalist and communist countries. Capitalist restoration in formerly communist countries, as mentioned, has inevitably led to a widening of wealth and income differences.

Figures on wealth and income distribution have political importance because the more there is an extreme polarization of income and wealth between upper and other classes, the less likely there will be political legitimacy and long-term social stability. Such data have economic importance because if the effective demand—income necessary to purchase commodities—of the majority of the population is too low, producers will not have markets and go out of business.

Governments have the power to alter distributions of income. Progressive taxation and funding of social programs (the social wage) function in the direction of equalizing incomes. Lowering tax rates for the rich, such as capital gains taxes, and cutting back social programs have opposite effects. In capitalist countries, conservatives and liberals differ over how much and in what direction state redistributive actions are necessary to maintain distributions of income within functional political and economic limits. Depending on who is in power, state policies affecting income distribution can seesaw back and forth.

TABLE 9–3
Redistribution of Household Income Upward in the United States between 1980 and 2006

Percent of Total National Income Received by	*1980*	*1992*	*2000*	*2006*
Poorest 20 percent	4.3	3.8	3.6	3.4
Second 20 percent	10.3	9.4	8.9	8.6
Third 20 percent	16.9	15.8	14.8	14.5
Fourth 20 percent	24.9	24.2	23.0	22.9
Richest 20 percent	43.7	46.9	49.8	50.5
Total	100.1	100.1	100.1	99.9
Richest 5 percent	15.8	18.6	22.1	22.3

Source: DeNavas-Walt, Cleveland, and Webster, U.S. Census Bureau (2003, p. 25)
Note: Totals do not equal 100 because of rounding.

The conservative Reagan and George H.W. Bush administrations in the United States (1981–1993) pursued policies that resulted in a redistribution of income upward as expected (see Table 9–3). The share of national income taken by the richest 5 percent of families increased by 17.7 percent, while that of the poorest 20 percent decreased by 11.6 percent. The Democratic Clinton administration (1993–2001) failed to reverse the trend. The richest 5 percent increased their share of national income further by 18.8 percent, while the poorest 20 percent decreased by 5.2 percent. Part of the reason was that conservative Republicans controlled Congress. Income inequality continued to increase during the Republican George W. Bush administration (2001–2009), though it was temporarily slowed by sharp decreases in stock market values—the main source of income for the rich—beginning in 1999 that did not recover until 2005. A main contributor to income inequality that offset the fall in stock market values was the Bush administration's aggressive pursuit of tax cuts for the wealthiest individuals and families.

RACE AND ETHNICITY

Within multiracial societies, there can be a clear correspondence between racial characteristics and the likelihood of having particular economic and social class positions. The more **racism**—the ideology that there are superior and inferior races—is institutionally ingrained, the more likely that such correspondences exist.

The origins of racism and racial tension within multiracial societies have been for the most part economic. Racism as an ideology usually develops to rationalize or justify exploitation or unfair economic treatment of one racial grouping by another. The enslavement of black Africans by whites of European descent is a particularly clear example. The labor needs of plantation economies in the Americas stimulated the African slave trade. Once blacks were in the Americas as slaves, a whole ideology of racism developed to rationalize and justify their unequal treatment.

The institutionalization of racism and racial tensions has, as is obvious, outlived the institution of slavery. African Americans in the United States are still disproportionately more likely to be members of the economic working class, less likely to be capitalists or new middle class, and more likely to be in the social working and lower classes than are whites. Racism as an ideology is reproduced intergenerationally by being both a cause and an outcome of economic discrimination against blacks. It is a cause of discrimination for obvious reasons, and the result that it produces inferior living conditions for blacks reinforces the racist rationalization of innate inferiority.

The intimate relationship of class and race in many, but not all, societies exists despite the concept of **race** itself being rejected today by most physical anthropologists as an adequate scientific basis for classifying people. Physical anthropologists gave up trying to develop taxonomies or classification schemes of discrete races in the 1940s. Among those who made such attempts in the past, there was never agreement even on what the number of supposedly different races was. For sure, there are physical differences among people, which can be called racial characteristics, with skin color variations between dark and light standing out the most. But it makes little sense to try to trace them to distinct races, and it makes much less sense to allege the existence of innately superior and inferior race. For discussions, see Simpson and Yinger, 1985, Chapter 2; Miles, 1989, Chapter 1; and Reynolds and Lieberman, 1993.

Among groups that share the same so-called "racial characteristics," there can be **ethnic** or cultural differences that correlate with the distributions of upper and lower positions in class structures. The related concepts of nations, nationalities, and national minorities describe peoples who share common ethnic characteristics that result in their developing distinct national identities, such as being French, Irish, English, or Russian. The most important characteristics of national identity are common language, land, culture, and history. The French, for example, have a common language, territory, culture, and set of historical experiences that are different from those of the English. French people, therefore, feel a common identity among themselves that they do not feel with English people. Peoples become national or ethnic minorities either when they migrate from their home territory to another where another nationality dominates (the Chinese in the United States are an example), or they are indigenous to the territory, such as Native Americans, but another nationality or ethnic group dominates.

In multicultural societies, one or more ethnic groups may disproportionately monopolize upper positions in the class structure and restrict access to them by ethnic minorities. Immigrant workers from southern and eastern Europe, for example, found themselves relegated to the economic and social lower positions in the United States at the end of the nineteenth and early decades of the twentieth centuries.

In multiracial and multicultural societies, where racial and ethnic prejudices exist and where the different racial and ethnic groupings generally only socialize within their own communities, a unitary economic class system may be accompanied by multiple social class systems. While the economic structure is integrated in the sense that there is one economy with its corresponding economic classes, the different racial and ethnic groupings who work alongside of each other may retreat at the end of the day into separate social existences within their own communities. If they lead separate social lives, do not see themselves as being on equal social terms with members of other racial or ethnic groups who share similar economic class positions, and do not intermarry with them, then they are in separate social classes despite sharing the same economic classes. White and black workers, for example, can be in the same economic class but different social class if they do not see and interact with each other as social equals.

CLASS AND RACE IN NORTH AMERICA

A comparative examination of the three countries of North America—the United States, Mexico, and Canada—reveals how class and racial dynamics can form in similar and different ways within neighboring societies.

The North American continent before the European conquest was home to a large number of indigenous societies. They varied greatly between classless hunting and gathering bands and the Aztec Empire, in which clear class differences existed between those who controlled the state apparatus and merchants, peasants, slaves, and others.

The conquest began in 1519 when Hernán Cortés landed on what today is the Gulf coast of Mexico. It took place in phases and in different parts of the continent for over three centuries, and it stopped further indigenous class development. As the Spanish and other European conquerors consolidated control of the various areas of the continent, they interlocked their own class systems onto the already existing ones of the Indians in densely populated areas, as in Mexico. In sparsely populated areas, such as New England and the United States and Canadian frontier areas, they simply constructed their own societies and class systems on tabula rasas (clean slates), so to speak. In either case, Indian class systems for the most part soon vanished. The only indigenous class position that substantially survived the conquest was that of the peasant, especially in Mexico, who continued to practice a form of subsistence-based horticulture regardless of who held power.

If in the pre-Columbian period societies had varied according to their level of technological development and degree of social complexity, in the colonial period they varied according to which European power was the colonizer. Spain, England, Holland, and France staked claims to different parts of the continent, and each instituted its own colonial set of economic and social class relationships.

Capitalism, feudalism, and slavery were the triangular poles that defined these colonial class structures. Since each power had its own institutions and was at a different level of capitalist development, what emerged during the colonial period reflected the differences between the European powers. Spain, the most economically backward of the powers, implanted semi-feudal class institutions. France, to a less extent, implanted semi-feudal class structures in New France. England implanted the most capitalistic relationships of the colonizing powers. Its areas were thus the least encumbered by feudalistic institutions and able to develop capitalistically at the greatest speed.

The Mexican class structure, which largely revolved around landlords and peasants, thus was closest to the feudal pole, while New England's, which revolved around market-oriented farmers and merchants almost from the beginning, was closest to the capitalist pole. At the same time, slavery, which revolved around the class positions of owners and slaves, was implanted, with its center in the south of what would become the United States but also in parts of the areas that would become Mexico and Canada.

Europeans implanted more than their economic and class institutions on North American soil. They also, most importantly, began world history's largest intermingling of racially different peoples since, in one way or another, the colonial and postcolonial drama threw together the European conquerors, the original indigenous inhabitants, Africans, and to a much smaller extent, Asians. Now four races and their mixed descendants would inhabit the continent. Never before in world history had so many racially distinct people been brought together on such a scale.

From the beginning of the colonial period, there developed clear correlations between class and racial position—black slave and white slave owner, Indian peasant and white landlord—that were rationalized by the ideology of racial superiority and inferiority—that is, racism. The world's races began to merge in North America, but in different class roles. They integrated, but vertically, with white Europeans at the top, directing the colonial enterprises in which people of color played subordinate parts. Class and race continued to be correlates in the postcolonial period down to the present in North America, though not as strongly.

By the end of the twentieth century, the United States and Canada had developed quite similar post-industrial economic class structures that were, at the same time, very different from those of Mexico. In economic class terms, the most remarkable difference is that over 90 percent of the labor forces of the United States and Canada are made up of employees, while a full quarter of the Mexican labor force is still self-employed. The twentieth century saw, in both the United States and

Canada, a steady driving out of business of independent farmers and storekeepers, and their, or their economic offspring's, repositioning as employees. For one generation, it was not uncommon to have been born on a farm but end up managing an office. In class terms, as what was called the "old middle class" of small-business owners declined, growing corporate and government bureaucracies opened up new positions for middle-level managers and professionals (the new middle class). Of course, not every descendent of the former majority old middle class ended up in a new middle-class position. The ranks of the urban working class also swelled with farm recruits.

The reason the economic class profile of Mexico is different is because the accumulation of capital, in the sense of large business driving out small business, has not proceeded as far. The Mexican countryside contains proportionately four or five times the number of farmers as does that of the United States or Canada. Similarly, Mexican cities contain proportionately about that many times the number of people who make their living from ownership of small businesses as do either of the other two countries.

In a number of ways, the Mexican economic class profile resembles that of the United States or Canada about 90 years ago. It follows that the future will see a steady erosion of the position of Mexican small farmers and other business owners as private corporations increase their shares of the market. Some, as happened in the United States and Canada, will move into newly created middle-class managerial and professional positions; most, as is already happening, will swell the ranks of the urban working class and poor or migrate out of the country.

If economic class development proceeds in an almost linear fashion toward the structures now shared in the United States and Canada—what the future holds for Mexico—social class history does not show so clear a progression. There are different ways in which social class configurations can develop around economic class structures. Thus, the social class profiles of Canada and the United States are not as close as are their economic class profiles. Canada has followed more redistributive policies that favor the poor than has the United States. Consequently, the size of its poor population is proportionately smaller.

In social class terms, the most outstanding difference between Mexico and its two continental neighbors is that its lower class of the poor makes up a much larger percentage of the profile. By one calculation, close to half the Mexican population lives in absolute poverty, compared to 13 percent in the United States and 7 percent in Canada. As a result of the disproportionately larger lower class, the Mexican middle class is disproportionately smaller, not exceeding 30 percent of the population, compared to about 44 and 47 percents of the populations of the United States and Canada respectively.[1]

The contemporary racial demographics of the three countries are strikingly different. Canada has proportionately the most whites, Mexico the most Indians, and the United States the most blacks. These contemporary figures follow logically from long-term historical developments. Canada had relatively little slavery in its history; hence, its black population is minimal. It has been a country mostly made up of European immigrants who, as in the United States, have had periods of ethnic conflict. Canada's Indian population, while proportionately larger than that of the United States, is much smaller than that of Mexico.

Mexico, historically the location of the Aztec and other indigenous empires, had the densest Indian population before the conquest and continues to have the densest population today. Over 98 percent of the Mexican population falls somewhere on a racial continuum between and including the poles of white and Indian. Blacks and Asians exist in Mexico, but to a much smaller degree than in the United States or Canada.

The United States is the most multiracial of the three countries, since there is significant representation of whites, blacks, and Asians, though it has proportionately the smallest Indian presence.

In all three countries there are substantial numbers of mixed-race persons. In Mexico, *mestizos*, who combine Indian and Spanish descent, make up nearly 80 percent of the population. In the United States, estimates of the proportion of blacks who also have European or Indian ancestors range between 60 and 90 percent (Davis, 1991). In Canada, the Métis population combines Indian with French and English descent.

In continental terms, mixed-race persons are the largest racial minority. However, they are culturally perceived very differently in the three countries. Mexico defines itself with pride as a mestizo society. Canada, though it has relatively few mixed-race persons, officially recognizes their existence, with the Métis being the most outstanding example. The

United States, with some exceptions in its history, has not identified mixed-race persons as such. They have been identified either as blacks in the case of mulattoes, or according to the majority part of their descent in the case of mestizos. There are, though, some indications that this cultural practice may be changing as the number of mixed-race persons who do not wish to negate or have negated part of their identity continues to grow in the United States.

Today, a half millennium after Europeans began their conquest of the indigenous societies of North America, whites continue to disproportionately occupy the top economic and social-class positions in the United States, Canada, and Mexico. In all three countries, racism and racial tension continue to be serious social problems, though with differing manifestations.

GENDER

The most primordial division within the human species—between males and females—has been the subject of considerable stratification research for the past several decades, in large part stimulated by the 1960s revival of feminism.

In most societies, males have more power than females, exercising greater dominance in economic production, political decision making, and over the domestic households within which they live. The original condition of this gender stratification is often called **patriarchy**—"rule of the father" literally, but male domination in a more generalized sense. Its most brutal expression is when male domination is imposed by physical force, as in cases of rape and domestic violence.

The concept of sexism is to gender inequality as the concept of racism is to racial inequality. Both represent attitudes that rationalize or justify the continuation of the inequality. They run the gamut from patronizing views of "the weaker sex" to raw misogynous prejudice.

The origins of patriarchy remain shrouded in controversy. Frederick Engels (1884) believed that there was an original period in world history of equality between the genders, but that once males began to accumulate private property and wealth, they consolidated their economic gains by imposing power over their households. Patriarchy then became institutionalized for all succeeding generations. Engels's explanation remains the leading hypothesis of the origins of patriarchy, but not without detractors who have either offered alternative explanations or found evidence of historical patterns that did not conform to the hypothesis.

There can be no doubt that, whatever its origins, male domination has been a salient feature of world history. The depth of its historical institutionalization is indicated by voting in most countries having been first restricted to men. It was not until the twentieth century that the franchise was extended to women in most countries, a century or more after men began voting.

The relationship between patriarchy and capitalism has shifted over time. In the early stage of capitalist development, most economic production continued to be centered within households for household consumption. Very little of it was destined for market sale. Patriarchal relations reigned within these households, mainly farm economies. But it would be difficult to argue that male labor produced more value than did female labor, since very little of either had a market value attached to it. Both were valuable not in the market sense, but in the sense of their usefulness to the survival needs of the household. Both genders worked hard at producing these survival necessities, which included food, clothing, housing, and child care and raising. There was a gender division of labor within production, but it was not necessarily an unequal one. At the same time, though, men were still the ultimate repositories of societal power. In colonial America, for example, only men could own property, vote, or give testimony in court (Ryan, 1979).

As capitalism developed, especially during the nineteenth century, a new stage emerged in which an increasing gender-related division opened between labor expended in the household for household use and labor expended in the outside market economy for wages or profits. Male labor began to be increasingly concentrated in the market economy, where it was valued in market terms. Female labor continued to be expended mainly within the household economy, where the type of value it produced, no matter how necessary or useful, was considered to be of secondary importance. This led Engels (1884, p. 158) to argue that "the emancipation of women and their equality with men are impossible so long as women are excluded from socially productive work and restricted to housework, which is private."

Engels's implication was twofold. First, women had to enter the paid labor force where market value was created; and, second, it would be possible to achieve, or at least begin to achieve, women's equality under capitalist conditions.

In the contemporary stage, though, the issue is no longer entry of women into the labor force. That has already substantially happened. Women today make up about 46 percent of the labor force of the United States and 40 percent of that of the total world economy (World Bank, 2006, Table 2.2). Rather, the issues are achievement of equality within labor forces and necessary off-the-job social services and support.

The participation rate of women in the United States and other labor forces grew in part because of the revival of feminism, which argued that for gender equality to occur, women would have to achieve positions of equality within paid labor forces. So long as their labor was performed exclusively within households, it was unpaid and did not generate economic power and equality, as also had been noted by Engels. However much feminist considerations spurred many women to seek jobs outside of the house, economic necessity was an undoubtedly more important stimulant. Up through the 1950s in the United States, it was possible for most middle- and working-class families to live moderately well on one income, but that is no longer possible for most families. It now takes two incomes to maintain most middle- and working-class standards of living. Whatever the relative weighing of the causes, the two-wage-earner family is now a firm social reality in many countries.

In the United States, women have not only increasingly moved into the labor force, but they have also begun to increase their representation in its middle-class managerial and professional strata. The advance has been of such magnitude that today there are proportionately more women than men in those occupations; 37.7 percent of full-time, year-round women workers were in professional or managerial occupations, compared to 32.5 percent of males (Hesse-Biber and Carter, 2005, p. 202). The impressiveness of that occupational advance, though, is tempered by its being concentrated largely in occupations such as teaching and nursing that have traditionally been open to women, and the reality that overall professional and managerial women workers receive only 70 percent of what males receive, with gender wage differentials continuing to exist at all occupational levels.

As many women have voluntarily or involuntarily assumed responsibility for providing household incomes, the extent to which men have been willing to correspondingly increase their responsibility for performing necessary domestic labor—child rearing, food preparation, cleaning, etc.—has varied. Many working women, thus, must endure a double shift—one in the paid labor force and one at home without help.

A growing proportion of women workers in most developed countries are the sole support of their own households. Rising rates of divorce, births out of wedlock, and women who choose to remain single have increased the number of female-headed households. In past historical periods, when traditional family households predominated, it could be assumed that there were as many women as men in each of the lower, working, middle, and upper social class categories. There were as many wives and daughters as there were husbands and sons in each of the households. Women enjoyed or were denied social class privileges, not on the basis of their gender, but on the basis of the household in which they were lucky or unlucky enough to be born or end up married into. But as more women-headed households have developed in the last few decades, income discrimination against women in the labor force, the failure of fathers to financially support their children, and the inadequacy of governmental income support programs has resulted in women being disproportionately below or just above poverty.

By the early 1980s, writers, activists, and social scientists began to note what they called an increasing feminization of poverty. Females today make up 51 percent of the population of the United States but 56 percent of the poor. The disproportion is greater if the adult poor alone are considered, which is a more important comparison, since it is adults who must provide the incomes that support families. Women make up 52 percent of adults but 60 percent of the adult poor. Altogether, women and their children make up nearly three-quarters (74 percent) of the population classified as poor in the United States (U.S. Census Bureau, 2007, Table POV01).

Although it is thus true that women are more likely to be poor than men, among women there are clear racial differences in terms of the likelihood of being poor. As Table 9–4 indicates, in the United States 26.2 percent of black and 22.6 percent of Latina women are poor, which

TABLE 9–4
Intersections of Class, Race and Gender Inequalities in the United States.
Percent Living Below Poverty, 2006.

	Male	*Female*	*All*
White	7.2	9.1	8.2
Asian	11.6	12.0	11.8
Latino	20.6	24.4	22.5
African American	22.0	26.5	24.4
All	11.2	13.7	12.5

Source: U.S. Bureau of the Census (2004a, Table POV01).

far exceeds the 9.3 percent of white women.[2] Since the poor population constitutes the lower social class, poverty figures such as these are indicators of the extent to which class, race, and gender intersect.

Key Terms and Concepts
(in order of presentation)

Stratification
Economic class
Social class
Capitalist, new-middle,
    small-business owners,
    working classes
Rentier
Upper, middle, working, lower,
    classes

Lumpen, Bourgeoise, Peasants
Personal wealth
Capital wealth
Distribution of income
Racism
Race
Ethnic group
Patriarchy

ENDNOTES

[1] I have made these calculations in James W. Russell, *Class and Race Formation in North America* (Toronto: University of Toronto Press, 2009), Chapter 8.

[2] Persons of Latin American origin in the United States, taken as a whole for statistical purposes, are variously labeled as Latino or Hispanic. The U.S. Census uses the latter label. Those who prefer the label "Latino" argue that the label "Hispanic" implies full Spanish descent, whereas most of this population is of mixed ancestry that includes Indian or African as well as Spanish roots. The existence of Indian or African ancestry in the majority of the Latino population indicates that most Latinos, in addition to being ethnically different, are also racially different from the dominant white majority.

Chapter 10

Organizations

Until relatively recently in world history, most people lived on farms and in small villages. They worked out of their houses. They did not go off to a factory or office. They did not attend school; such education as there was took place in the home. The most contact that they had with formal organizations was in attending churches and as subjects of states that demanded that they pay taxes and obey laws.

As capitalism developed and feudalism declined, private profit-oriented companies grew in size and power to the point where they began to employ significant proportions of labor forces. Economic activities began to increasingly take place in formally organized factories, stores, and banks. Localized economies gave way as the scale and location of economic life shifted from isolated rural households to centralized urban organizations. In a parallel manner, large-scale **formal organizations** emerged as the locations within which educational and other societal activities increasingly took place.

Both Karl Marx and Max Weber noted the importance of the shift from household to organizationally based economic and social life. In precapitalist societies, formal organizations, like commodities, existed only on the peripheries of social life. As capitalism developed, the number, size, and importance of formal organizations in social life increased at an exponential rate.

Today, formal organizations are social actors themselves, in the sense that their actions are not wholly reducible to the will of the individuals within them. Much is done in the name of particular organizations rather than particular individuals. As structures, formal organizations can out-live their particular human creators. Members pass into and out of orga-nizational roles while the organization itself remains.

Sociologists thus see societies as being composed of distributions of organizations as well as other groups. In order to grasp how a city or a country functions, they must identify and analyze its key organizations. To a large extent, the character of a society depends on the character of its organizations, which can be structures for dominating or for facilitat-ing freely cooperative and democratic endeavors.

ORGANIZATIONAL FUNCTIONING

In analyzing an organization, sociologists distinguish between how it functions internally, in terms of the performances and interactions of its members and various departments and units, and how it functions as a whole, in relation to other organizations or individuals under given eco-nomic, political, legal, and other conditions. One type of sociological study might analyze problems of low morale and productivity within a particular corporation; another might analyze the influence exerted by a particular lobbying organization on legislators. In either case, what is at issue is how effectively the organization functions in terms of its goals.

Analyses of the internal functioning of organizations focus first upon structures of interaction. Every organization of any size has a formal di-vision of labor. Members perform different specialized roles that carry with them different levels of authority and power. Such structures can ei-ther facilitate or hinder the accomplishment of organizational goals. What may have been an appropriate structure at one point in time may no longer be so if conditions have changed. If such structural deficien-cies are found, then the need for reorganization is indicated.

But analysis of how an organization is formally structured is usually not sufficient to fully reveal how it actually functions. Sociologists have found that most large-scale organizations have significant informal struc-tures of interaction that exist alongside of their formal structures. Jobs overlap. People bend rules. Some individuals accumulate far more power and influence through personal relations than indicated by their formal titles. In short, informal arrangements supplement formal arrangements in organizations. They may supplement them in ways that enhance overall organizational functioning and accomplishment of central goals, or they may contradict them in ways that lead to malfunctioning.

In analyzing particular organizations, sociologists thus distinguish formal and informal structures of interaction. By **formal structure** they mean the intentional way in which the organization's division of labor is defined, both in terms of specialization for the various job or other titles and in terms of structures of authority. By **informal structure** they mean regularly occurring and significant interaction patterns that have not been defined by formal rules.

For any organization to function well as a whole in terms of accomplishing its central goals, it must successfully navigate the waters of its external **environment**. Profit-making businesses, in addition to being mindful of competitors, need to be aware of changes in their markets and relevant public, legal, political, and other conditions. Nonprofit organizations as well are affected by outside conditions. Budgets of public agencies are controlled by legislatures, which themselves are affected by shifting political conditions. In all cases, the survival of organizations depends on how well they are able to strategically adapt to or overcome external conditions.

TYPES OF ORGANIZATIONS

Organizations differ according to their size—whether they are large or small—and how they are controlled—whether ultimate power is democratically vested in their members as a whole or formally restricted to owners or managers. These differences, which are interrelated, have sociological consequences. Interrelating the variables of size and mode of control yields a typology (Figure 10–1) of four fundamental types of organizations: (1) small-scale, owner-controlled organizations, (2) small-scale, member-controlled organizations, (3) large-scale, owner- or manager-controlled organizations, and (4) large-scale, member-controlled organizations. For convenience, we will call them, respectively, small businesses, cooperatives, bureaucracies, and membership associations.

MODE OF CONTROL

		Owner/Manager	Members
S	Small	1 Small Businesses	2 Cooperatives
I			
Z		3	4
E	Large	Bureaucracies	Membership Associations

Figure 10–1   Typology of Organizations

Small Businesses

Small businesses, which are large enough to have employees besides the owners, are the clearest and most common examples of small-scale, owner-controlled organizations. Their owners have exclusive power to make all significant decisions, given the prerogatives of ownership in private property systems. Their employees are expected to carry out the owner's wishes.

Medieval guild-organized shops were the prototypes of modern small-scale, owner-controlled businesses. Master craftsmen had complete control over journeymen and apprentices that they employed. The small-scale, autocratic organization was patterned after the patriarchal family, in which the father had exclusive power to rule over the women and children of the household. Most early small businesses were, in fact, operated out of households, with the father running the business as well as the family, and with women and children being subordinates in both.

In small-scale, owner-controlled organizations, superiors and subordinates work close by each other. This led Durkheim (1893, p. 354), among others, to the conclusion that small-business working relations were less alienating than those of bureaucracies, where the social and physical distances between employees and workers are much greater. But despite occupying the same physical spaces, small-business owners and employees occupy fundamentally different roles. They may perform the same tasks, but one has ultimate power over the other. The superior has the power to set the terms of work and to hire or fire the other.

Working together in close quarters requires superiors and subordinates to develop a working relationship in which the superior has the power to set the terms. The superior can be a petty tyrant who bosses people according to whim, a paternalist who treats employees as children with alternating doses of kindness and sternness, or an owner who treats employees as co-workers and otherwise equals. Subordinates, in turn, must either adapt to the terms of the relationship set by the owner or leave. If they adapt, it can be either willingly or only on the surface while harboring submerged resentment or rebellion.

For owners and employees alike in developed countries, working in small businesses carries a number of disadvantages. Small businesses generally have low profit margins and consequent low levels of income for owners and pay and benefits for employees. Owners often have to work longer hours than middle-level corporate and state managers to attain the same levels of income. There are few if any intermediate positions between entry-level positions and that of the owner, limiting possibilities for employee career advancement. Employees of small businesses are less likely to be organized into unions, further limiting their levels of pay and other financial compensations.

Cooperatives

There are many areas of social life where small groups of people combine to form organizations that they jointly control in principle. They make all decisions through consensus, majority votes, or other forms of membership control or consultation. They may have elected leaders or function without a separate leadership body.

There are many **cooperative**-type organizations that exist on an ad hoc basis alone. People organize themselves around a particular momentary issue. A group of neighbors comes together to put pressure on a city government to put a traffic light at a dangerous intersection. The organization ends with the attainment (or with the giving up on the attainment) of its founding objective. Or, once organized, the people go on to pursue other common interests.

Other small-scale, democratic organizations have more permanent, long-term existence. A group of neighborhood business owners comes together to form an organization that meets regularly to discuss and act on common issues. Groups form to study the Bible, stock market investment strategies, or public issues. Softball players organize themselves into teams and leagues that reappear each summer.

Cooperative organizations exist so long as they fulfill a useful function, and function in an acceptable manner in the eyes of their members. Their existence can also be encouraged or prohibited by governments. State authorities can facilitate formation of local cooperative organizations by making available public meeting places and providing other forms of aid. They can also restrict or drive underground local organizations of the population through legal, police, and other repressive measures.

Bureaucracies

There is a vague uneasiness felt by many people about the power of **bureaucratic** organizations to pattern how they work and live. More and more people work within bureaucratic state or private organizations; and even if they own their own business, they have to deal with tax, legal, and regulatory bureaucracies. As citizens, each person comes in contact with educational and other governmental bureaucracies. No one is free from being affected by decisions made by and rules emanating from bureaucratic organizations. The image that many have in mind when they speak disparagingly of bureaucrats is of tyrannical officials whose work lives and seeming pleasures are based on the enforcement of overly rigid and maddeningly petty rules. For many, the very idea of bureaucracies is repulsive. American populism has long taken aim at "Washington bureaucrats." Libertarians and anarchists recoil at the thought of bureaucratic control over private citizens, but others associate bureaucracies more positively with modernity and efficiency.

In bureaucracies—including private corporations and state administrative agencies—ultimate rights over leadership selection and decision making are vested at the top. Base members or employees do not, in principle, have any formal right to be involved in those decisions. Their job is to carry them out.

The term bureaucracy (from the French *bureau*, or "desk," and Greek *kratos*, or "rule of") first appeared in the nineteenth century to describe the administrative officials and their staffs of European governments. The business of government was divided up into bureaus or departments, such as finance, public works, education, and foreign affairs, with an official put in charge of each. In turn, the official in charge had a staff of subordinate officials who oversaw the work of lower-level employees.

For most of the nineteenth century this usage prevailed, with the term *bureaucracy* being identified with the administrative apparatuses of governments. But by the twentieth century the term took on a more generalized meaning, becoming synonymous with any large-scale, management- or owner-controlled public or private organization.

Bureaucracies are not intended to be democratic organizations, since ultimate control rests at the top in the hands of managers, owners, or other overseers, and base employees do not have the right to choose their managers or have final say over policy. The more that key economic and political organizations have a hierarchical bureaucratic form in a society, therefore, the fewer the areas of direct democratic control within that society.

Managers perform the key leadership roles in all private or public bureaucracies. They are responsible for coordinating and administering the factors of production from planning to budgets to production. While the functional importance of managers has grown, they do not hold ultimate power. Corporate managers are ultimately beholden to corporate owners; state managers are ultimately beholden to political authorities.

In the most neutral of senses, managers simply perform the function of efficiently coordinating the work of large-scale organizations. The true function of managers is to make sure that an organization's product or service gets produced in the most efficient and effective manner possible. To do that, they must have command over the labor force that is involved in directly producing that product or service.

Top managers, it is often pointed out, rarely know how to actually make the organization's product. Rather, they know how to direct the people who do know how to make it. A top automobile executive is as unlikely to know all of the skills involved in assembling a car, as the president of a university is unlikely to know how to teach all of the subjects. Between top managers and productive laborers there are intermediate managerial layers. The larger the scale of the organization, the more likely that such new middle-class positions will exist.

Since most large-scale organizations have some features in common, top managers can often circulate between seemingly very different types of organizations. In the United States, top directors of public sector bureaucracies, such as the Departments of Defense, Interior, Education, and Housing, are often drawn from the top managerial ranks of the private corporate world. The career of former President Dwight D. Eisenhower was a classic in this respect. After leaving the military as a general and before being elected president, he was a member of a number of corporate boards of directors and briefly president of Columbia University.

The common features of all bureaucracies have given rise to attempts to develop common principles of management. Frederick Taylor (1856–1915), a turn-of-the-century American engineer, originated the first comprehensive management system, which he called **scientific management**. Taylor observed that there was a large gap between the actual and the potential productivity of workers. He called upon managers to hire experts to study the work process itself and devise methods to make it more efficient, and thereby close the gap between actual and potential productivity. Taylor and his associates subjected work processes to intense scrutiny and then recommended changes in order to increase worker productivity.

They developed the now famous **time and motion studies**. Using stopwatches, they timed how long it took workers to complete a task and studied the motions they went through. On the basis of these observations, they proposed faster ways to accomplish the same work that involved fewer or shorter motions on the part of the worker.

One of Taylor's earliest successes was at a Pennsylvania steel mill. The mill was powered by coal that arrived intermittently by train. To get it unloaded, the managers had put out notices soliciting temporary day laborers, with the requirement that they bring their own shovels. They then hired in order of application. Taylor observed this practice and concluded that it was inefficient and unnecessarily costly. It was possible to get the coal unloaded faster with fewer men and therefore at less cost to the company. He made two recommendations that followed from the principles of his scientific management. First, managers should selectively hire according to appropriateness for the job, rather than simply on the basis of order of application. To unload coal, a big, strong man is preferred to a smaller, weaker one. Second, management should supply the tools (the shovels in the coal-unloading example) to make sure that they are the most appropriate and efficient for the task to be done. Taylor observed that many of the day laborers brought small shovels, which resulted in each of their shoveling motions being less productive and more strenuous.

Taylor's advice on how to get coal unloaded may seem to have been no more than common sense and almost comical in retrospect, but it typified an approach that was to be highly influential in managerial circles and that would profoundly reshape the workplace. Before Taylor, managers had essentially been content to oversee production, leaving decisions about how to get the work done to the workers themselves, so long as it was done. Taylor urged managers to wrest from workers control over the design of the work process. Managers and workers had different interests. The goal of management was to produce as high a profit as possible, and that required keeping labor costs down by streamlining the production process. Workers, on the other hand, were more interested in keeping the strenuousness of their jobs within tolerable limits.

Taylor also observed that the vital knowledge of how to perform many production processes was the exclusive domain of skilled workers. The craft of steel making in the nineteenth century, for example, was held and passed on by experienced workers on the plant floors. Managers only knew how to hire people who knew how to do the work. They themselves did not know the production secrets. That left management vulnerable in a double sense. If the worker or workers who knew the craft secrets were to die or otherwise leave, production would have to halt until suitable replacements were found. Similarly, in periods of industrial strife such skilled workers had inordinate power to shut down production. Taylor, therefore, urged managers to gain control over the craft secrets. The major device for doing that was to co-opt the possessors of those secrets, in particular engineers, into their own ranks. Engineers in the nineteenth century had been more like skilled workers than professionals with university degrees. By elevating their status and pay, managers were able to shift their identity and loyalty from workers to the company.

Of the scientific management school that Taylor founded, Max Weber commented:

> With the help of appropriate methods of measurement, the optimum profitability of the individual worker is calculated like that of any material means of production. On the basis of this calculation, the American system of "scientific management" enjoys the greatest triumphs in the rational conditioning and training of work performances. (Weber, 1922, p. 213).

But these triumphs of scientific management exacted high human costs in Weber's judgment:

> The psychophysical apparatus of man is completely adjusted to the demands of the outer world, the tools, the machines—in short, to an individual's "function." The individual is shorn of his natural rhythm as determined by the structure of the organism; his psychophysical apparatus is attuned to a new rhythm through methodical specialization of separately functioning muscles. (Weber, 1922, p. 213).

Weber's view that the scientific management school operated on the basis of a machine model of the workplace is widely shared today. Taylor essentially viewed workers as mechanical parts to be fitted into a smoothly functioning machine. Their feelings and emotions—in short, their human qualities—were of little importance to him. What counted was that they got the job done in the shortest, most efficient, most profitable manner possible.

The pejorative term **Taylorism**, as used today, is associated with workplace alienation and managerial strategies to pump as much work as possible out of workers without regard for their human needs. Taylor's name continues to be accorded classic status in managerial studies literature, but largely as a foil for more contemporary theories. The great fallacy of Taylor, according to much contemporary commentary, was that he did not give due regard to the human qualities of workers. By treating them as parts of a machine, he fostered as much alienation as efficiency, and in the long run, worker alienation undermined efficiency.

After Taylor, managerial experts became more concerned with winning the worker's loyalty to the company and improving workplace morale. But, as Harry Braverman (1974) observed, although Taylor and his ideas are no longer openly esteemed in managerial literature, it is not because they have been abandoned. Rather, they are now, for the most part, largely taken for granted. Taylor set in motion a series of managerial reforms in the design of the workplace that are still in place. His ideas have been supplemented by schemes to win the worker's loyalty and increase morale, as well as performance.

Membership Associations

Membership associations, as we are using the term, are large-scale organizations in which all members are vested with the formal right to participate in at least leadership selection and often major decision making. As such, they are contrary to bureaucracies, in which members or employees have no vested democratic rights. Labor unions and political parties are examples of large-scale organizations that often are structured as membership associations.

The associational form, in principle, enables democratic participation in society in a double sense. First, it enables people with common interests to come together in organizations that are large and powerful enough to effectively promote those interests. Second, by being democratically constituted, associations enable people to participate in decision making and leadership selections that directly concern them. In a very real sense, the growth of functioning associations and societal democratization go hand in hand.

An organization can be judged to be formally democratic when it has within its constitution adequate mechanisms for membership control such as provisions for voting, referenda, and recall elections. Nominally democratic organizations, though, have different types of formal provisions for membership participation in decision making, which can be judged comparatively in terms of degree and type of democratic participation by members that they allow (see Lembcke, 1988). However, just as sociologists have found that organizations contain informal as well as formal structures, they have found that the existence of formal democratic provisions is no guarantee that an organization actually functions democratically.

In any large-scale association, holders of top offices have innumerable advantages over rank-and-file members in terms of power to affect decisions. Robert Michels (1876–1936), in a classic analysis (1911), went so far as to argue that there is an **"iron law of oligarchy"** that operates in all large-scale organizations leading to undemocratic leadership domination, regardless of formal intentions or pretensions. Thus, according to him, substantive democratic control is impossible in any large-scale organization.

Michels may have overstated the case, but he did draw attention to the clear danger of leadership domination supplanting membership control of associations. It continues to be the case that associational functioning is always at least potentially problematic. To some degree, size does constrain the possibilities for direct democratic control over any type of organization. The larger the organization, the less likely that it is possible for all members to be directly involved in the making of all decisions.

There can be tension or contradiction between democracy and efficiency in an organization. A large-scale organization would be paralyzed if it required that all decisions be made by consensus. It would also be considerably slowed down if it required that there be membership votes on all decisions. At best, therefore, members of large-scale associations can only periodically vote on leaders and policy. In the meantime, daily decision making must be delegated to elected representatives who presumably act on behalf of, and in the interests of, their constituents. The democracy that exists in any given association is thus always a matter of degree.

Mixed Types

Many organizations overlap rather than fit clearly into one or another of the above categories. Organizations can combine both associational and bureaucratic features. A labor union may be organized so that members, but not clerical staff, democratically participate in the selection of leaders. The relationship between union leaders and members is associational, but the relationship between leaders and clerical staff is bureaucratic. For that reason, clerical workers for unions are often members of, and represented by, different unions. A university may be organized so that faculty democratically control most of their departmental decision making but have no formal right to participate in the selection of their top administrators and boards of trustees. The relationship between top administrators and faculty is thus partly associational and partly bureaucratic. Meanwhile, the relationship between top administrators and clerical and maintenance staff is fully bureaucratic.

Key Terms and Concepts
(in order of presentation)

Formal organization
Formal structure
Informal structure
Organizational environment
Small business
Cooperative

Bureaucracy
scientific management
Time and motion studies
Taylorism
Membership organization
Iron law of oligarchy

Chapter 11

The Family

There is a tendency to see contemporary family life as a haven from the tensions of the economic world. There, warmth and affection await people weary from the cold calculus of economic life. Indeed, sociologists consider families to be primary groups in which interaction is personal, with individuals being treated as whole persons, unlike in society's multiple secondary group settings, like classrooms and workplaces, where interaction is more impersonal and individuals are treated more in terms of just their particular roles. But it is deceptive to see a great divide between family and economic life, for family life is greatly affected by what happens economically. The ability of a family to have enough to eat, decent shelter, and other necessities for a comfortable existence within which warmth and affection can reign depends greatly on whether it has an adequate income. The relationship between family and economic life also runs the other way, with economies being dependent on the existence of family units or their institutional equivalents to provide necessary sustenance for labor force participants.

FAMILY, ECONOMY, AND SOCIETY

Family life has been a necessary condition of economic production. Families are production units themselves that function within the total production of societies. Economic production includes reproduction of the species itself, as well as production of goods and services. People must make themselves as well as the means (goods and service of their survival. Reproduction of the species is the absolutely necessary complement to the production of goods and services. Neither type of production could exist without the other.

Families produce and maintain the energy of present and future laborers. They expend efforts so that their members who are in the labor force can eat, sleep, and be cured of illnesses. Without that family labor, those workers would not be able to return to work each day. Children, in cold economic language, are future workers who must be nourished, cultivated, and trained so that they can grow up to work. Families, in this sense, are like workshops for the production of future laborers. Labor forces could not be replenished without the family labor that is performed in bringing up future workers.

Put in a broader social sense, the **family** historically has been the primary institution responsible for the physical, emotional, and moral development of children. Families reproduce the members of societies by child rearing as their primary function. For sure, families without children also have functional importance for societies; adults within them receive necessary emotional and other forms of support. But in the most historical and objective of senses, the family's greatest importance to society rests in its mission of child rearing. Historically or in the present, no other institution has been as directly responsible for the welfare of children. Without enormous labor on the part of responsible adults within households, children and societies themselves could not survive.

Babies come into the world physically helpless, dependent upon household and family labor for their survival. They require that adults be constantly present to feed, clothe, clean, and cure them of illnesses. Babies can suffer death or life-long damage—especially in brain development—if they do not receive adequate food intake. It is true that medical specialists play a role in the physical development of infants, but family or household adults play the more primary, absolutely necessary roles, roles that extend beyond infancy to the onset of adulthood.

Within family households children develop emotionally. They learn from and adapt to the mental life of the household. Early childhood and adolescence are critical periods in emotional development. It follows that the more emotionally healthy the household, the more likely that children will grow up into emotionally stable adults. Conversely, the more mentally unhealthy and unstable the household environment, the more likely that the emotional development of children will be harmed. Emotional health, of course, is only influenced by, but not totally dependent upon, family environments. Emotionally troubled persons can grow up in otherwise stable households, and mentally healthy adults can come from emotionally unstable homes.

Families and households are also the environment within which children develop morally. They acquire values and the fundamental sense of how to differentiate right from wrong. It is there that the superego—the part of the mind where judgments of right and wrong are made, according to Sigmund Freud—develops. Children are profoundly influenced by the explicit or implicit values of their household. There are strong possibilities that they will internalize those values and reproduce them in their own families as adults. But here, as with mental and emotional health, it is only possible to speak in terms of probabilities and tendencies. There is no certainty that children will necessarily follow the values of their families. They can also modify or completely rebel against them. Whatever the outcome, though, the values spoken and practiced within the family household originate the moral development of children.

The family thus performs key economic and social functions. Economically, it is a unit of labor for the production and maintenance of labor itself. Socially, it is the institution most directly responsible for the physical, emotional, and moral development of children.

FAMILY SOCIAL PROBLEMS

In an ideal world, all children would be born into families where they would receive the best possible physical, emotional, and moral care, but this world is far from ideal. Contemporary family life is beset by a large number of problems that have detrimental consequences for children and, of course, adults too. Among them are poverty, divorce, alcoholism, violence, and absence of adequate child and health care.

Poverty

The most serious problem directly affecting the physical development of children is poverty, which is especially widespread in developing countries. In conditions of poverty, children are less likely to have adequate food intakes, which are necessary for healthy physical development. No matter how responsible their parents may be, children will suffer the physical consequences of inadequate food intakes if they are born into conditions of poverty that are not mitigated by government or charitable food distribution programs. The United Nations Children's Fund (UNICEF, 2007, p. 4) estimates that 143 million children under five in the developing world suffer from undernutrition.

In addition to malnutrition, poverty causes other unhealthy living conditions for children. Diseases, which usually strike children the hardest, are more likely to start and spread where the poor live without plumbing for potable (safe drinking) water and toilets. When children of the poor are sick, they are less likely to have access to doctors and health facilities. A leading cause of death among children is dehydration, which results from chronic diarrhea. It is easily cured by doctors and other trained personnel, but they are not available to many developing country poor children, whose deaths are as unnecessary as they are tragic.

Overall, according to UNICEF (2004a, p. 17) 3,900 children die each day because they do not have safe drinking water and adequate sanitation. Two million children die before the age of five because they lack immunizations. Seventy percent of deaths under the age of five in the developing world result from acute respiratory infections, diarrhea, measles, and malaria, with malnutrition contributing to about half of the deaths. These are easily preventable or treatable causes that rarely cause death in the developed world.

Divorce and Family Reorganization

The traditional **nuclear family** includes two biological parents and their children. However, worldwide, very large numbers of children do not live within that form, living instead in single-parent, step-families, or adoptive families. When the proportion of a society's children living within the traditional form of the family suddenly decreases sharply, a series of generally unplanned-for consequences arises.

In the United States between 1960 and 1990, the proportion of children under eighteen years of age living in families where both of their biological parents were present dropped precipitously from nine out of every ten to six out of every ten (Norton and Miller, 1992). That percentage stabilized somewhat in the 1990s, so that in 2002 61.9 percent of children lived with both biological parents (Acs and Nelson, 2003).

Rising divorce rates were the leading cause of the steep decline of the two-biological-parent form in the United States. Between 1960 and 1980, the divorce rate more than doubled, so that by 1980 one out of every two marriages could be expected to end in divorce (Castro Martin and Bumpass, 1989). The United States is not unique in that respect. Across developed countries divorce rates have doubled and tripled since the mid-1960s (Furstenberg and Cherlin, 1991).

Legal changes paved the way for the increase in divorce rates in the United States. In the past, divorces could be granted only when serious fault, such as infidelity, abandonment, or insanity, was found in one of the partners. But beginning in California in 1969, states rapidly enacted statutes so that a divorce could be granted on the simple basis of incompatibility. By 1985, all of the states had enacted such no-fault divorce statutes.

There is considerable disagreement over what the rise in the divorce rate reflects. Some argue that it reflects increasing unhappiness in families. Others counter that family unhappiness may not have increased. They contend that in the past, when divorce was legally difficult, couples stayed together unhappily or separated while remaining legally married. There is also disagreement over whether the rise of divorce is a good or bad development. Some argue that no-fault divorce can strengthen the institution of marriage by allowing people to get out of bad relationships and into sounder, longer-lasting marriages. No-fault divorce also allows needed flexibility for people who are happier with two or more short-term marital commitments than with one exclusive long-term commitment. Others argue, though, that the rise in divorce rates has undermined the capacity of families to fulfill critical social functions. In particular, divorces are likely to be traumatic events for children, resulting in the destabilization of their upbringing.

In the early 1970s, as divorce rates began to rise, most professionals assumed that what was good for the parents was good for the children. If the parents wanted to divorce, it was assumed that this would be in the long-term interests of the children, because the old unhealthy, unhappy family would be dissolved, and eventually better arrangements would be found. It was optimistically assumed that although children would initially suffer discomfort in the breakup, within two to three years they would adapt to their new living arrangements. Subsequent research (Wallerstein and Blakeslee, 1989), however, cast doubt on that sanguine assessment. Disproportionately high numbers of children of divorce were found to suffer long-term emotional consequences that continued to affect them as adults. Negative consequences include distrust of and difficulty in forming close and intimate relationships on their own as adults and failure to fulfill their own educational and career potentials.

Certainly, there are also children, possibly the majority, who adapt very well to divorce and do not suffer negative psychological consequences. There are also, undoubtedly, children who benefit positively from divorce, especially when the original family situation was particularly bad. But there is a growing consensus that early estimations of the effects of divorce on children were overly optimistic. Many children have great difficulty in adjusting to divorce, difficulties that can continue to plague them into adulthood.

Children are also likely to suffer financially from divorce. It is not uncommon for them to be plummeted into poverty. Most women continue to be awarded custody of children by the courts, but they as a whole earn less money than men. As a result, the living standard of children can fall after a divorce. Most court decisions attempt to compensate for the lower income by requiring that the divorced father make child support payments. But, unfortunately, 63.2 percent of noncustodial fathers did not make full payments, and 23.9 percent did not make any at all in 2005. Noncustodial mothers—16 percent of noncustodial parents—had a similarly poor record of meeting their obligations (Grall, 2007, Table 1). As a result, the courts, the United States Congress, and a number of state legislatures have had to develop special measures to enable the collection of child support payments from negligent parents. These measures, however, have yet to fully resolve the problem. They often require that the custodial parent, overwhelmingly women, initiate and pursue protracted legal actions, actions which many women, for a variety of reasons, are reluctant to do.

In part, due to the increasing realization of the negative impact that divorce can have on children, family therapists and marriage counselors began to shift the thrust of their advice in the 1980s (see Lear, 1988). In the 1970s, most counselors stressed that what was important was that each partner in a marriage be able to fulfill personal needs. If either one or both could not do it in the present relationship, they should dissolve that relationship and live alone or find another, more fulfilling one. In the 1980s, the advice shifted to trying to find out what was positive in the relationship and what was needed to overcome problems.

Whether because of divorce, death of a parent, or birth out of wedlock, increasing numbers of children in the United States now live in households where only one parent—almost always the mother—is present. In 1960, fewer than 10 percent of children under eighteen lived in single-parent households; in 2007 the proportion was 25.8 percent—more than one in every four children (U.S. Census Bureau 2007b, Table CH1). In the case of African Americans, the single-parent household has become the largest single form of the family for raising children. Some 53.8 percent of all African American children under eighteen years of age live in single-parent households (U.S. Census Bureau 2007b, Table C3).

Single-parent families are more likely to be poor than are married-couple families, which include both two-biological-parent families and stepfamilies. Thirty-seven percent of children under eighteen years of age in 2007 in the United States who lived in single-parent households were poor, compared to 9.5 percent who lived in married-couple households (U.S. Census Bureau, 2007b, Table C8). For children under three, the contrast is even greater.

The strong correlation between the single-parent form and poverty led a number of analysts, most notably Moynihan (1965), to argue that high percentages of out-of-wedlock births and family instability, especially among African Americans, were impeding declines in poverty and other social problems. Moynihan's conclusion touched off a fierce debate, with his detractors arguing that institutional racism was a more important cause of black poverty than family patterns.

In addition to a rise in the number of children living in single-parent households, there are also increasing numbers of children living in **stepfamilies**. When a single parent marries or remarriesor, when a just-divorced parent remarries, new stepfamilies are created in which there is one biological and one stepparent. The proportion of stepfamilies has grown dramatically with the increase in the divorce rate, making it now a major subtype of the family. Of children living in the United States, 7.4 percent live in stepfamilies (U.S. Census Bureau, 2007b, Table C9). But many of those now living in two-biological-parent and single-parent families eventually will live in stepfamilies, as currently married biological parents divorce and remarry, and as single parents marry or remarry. As many as one out of every three children will live at one time in a stepfamily situation.

Stepfamilies have unique problems. Interaction between stepparents and children can be problematic. Stepparents do not have the same degree of cultural legitimacy as biological parents in the eyes of children and others, and there is much that suggests that the role of the stepparent continues to carry considerable social stigmatization. Many childhood stories, such as *Cinderella* and *Hanzel and Gretel*, portray stepparents as evil or wicked to children. Yet stepparents are expected to assume the same responsibilities as biological parents for children's welfare. As the number of stepfamilies has grown, there has been a growing realization that they are prone to unique types of tensions (Maddox, 1976; Furstenberg and Cherlin, 1991; Stewart, 2007). In part, that is because stepfamilies, despite being increasingly common, are still stigmatized culturally and viewed as abnormal. However, large numbers of stepfamilies function well, indicating that it is possible for children to thrive in them as well as in more traditional two-biological-parent families.

Alcoholism

If one or both parents in a household are alcoholics, children are likely to suffer from an unstable emotional environment. Families that contain active alcoholics are beset by large numbers of destabilizing problems. Excessive drinking by one or more parents impairs their ability to perform necessary work and household roles. They can lose their jobs, causing family income to plunge. They can lose their ability to parent, causing children to be set adrift in a sea of emotional chaos. The destabilizing effect of alcoholism on families is a significant international problem, with the exception of the Islamic countries, where alcohol sales are prohibited. About 7.7 percent of the United States population suffers from alcoholism (Substance Abuse and Mental Health Services Administration, 2007). Extrapolating that figure and earlier estimates (Berry and Boland, 1977, p. 52), as many as one in four households contains at least one alcoholic adult.

Most professionals today view **alcoholism** as a disease, not a moral condition, with mental and possibly physical sources. Alcoholics have a deep-seated mental and possibly physical compulsion to drink that results in the impairment of their abilities to function physically or socially. No matter how much they may want to stop drinking, it is not easy. They must overcome an extraordinarily powerful compulsion. Alcoholism is thus a difficult problem to treat, both for the alcoholic who wants to recover and for family members who want to regain household stability. Yet it is not an impossible problem, since many alcoholics and their families have been successful. Though no one approach to treatment can claim perfect cure rates, treatment programs and community-based self-help groups such as Alcoholics Anonymous have often proved to be helpful.

Domestic Violence

In recent years, social research in many countries has documented alarmingly high rates of domestic violence. Far from being nests of tranquility, many families are caldrons of tension that boil over into emotional and physical violence. The victims of domestic violence are usually children and women, who are physically weaker than parents and males, respectively. Smaller subsets of domestic violence involve women and children as perpetrators. Domestic violence causes incalculable emotional damage to children, who grow up either as its direct victims or who witness it between parents.

Gelles (1985) defined as abusive and violent domestic interaction "kicking, biting, punching, hitting or trying to hit with an object, beating, threatening with a gun or a knife, and using a gun or a knife." Based on data gathered from a national sample in the United States, he concluded that "3.8 percent of women living with men are abused each year," and "child abuse involves 3.6 percent, or 1.6 million children aged 3 to 17." This undoubtedly was a conservative estimate. It relied upon the truthfulness of respondents, who were being questioned about a subject that, like alcoholism, many people are reticent to admit openly or discuss openly.

According to more recent studies (ACEP, American College of Emergency Physicians, 2005), two million children a year are abused in the United States, resulting in one thousand deaths; and 20 percent of children are sexually abused before becoming adults.

Parents may use physical force spontaneously against children out of uncontrolled frustration or rage. There is little disagreement that this constitutes child abuse. They may also use physical force as calculated punishment to control and discipline children. Here there is widespread disagreement regarding how much physical force can be legitimately used. Spanking is acceptable in many cultures, though not slaps, punches, or stronger measures. Other societies, such as Finland, consider spanking and any other form of striking children to be unacceptable and illegal. Finnish parents who lay a hand on their children for any reason, including spanking, can be arrested and fined.

More widespread than child abuse is the practice of men using physical force to dominate their wives and girlfriends. Intimate partners can become intimate enemies, with love and violence becoming intertwined in pathological forms. Social research has conclusively documented widespread wife and girlfriend battering in the United States. One study (Stark and Flitcraft, 1988) concluded that women abused by their husbands or boyfriends accounted for one out of every five trauma admissions to hospital emergency rooms. Yearly in the United States, domestic violence accounts for batterings of between two and four million women and two thousand deaths. It is the single largest cause of injury to women between the ages of 15 and 44 (American College of Emergency Physicians, 2005).

In the 1970s, organized women's groups increased public awareness in the United States of the extent of violence against women within families. That campaign established the need for battered women's shelters, where women could flee and find refuge. Those shelters, which exist now in most areas of significant population size, are unfortunately almost always busy, reflecting the dismal underlying social reality of considerable family violence.

Domestic violence within couples seems to move in cycles. Tensions set off an argument that escalates into violence. A cooling-off period follows. The husband or boyfriend realizes what he has done, apologizes, and begs for forgiveness. Daily routines of work and family life resume until tensions trigger another violent episode. Studies of women who seek refuge in shelters show that many of them have endured years of periodic physical abuse before fleeing. They stayed in the relationship out of a combination of hope that things would somehow get better and feeling that they were trapped without economic alternatives to take care of themselves and their children.

Domestic violence exists in all economic and social classes, but the most serious form of it—murder—occurs disproportionately in lower social classes (Pelton, 1981). The harshness of lower-class living conditions may be responsible for breeding greater family violence as well as general violence. It follows that if harsh living conditions increase the likelihood that there will be violent tensions within families, it may be that family violence is even more widespread in developing countries, where levels of poverty and absolute misery are much higher than in developed countries.

In the United States, all social classes are exposed to the rampant violence portrayed on prime-time television. Violence is projected on television as a normal, indeed preferred, response by heroes and villains alike to conflicts. While lower-class life is in reality more violent than that of other classes, all classes to some extent live in the television-engendered vicarious climate of violence. Both forms of violence—real and vicarious—may create a climate that increases the likelihood that physical force will be resorted to in family disputes.

Child Care

Until relatively recently in history, most people lived and worked on farms where the location of home and work in the same physical space facilitated the care of children. The developments of capitalism, factories, and urbanization increasingly separated the physical locations of home and work life. But there was little resulting problem in child care because the gender division from the farm was reproduced in the city: men went off to work in the paid labor force, while women labored at home taking care of households and children.

However, now with greater numbers of women being forced to find paying jobs to make financial ends meet at home—the rise of the **two-wage-earner family**—it has become increasingly difficult to maintain this traditional division of labor. The mobilization of women's labor into paid labor forces has left young children without the possibility of being cared for by their mothers at home. By 1990, 47.5 percent of all children under three in the United States were being cared for during the workday in a child-care center or by someone other than their parents (Hofferth, et al., 1991).

A number of European and Scandinavian countries, such as France, Sweden, and Finland, which have experienced the massive entrance of women into their paid labor forces, have developed comprehensive programs to cope with the resulting gap in child care. But most other countries, including the United States, have not. In these latter countries, working parents confront a patchwork of mostly less than satisfactory solutions, which range from an informal economy of neighborhood mothers who take in other children during the day to high-quality but highly expensive preschools that cater to upper-middle- and upper-class families.

Most workers in established child-care centers—especially those that most middle- and working-class parents can afford—receive low wages. In the United States it is often the case that a person can make more money taking care of animals than taking care of small children. As a result, there is a high turnover of the labor force in these centers. Many take low-paying child-care jobs as stopgap measures until they can find better-paying positions. With there being little incentive for workers to develop experience and professional careers in child care, children are taught and taken care of by a constantly shifting group of adults. Most working parents thus find the quality and affordability of available child care to be inversely related: what they can afford is unsatisfactory, while what they would like for their children is beyond their financial reach.

Health Care

Families are directly concerned with the health of their members. When young or adult members are very sick or suffer serious injuries, they must rely on the help of other household members. Similarly, it is the family unit that is responsible in most cases for absorbing the financial costs that result from sicknesses or injuries.

The original health-care dilemma for a society and its families is that there are unequal needs. Sicknesses and injuries are not equally distributed. Sicknesses strike some groups, such as older people and those with inherited or acquired medical conditions, more than others. Injuries happen unexpectedly to otherwise healthy persons when accidents occur. Because of having unequal incomes, families have different abilities to pay for the resulting costs of sicknesses and injuries. It follows that if access to health-care services was completely determined by ability to pay, many families would have to go without.

Societies have resolved this dilemma by spreading the financial costs of illness and injuries among larger and larger groups. In the past, families stricken by sudden medical crises had to rely on financial help from relatives, neighbors, or other members of their communities. Occasionally in the nineteenth and early twentieth centuries, membership unions and immigrant organizations in the United States contributed regular payments to special funds that could be disbursed to pay medical bills. These were forerunners of private insurance policies that spread the medically related financial risks of illnesses and injuries among a larger population base of premium-paying families and individuals. But the ability to afford insurance policies varies from family to family. While private insurance programs significantly improved access to health care, they were not sufficiently affordable to ensure universal access.

As a result, by the 1990s all developed countries, with the notable exception of the United States, had comprehensive government-sponsored health-care programs to cover all of their citizens. By socializing—that is, spreading out and equalizing—the risks and costs of illnesses and injuries among all citizens, they essentially resorted to a socialist solution to a capitalist problem. Rather than having effective demand determine access to health care, as would occur under purely market conditions, they made health care, like public education, a right to which all citizens were entitled.

A Commonwealth Fund (2008, p.15) study found that the United States has the most expensive health-care system in the world. On a per capita basis it is over twice as expensive as those of other developed countries. Yet 47 million people in 2006, 15.8 percent of the population (DeNavas et al., 2007, Table 6), remain uninsured. Many more are underinsured, and the quality of the U.S. health-care system is last among developed countries. It has more preventable deaths—that is, deaths that could have been avoided with adequate health care—than in any other developed country (Commonwealth Fund, 2008, p. 19). Overall, the World Health Organization (2005) ranked the quality of the U.S. health-care system 37th in the world, below that of all other developed countries and a number of developing countries as well.

The United States, for reasons that have most to do with its historical and political development, continues to use market forces to determine access to health care. Most of its families obtain it through private insurance programs that they receive as employer-supplied benefits. But because unemployed persons do not have access to these benefits and many employers do not offer them, a significant and growing number of citizens have no insurance at all. To compound matters, there are significant differences in insurance programs, with some covering much more illness- and injury-related costs than others. As a result, families in the United States, unlike those in other developed countries, continue to have highly unequal access to health care.

FAMILY SOCIAL POLICY AND LEGISLATION

It is unlikely that there ever was a past golden age of family life in which all children were happily well taken care of by their parents. For much of the past, there were undoubtedly significant numbers of family conflicts and children who suffered poor physical and emotional living conditions. One of the reasons why present conditions may appear much worse than those of the past is simply that more attention is being directed toward them. Contemporary social research and advocacy groups have played key roles in uncovering and publicizing family problems, such as child abuse and wife battering. It is thus always necessary to distinguish between the objective existence of a problem and the extent to which there is public awareness of it. Serious social problems can exist without drawing much public attention. Similarly, less serious problems can be the focus of inordinate amounts of attention.

Nevertheless, there are a number of trends that have aggravated family problems. The rise of the two-wage-earner family has drained family labor time away from the care of children. Rising divorce rates have resulted in children having to emotionally adjust to new family living arrangements, adjustments that have proved to be much more difficult than anticipated by professionals in the field when divorce rates began to rise in the early 1970s.

Nearly all commentators agree that the family is under pressure, but they disagree about what, if anything, governments should do to relieve it. Conservatives in the United States argue that government programs have weakened the family by removing incentives for family units to be self-reliant. According to them, the more governments subsidize health care, child care, and other living costs, the more families lose their functional importance. Conservatives believe that family living conditions ought to be largely determined by how the family's breadwinner or breadwinners fare in the economic marketplace. The more money they made, the more comfortable the family's living standard will be. According to conservative theory, dependence of their family's as well as their own living standards on their income gives heads of households extra incentives to work hard and produce, which ultimately benefits society as a whole with a strong economy.

Liberal, social democratic, and socialist theories, in progressively greater degrees, maintain that state aid is necessary to support families. State-financed education, health insurance, child care, and other programs socialize and equalize the costs of bringing up children. They ensure that all children, regardless of family income, have access to vital services. If the distribution of such services were left up to what families could individually afford, large numbers of children would go without in varying degrees, and family living conditions for the poor would approach absolute misery. If governments did not provide food and income subsidies, babies from poor families would not have enough to eat or access to health care, resulting in higher infant mortality rates.

Working- and middle-class families are also in need of state-subsidized programs. Public education, which benefits all classes, is greatly subsidized. Student loans and grants for college education are often state supported. There are federally backed housing loans. There are state-supported crisis intervention and disaster programs that are available to all families in time of need. Employer- or government-financed paid leave from work for new parents, which exists in many developed countries, benefits all classes.

There are two additional reasons that advocates of government support for families cite. First, whatever the merits or defects of their parents, children cannot be held responsible for the living conditions into which they are born. Any doctrine of fairness would dictate that all children deserve equal access to health, education, and other necessities. Second, children are the future of societies. Those societies that do not invest in their upbringing will surely pay the consequences. If generations of poor children are brought up in squalid, alienating conditions, which lead them to drop out of school, there will be future social costs of increased crime, inadequately trained labor forces, and unplanned-for pregnancies, among other problems.

Whatever the future form of the family, children will always be present in society. What is socially done to protect and promote their potential development will positively benefit the development of society itself. There are great social risks involved in leaving the fate of children completely up to chance or the financial abilities of individual families. The key question for public policy is whether society as a whole, through government action, will take more responsibility for the welfare of children. If it does not, it will have to pay for the economic and social consequences in the future.

Key Terms and Concepts
(in order of presentation)

Family	Stepfamily
Nuclear family	Alcholism
Single-parent family	Two-wage-earner family

Chapter 12

Population

Demography is the specialization within sociology that studies the sizes, distributions, and rates of change of populations. Demographers derive their basic data from censuses, vital statistics (of births, deaths, and marriages), and population sample surveys. Demographic information is used to describe and analyze particular societies and their components. Governments use population counts to determine allocations of services such as public schools. Businesses use them to determine potential markets. Social scientists use information on the internal distribution of populations as raw material for empirical studies.

In one respect, demography is a fairly straightforward and technical specialization devoted to the noncontroversial task of making counts, but behind that appearance, as with all parts of the social sciences, rests a series of controversial issues.

MALTHUS AND OVERPOPULATION THEORIES

Among the most important and controversial issues that demographers address is whether the world and the countries within it are overpopulated. Theories that the world is headed for an overpopulation catastrophe go back two centuries to the 1798 publication of *An Essay on the Principle of Population* by the English clergyman and political economist Thomas Robert Malthus (1766–1834).

227

Malthus argued that population grew at a faster rate than the production of food and other necessities, resulting in the long-term tendency for absolute increases in starvation and other forms of human deprivation. He concluded that populations double every twenty-five years, with increases in production of food and other necessities lagging behind. In Malthus's (1798, p. 86) famous formulation, "population, when unchecked, increases in geometric ratio. Subsistence increases only in an arithmetical ratio." Consequently, over time, in his reasoning, the gap between population size and means of subsistence would grow at an accelerating rate:

> Taking the whole earth... and supposing the present population equal to a thousand millions, the human species would increase as the numbers 1, 2, 4, 8, 16, 32, 64, 128, 256, and subsistence as 1, 2, 3, 4, 5, 6, 7, 8, 9; in three centuries as 4096 to 13, and in two thousand years the difference would be almost incalculable (Malthus, 1798, p. 86).

Malthus's projection of an impending overpopulation apocalypse directly countered the central argument of utopian reformers and the ideologists of the still-unfolding French Revolution that humans had the capability to rationally perfect their societies. No matter what they did, according to his dire prediction, humans would face a bleak future of accumulating food shortages that would undercut any possibility of improving the quality of life.

Malthus's hypothesis was based upon speculative reasoning, since in 1798 there was very little valid empirical information about contemporary or past population sizes. Very few countries had accurate censuses of their population. That type of information only became available in the twentieth century as countries developed accurate censuses and the field of historical demography was able to construct estimates of population sizes in earlier historical periods. As a result, it is now possible to test Malthus's central hypothesis that populations grow at a geometric rate, doubling every twenty-five years.

Figure 12–1 represents how Malthus believed world population grew. Figure 12–2, based upon current estimates of how world population has actually grown (Table 12–1), shows that world population grew at a fairly low rate until the 1600s, the beginning of the modern era, when it began to accelerate sharply. It did not grow at a steady geometric ratio, as had been hypothesized by Malthus.

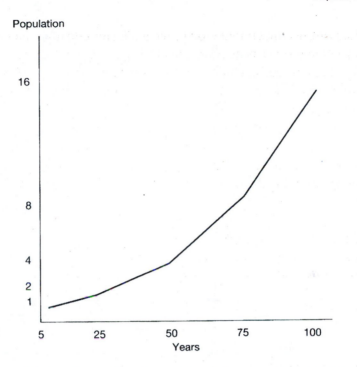

Figure 12–1   Population Growth in Billions as Hypothesized by Malthus

TABLE 12–1
Growth of the World's Population

Year	World's Population (in millions)
23,000 B.C.	3.34
8000 B.C.	5.32
4000 B.C.	86.5
1 A.D.	133
1650	545
1750	728
1800	936
1900	1,610
1950	2,400
2000	6,052
2003	6,272

Sources: Deevey (1960); World Bank (2004)

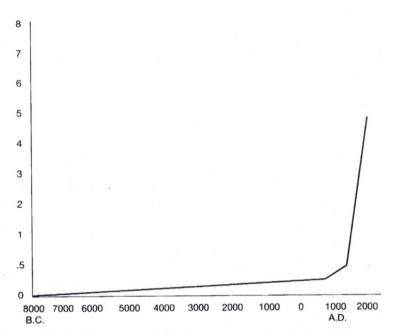

Figure 12–2   World Population Growth in billions from 8000 B.C. to Present

However, Figure 12–2 is partially misleading because it does not include data from the period prior to 8000 B.C. In an influential article, Edward S. Deevey, Jr. (1960) replotted the growth of world population using logarithms instead of numbers. This enabled him to construct axes that handled longer periods of time and more people. As Figure 12–3 shows, world population has grown neither at a steady geometric rate, as predicted by Malthus, nor in the manner suggested by Figure 12–2. Rather, it has grown in three distinct stages characterized by periods of surges and levelings off.

According to Deevey's general interpretation, each new stage was initiated by a technological advance that increased the amount of people who could be supported. The discovery and spread of horticulture and later agriculture initiated the second stage around 8000 B.C.; and the scientific-industrial revolution initiated the third stage around 1650. Deevey suggested that the current period of high population growth rates would eventually taper off as the maximum number of people who could be supported by industrial technologies was reached. That maxi-

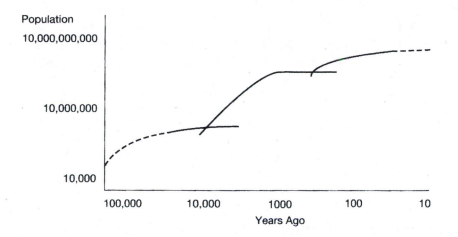

Figure 12–3   Logarithmic Growth of World Population from 23,000
B.C. To Present
Source: Deevey (1960)

mum would be, he estimated, at least several times as large as the current world population.

Deevey's and similar interpretations suggest that the great error of Malthus was that he considered population growth rates as developing in isolation from economic and technological developments.

CONTEMPORARY WORLD POPULATION CONDITIONS

Despite Malthus's misconception of how populations grow, **neo-Malthusians** hold that it is still valid to see overly rapid population growth rates outstripping resource bases (particularly food) and portending global disaster. Aldous Huxley (1958) once warned that over-population was the second greatest problem facing humanity (the threat of nuclear war being the first). It is widely assumed in the developed countries that overpopulation is one of the primary causes of poverty in developing countries.

Current discussions of population and possible overpopulation start with two observations. First, world population, which had been growing at a rapid rate, began to grow at an even faster rate after 1945. That produced a surge within the surge associated with industrialism, as shown by Deevey above. By 2000, world population stood at six billion one hundred thousand, compared to two billion four hundred thousand in 1950—two and a half times as high. Second, developing country populations are growing at much faster rates than those of developed countries. The reverse had been true before 1920.

Demographic transition theory is particularly useful for interpreting these observations. According to it, population growth rates within countries go through three phases: an initial phase in which there are both high birth and death rates, resulting in population growing little or not at all; a period of declining death rates when birth rates remain unchanged, resulting in a surge in population growth; and a final period when birth rates decline, resulting in a leveling off of population growth rates. Put more succinctly, a demographic transition is "the process of change from high birth and death rates to low birth and death rates" (Kammeyer and Ginn, 1986, p. 254). The developed countries have all completed this transition and currently have low population growth rates.

The year in which Malthus made his dire projection, 1798, was during the surge phase of the First World demographic transition. It appeared that population growth rates were soaring because they were. But what Malthus could not see was that they were destined to level off. For that reason, it is always hazardous to predict future population developments from present trends. Statements such as "if present rates of growth continue…" are always fraught with potential error. Future rates of growth will be greatly affected by factors that do not yet exist.

The reason why today both developing country and overall world population is growing rapidly is because developing countries are in the surge phases of their demographic transitions, surges that are sufficiently large to accelerate overall world population growth rates. The surge in developing country population growth rates was largely caused by the post-World War II international diffusion of vaccines and other means of combating infectious diseases. Dramatic reductions in deaths caused by infectious diseases resulted in more babies surviving infancy and more people growing to older ages. At the same time, birth rates have not declined enough to offset decreases in death rates and move countries into the leveling-off phase of the demographic transition. It is most likely that by 2020 the size of annual increases in the world's population will peak (Livi-Bacci, 1992, p. 202), inaugurating the beginning of the leveling-off phase of this latest demographic transition phase in world history, as predicted by Deevey above.

There are a number of reasons why developing country birth rates have remained higher than those of developed countries. They have proportionately more people working in rural areas than do developed countries, resulting in large families continuing to be economically functional, at least in the short run. Even those families that have been forced by landlessness and rural poverty into moving to the mushrooming Third World urban centers find that children are productive at early ages in cities in countries where child labor has not yet been made illegal. As any visitor to a poor Third World city knows, many children work at selling newspapers and gum, washing windshields of cars, doing odd jobs in workshops, and picking rags rather than attending school. In developing countries, privately funded pensions and state-subsidized social security programs for retired workers are rare. Old people are supported by their families, which results in an added incentive to have large families. Finally, in much of the Third World, building a large family is as much a mark of prestige and success as building a large fortune, especially when the latter is virtually impossible for the vast majority.

Despite these obstacles, developing country birth rates have been declining dramatically since the 1960s, when family-planning information and contraceptive devices began to be spread. The proportion of couples who use contraception for birth control is now approaching that of developed countries. Fertility rates for women fell dramatically between 1970 and 2005 from 5.4 to 2.9 children per mother (UNDP, 2007, Table 5). Thus, though developing country birth rates remain higher than those of developed countries, the gap has been closing rapidly.

It is abundantly clear that family planning, beyond its importance for lowering overall birth rates, has the effect of improving the prospects for a family's standard of living, especially in developing countries. The fewer the number of dependents in a household, the greater the per capita income of each. Parents can care for two or three children much better than they can ten.

The reality that relatively high population growth rates remain in most developing countries does not necessarily mean that they are absolutely overpopulated or that they must inevitably endure starvation and malnutrition. India, which is often pointed to as a greatly overpopulated country, has a similar **population density** (people per square kilometer) as those of Belgium and Japan, and a lower one than the Netherlands, countries never considered to be overpopulated (World Bank, 2007, Table 1). Bangladesh, whose people suffer greatly from high rates of malnutrition, has one of the world's most lush food-growing areas.

These demographic facts indicate that developing country population growth rates or relatively large family sizes cannot be the sole explanation for why there is so much starvation and malnutrition. An alternative and more plausible explanation of poor country malnutrition is that it results primarily from unequal distribution of the world's food resources. Each year more total food is produced in the world than total necessary consumption needs, and the excess has consistently grown since at least 1964, for which figures are available. In 1999, for example, world food production allowed an average per capita consumption of 2803 calories, well above the 1720–1960 threshold for adequate nourishment. That consumption, though, was unequally distributed. Developed countries on average consumed 3380 calories, while developing countries consumed 2549. Sub-Saharan African countries consumed 2185 (FAO, 2002, chapter 2). It follows that if world food resources were more equitably distributed between and within countries, malnutrition would diminish regardless of rates of population growth.

Unfortunately, the misperception that overpopulation is the root cause of Third World poverty is continually fed by First World media images, which constantly focus on crowds and crowded conditions for story backdrops. Television features about poverty in Mexico continually reinforce the image that the country is overpopulated by focusing on crowded shanty neighborhoods. The image would be different if the camera focused on vast stretches of uninhabited land owned by the rich or controlled by First World-based agribusiness corporations. This media practice results in stereotyping and exemplifies what sociologists refer to as the distinction between reality and the perception of reality. Perceptions of reality do not necessarily have to be produced according to what the actual underlying reality is (see Table 12–2).

In studying such phenomena, it is always necessary to keep in mind why perceptions can vary from realities. The perception that overpopulation is the root of developing country problems in large part serves First

TABLE 12–2
Overpopulation: Perception and Reality—Some Examples

	Population Density (people per square kilometer)
Perceived as overpopulated	
Mexico	55
India	373
Not Perceived as overpopulated	
Belgium	347
Japan	350
Netherlands	483

Source: World Bank (2007, Table 1).

World and Third World elite ideological needs. Blaming the appallingly miserable living conditions that prevail in developing countries on overpopulation shifts the focus from how resources and products are distributed within the world economy, which disproportionately benefit developed countries and the Third World rich at the expense of Third World majorities. The not-so-hidden message of the overpopulation argument is that the poor cause their own poverty by having too many babies, a message that amounts to what sociologists call "blaming the victim."

It can thus be safely concluded that overpopulation is not the underlying cause of Third World misery. While there continue to be families that have more children than they can adequately support, some areas may be overcrowded, and high population growth rates may slow economic development, there is no evidence that developing countries are absolutely overpopulated, in the sense of having more people than could be supported with an equitable system of resource and product distribution.

POPULATION CONTROL AND DEVELOPMENT

Since the 1950s there has been a growing controversy regarding population control programs designed to lower developing country birth rates. Population control advocates argue that Third World growth rates undermine development in those countries in the short run and world stability in the long run.

Up until the middle 1960s, the United States government largely avoided involvement in population control programs. The issue of government-encouraged birth control was politically controversial, given the Catholic church's historical opposition. Advocacy of population control programs for developing countries was largely in private hands, with the Rockefeller Foundation and other private concerns taking the lead. By 1965, though, the Johnson administration had become convinced that the U.S. government had to underwrite population control efforts in developing countries. On June 25, 1965, President Johnson told the United Nations General Assembly that "$5 invested in birth control is worth $100 invested in economic growth" (cited in Barclay, Enright, and Reynolds, 1970, p. 2). The government replaced private foundations as the leading funder of such Third World population control programs as educational campaigns and birth control clinics. By the late 1960s, the United States Congress increasingly attached to bills authorizing foreign aid to particular developing countries the requirement that they have population control programs (Mass, 1976, p. 58). (Ironically, the United States government, which was the leading advocate of population control programs in the Third World during the 1960s and 1970s, stopped forcefully advancing that position during the 1980s and early 1990s because of the ascendancy into the White House of conservative Republicans who were committed to outlawing abortions. China, which had vehemently criticized Western programs to control population growth rates in the Third World during the 1960s, instituted the world's strictest population control program. Two of the major proponents in the international debate over population growth in the Third World thus essentially switched sides.)

Behind the well-meaning belief that cutting population growth rates would benefit the Third World poor were political fears and concerns that verged on racism. Politically, in a time when the Vietnam War, which pitted a First World power against a communist-led insurgency, was still raging, many believed that overpopulation caused poverty, and that poverty bred communism. The not-so-subtle racial fear was that Third World nonwhite people were increasing much faster than First World whites. One 1969 newspaper ad advocating population control (cited in Barclay, Enright, and Reynolds, 1970, p. 7) bluntly stated, "The ever mounting tidal wave of humanity now challenges us to control it, or be submerged along with all our civilized values."

The intersection of racist motives and population control goes back to the late-nineteenth-century upper-class **eugenics** movement in the United States. Eugenics was founded on the belief that countries ought to practice selective breeding of their populations in order to maximize strong over weak genetic traits. Not surprisingly, in the climate of those times, strong traits were associated with whites from Northern and Western European backgrounds, while weak traits were associated with nonwhites and Southern and Eastern Europeans. The eugenicists advocated national quotas on immigration (to maximize entry of people with "strong" traits) and sterilization of the mentally incapacitated.

By the 1930s and 1940s, eugenicism died out in the United States, largely in reaction to Nazi practices that had been founded on similar beliefs in the genetic superiority of particular races and peoples. Many leading eugenicists, however, transformed their concerns into the more broadly conceived concern for Third World population control to avoid worldwide overpopulation (Barclay, Enright, and Reynolds, 1970).

In the 1960s' rush to cut Third World birth rates, many abuses occurred. Poverty in Puerto Rico was blamed on overpopulation, and Puerto Rican women were urged by a well-financed campaign to reduce the number of their pregnancies. Doctors advocated that women undergo sterilization as the ultimate solution to birth control. By 1965, 35 percent of the women of childbearing age in Puerto Rico had been sterilized. Two-thirds of them were still in their twenties when the operation was performed (Mass, 1976, p. 95). In some countries, men were offered portable radios or cash if they would have vasectomies. In the domestic United States, nonwhites (blacks, Latinos, and Indians) were also subjected to a barrage of appeals to limit their birth rates.

NATIONAL POPULATION POLICIES

Governments can either have intentional or laissez-faire population policies. They can either intentionally seek to plan growth rates, or they can avoid involvement and leave the course of growth rates up to fate. Racist and political motives aside, there are legitimate reasons why countries can adopt policies that intentionally seek to decrease or increase their population sizes. Developing countries may conclude that the pace of population increase is dysfunctional for their development needs and seek to slow it. Other countries may conclude that their population bases are either not growing fast enough or are actually decreasing, and seek to stimulate population growth. The United States in the nineteenth and early twentieth centuries pursued policies to attract people to the country. A number of Eastern European and Scandinavian countries today deem themselves to be underpopulated and have policies aimed at increasing the number of people within their borders. The majority of countries in the world, though, do not have intentional population policies. Either they take the laissez-faire attitude of allowing growth rates to develop as they will, or they are in the preliminary stages of developing population policies.

Three variables—birth rates, death rates, and migration patterns— determine population growth rates and therefore form the areas available for national population planning. Governments can stimulate birth rates by offering incentives to parents, such as tax breaks, paid leave, and other social benefits. Birth rates can be lowered in the most benign way by making birth control information and low-cost or free contraceptive devices available. Repressive approaches to lowering birth rates can impose a variety of penalties to discourage pregnancies. China, for example, began a strict program in 1980 to limit families to one child. Among the negative sanctions used was to deny the right of free education to a third-born child (Peters and Larkin, 1983, p. 183).

Only the most draconian national population policy would intentionally attempt to increase death rates in order to lower population growth rates. However, past First World inaction toward famines and other death-causing disasters in the Third World was sometimes justified by the argument that such disasters are not wholly bad, since they serve to decrease population sizes (for a critique, see Baran, 1957, pp. 237-248). In a more positive light, all national public health programs have the effect of decreasing infant and general mortality rates, and therefore serve to stimulate the growth of population. Withholding such programs would have the opposite effect, whether intended or not.

National governments can either encourage or discourage migration into their countries as a means of affecting population growth rates. As mentioned, the United States filled up what was largely a sparsely populated country by allowing almost unlimited immigration up until the early twentieth century. (The Chinese were excluded after 1882—the beginning of racialist-oriented national quota systems.) The U.S. borders were closed to large-scale immigration only after the Immigration Act of 1921. Australia and New Zealand are countries today that are trying to increase their population sizes by encouraging immigration, though they are highly selective in who they admit.

MIGRATION AND URBANIZATION

People migrate within and between societies. In both cases, a series of what demographers call **push-and-pull factors** affect their decisions. Conditions such as economic deterioration, famine, or war influence decisions to leave one location, to push people out. Other conditions, such as perceived economic opportunities, greater prosperity, or peace, can attract or pull people to other locations.

Economic misery and warfare are the primary push factors that today account for legal and illegal migration from developing to developed countries. The latter economies, in turn, pull Third World migrants by their relative prosperity and often the availability of low-wage jobs. The main international direction of both legal and illegal labor migration is thus from relatively poor to relatively prosperous economies, with people leaving developing countries for perceived better living conditions in Western Europe and the United States.

The effects of such migration on Third World development are mixed. On the one hand, lack of land and jobs drives peasants and workers to search abroad for income opportunities. They often send money back to their families who remain at home. These remittances can be a considerable source of income to the national economy. On the other hand, professionals such as doctors and engineers leave not because they cannot find work, but because they can make more money in developed countries. Developing country governments have often subsidized their education with grants to study internally or abroad, only to see them leave the country or stay abroad permanently once the degree is obtained. This so-called "brain drain" from the Third World has obvious negative consequences for development. The postwar communist governments faced the same dilemma and responded with a repressive policy of forbidding out-migration by trained labor-force members.

Within societies, people have responded similarly to deteriorating economic conditions by moving to other areas where opportunities are perceived to be better. By far, the greatest type of internal migration in the modern era in almost all parts of the world has been from rural to urban areas, producing the long-range trend of **urbanization**. Increasing agricultural productivity made it possible for smaller numbers of farmers and rural laborers to produce enough to feed growing city populations. As agriculture became more capital intensive, small farmers and rural laborers found themselves unable to compete under the new conditions and were forced off the land and into expanding urban occupations.

The shift of people from rural to urban areas, however, has seldom been a smooth process in which people simply changed types of jobs and household locations. Rather, in actuality, it has usually been unplanned and accompanied by severe dislocations, leaving a wake of subsequent social problems. In most cases, people have been pushed off the land at a faster pace than the creation of new urban jobs, resulting in large-scale unemployment. Examples of massive unemployment and its corollary problems brought about by deteriorating rural economic conditions that forced people off the land go back to fifteenth-century England and are rampant in many developing countries today.

The rural-to-urban shift has long been noted by sociologists as producing its own set of social problems, including alienation, family breakdown, and criminality. When people move, they not only leave one area and type of occupation for another, they also leave ways of life that provided accustomed forms of social stability. Families that for generations had been in the same rural area had developed elaborate social networks of support among relatives. Most children grew up interacting with—and being controlled by—extended families and deeply rooted local institutions such as churches. But moves to urban areas produced radical breaks with these institutions that had produced social stability, albeit in contexts of deteriorating economic conditions. In the absence of compensating new institutions, children were socially cut adrift. When the urban experience fails to provide the hoped-for economic improvement, the problem is compounded. It is often then that juvenile delinquency, gangs, and other forms of criminal behavior tend to increase in urban neighborhoods made up of new domestic or international immigrants.

At one time or another, both African American neighborhoods and those made up of immigrants have been perceived to be dangerous in United States cities. What both had in common is that they were made up of uprooted populations. African Americans were uprooted from rural southern communities in the first part of the twentieth century, and immigrants were uprooted largely from peasant communities in Europe and Latin America. When the immigrant group is perceived to be racially different from the already established population—as were blacks and most Mexicans who moved into U.S. cities—then racism and racial antagonism can exacerbate the problems of the uprooted population.

Even more socially disruptive has been migration propelled by warfare. Over the last three decades, local and regional wars—such as those in Central America, the continent of Africa, Afghanistan, Iraq, and parts of the formerly communist countries—have increasingly produced forced migrations of refugees to locations either within or outside the borders of their countries. The number of such displaced persons more than quadrupled since the 1970s, causing the United Nations High Commissioner for Refugees (2008, p. 2) to report that worldwide in 2007 there were forty-two million refugees and conflict-caused internally displaced persons. In most cases, the host areas have been ill prepared to absorb the new immigrants, resulting in overcrowded refugee camps, inadequate supplies of food, and rampant disease.

Key Terms and Concepts
(in order of presentation)

Demography	Eugenics
Neo-Malthusians	Push and pull factors
Demographic transition	Urbanization
Population density	

Chapter 13

Social Research

The purpose of social research is to produce valid understandings of how societies and their constituent parts develop and function. Researchers based in universities, government agencies, and private businesses investigate two types of problems: those that involve current public issues, such as drug abuse, homelessness, and family violence, and those that arise from intellectual issues within the general body of social science literature, such as the role of Protestantism in the development of early capitalism, the origins of racism, and the causes of class mobility. Research products appear in such forms as books, lectures, articles, documentary films, and applied social programs.

Understanding the general principles of social research is obviously essential preparation for careers that require its production. They include college teaching and a variety of research-oriented positions attached to government agencies and private businesses. Only a minority of sociology students, though, pursue careers that ever involve the production of research. For them, the importance of understanding social research principles is to be able to be critical consumers who can, as professionals and citizens, intelligently evaluate research claims. Teachers and social agency professionals need to be able to make sense of and evaluate studies that relate to their work problems. Citizens should take an interest in and be able to understand the importance and limitations of social science studies reported in the general press, such as pre-election surveys and studies of the long-term effects of divorce on children.

Social research develops through definitions of problems, reviews of appropriate literature, selections of research designs for the collection of pertinent information or data, and analyses of problems with the aid of the newly collected information. Accomplishment of these tasks does not necessarily proceed in strict chronological order. Researchers often, for example, redefine their problems according to the information that they have collected.

Sociological theory is involved in all stages of research development. The theoretical premises of researchers, consciously or unconsciously, influence the types of problems selected, literature consulted, research designs chosen, and analyses and interpretations of results produced. Ethical issues can also be deeply involved in any of the stages of research.

DEFINING RESEARCH PROBLEMS

There is an inexhaustible supply of possible research problems. In addition to areas that have never been researched, old research topics and results are constantly being reexamined and challenged. As societies develop, they constantly reinterpret their past, make projections about their future, and have to deal with the social problems in their present.

There are a number of ways to identify contemporary research problems. Quality daily newspapers are the best, though not infallible, sources for gaining quick overviews of the range of contemporary social problems that have become social issues. They spotlight instances of contemporary social problems (drug-related murders, wars, corruption trials, family violence episodes, prison riots, famine-related deaths, and so on), and they cover the related perceptions of commentators and political figures. Journals and books are the best sources for gaining familiarity with other general problems, such as the causes of economic underdevelopment, the consequences of different population growth rates, and the origins of discrimination. Government agencies and private foundations also advertise for research proposals for particular types of problems whose investigation they are willing to fund.

REVIEW OF THE LITERATURE

Once the problem has been identified and defined, the researcher locates relevant existing research and commentary in libraries or online in order to find out what is already known or at issue. Finding background information in libraries is somewhat of a science itself.[1] The first step is to define the problem in such a way that it conforms to the classification systems used by libraries. This is done initially by scaling down the general topic or research problem to a key word or two, such as alienation, prison behavior, French politics, drug addiction, and so on. With the key words at hand, three types of publications can then be searched: reference works (encyclopedias and dictionaries), books from the general collection, and periodicals and journals.

Encyclopedias and specialized dictionaries are good resources for introductory, general, and often up-to-date overviews of topics. They also often contain bibliographic information for further reading.

Online and, still in some locations, card catalogues contain complete files of library collections of books. Searches can be done according to author or title of a book, or subject headings such as slavery or alcoholism. If there is no subject heading for the topic of interest, chances are that there may be a different subject heading that contains closely related material. The *Library of Congress Subject Headings*, which cross-references all subject headings contained in online and card catalogues, can be useful in this case.

Articles in journals, magazines, and newspapers are not listed in online and card catalogues. For them, libraries keep indexes—such as *Social Science Citation Index* and *The New York Times Index*—that usually categorize articles topically. A useful index is the *Essay and General Literature Index*, which accesses articles in edited collections. Another is the *Public Affairs Information Services*, which lists pamphlets and government reports as well as selected journal and newspaper articles. Libraries also have collections of abstracts—such as *Abstracts in Anthropology* and *Sociological Abstracts*—that list articles by subject areas and, in addition, contain a paragraph or more describing the article.

Many libraries today also have computer access to data banks that contain listings of articles and books. These can be accessed through key words—for example, slave revolts in nineteenth-century Georgia. Listings that contain the key words will be printed out for the client.

RESEARCH DESIGNS

Once the review of the literature has been completed, the researcher chooses a suitable **research design**, which is made up of one or more techniques for collecting appropriate new information or data. Sociologists generally collect data that already exists from a variety of possible sources or, when necessary, create it themselves with surveys, field studies, or experiments.

Sources of Existing Data

Each year, governments and other organizations release large amounts of statistical information of potential use to social scientists. The census of any country is one of the most vital sources of information available to sociologists. The U.S. Census Bureau publishes its census report every ten years that contains information on population sizes, birth and death rates, housing, income, and a range of other subjects. It also continually issues supplemental reports and estimates of changes since its last official ten-year report. The *Statistical Abstract of the United States*, which is issued yearly and is available online (*http://www.census.gov/compendia/statab/*) and in most libraries, is the best single compendium of U.S. official statistics. In Canada, Statistics Canada publishes census information every five years, with supplemental reports in between. The *Canada Year Book* is the best single compendium of governmental statistics. Statistical information from nongovern- mental business and community organizations is also often available and of potential use. Of these, the World Bank's *World Development Report*, issued annually, is of especial use for comparative economic and social data on most of the world's countries. The United Nations and other international organizations also publish useful compendiums, including its *Human Development Report*, of international statistics.

Many research projects rely on the collection of already existing qualitative types of information. A researcher, for example, interested in the conceptual development of a particular school of social theory, such as functionalism, would collect as information quotations, paraphrases, and summaries of ideas taken from the works of those writers.

There are other projects whose purpose is to reveal the types of themes conveyed in newspapers, books, radio, television, movies, songs, and other communications media. Is media coverage of a particularly controversial issue biased? What do the lyrics of popular music reveal about cultural values? The researcher collects examples from the type of media of interest that can then be analyzed.

Interviews and Surveys

There are two basic types of interviews for collecting information: **interviews** of knowledgeable informants and **survey** interviews. In the first, the sociologist, like a reporter, seeks out knowledgeable informants about the issue at hand and interviews them to gather information. A researcher who was studying upper-class social life in a particular city might seek an interview with the local newspaper's society editor. It can be assumed that society editors have special knowledge about upper-class social life.

The purpose of survey interviews is somewhat different. It is to determine the distribution of a variable or variables of interest, such as attitudes, party affiliations, or income, among a population. Survey interviews involve administering standardized questionnaires to groups of respondents and then tabulating the results.

In surveys and other research techniques as well, a distinction is made between universes and samples. **Universes** are the ultimate focus of the research. The sociologist hopes to gather data that indicate, for example, the distribution of income in the United States as a whole—her or his universe. **Samples** are the actual groups from which data is collected. In some cases, such as national censuses or small-scale research, the sample and the universe coincide. But for most research, it would be prohibitively expensive and time-consuming to actually survey *all* members or cases in a universe. In that type of research, the sample must be drawn so that a plausible case can be made that its characteristics are **generalizable**—the key word in this type of survey research—to the universe of ultimate interest.

Sociologists use the statistical probability technique of **randomization** to create generalizable samples. Pre-election surveys are the best-known examples of this technique. If done well, their results have a high degree of accuracy for predicting actual outcomes. Their use is now a commonplace part of the political landscape. What is remarkable about such polls—and a mystery to many people—is how on the basis of interviews with as few as 1,200 people, they can accurately predict outcomes for elections with over 100 million voters.

The secret of that success has been the application of mathematical probability theory to social science problems. According to probability theory, if a sample is carefully drawn out of a population or universe, the range and internal variations in its characteristics will closely match that of the larger population. In order for the two to match, members of the sample must be randomly drawn, meaning that each has an equal chance of being selected. If each is randomly selected, then little or no bias will exist to distort the distribution of characteristics within the sample.

Most pre-election surveys today use computers to create randomized lists of telephone numbers, and those homes are then called for the survey. This technique has worked well in the United States, since most voters have telephones. There is, though, some question about whether the growing use of unlisted cell phones and call blocking is making it more difficult to create valid samples.

The technique did not work well in earlier periods when substantial numbers of low-income people could not afford telephones. For that reason, numerous pre-election surveys in 1948 erroneously predicted that Thomas Dewey, the Republican, would defeat Harry Truman for the presidency. Because Democratic voters tended to have less income than Republicans, they were less likely to have telephones. The sample, drawn from telephone books, was biased because it overrepresented Republican voters. For the same reason, telephone polling would not work for contemporary developing countries where substantial parts of the population still do not have phone service. Where telephone polling is inappropriate, mail and in-person surveying must be used.

While election polls are the best-known example of the use of the technique of survey sampling to efficiently learn about the characteristics of a large population, there have been a wide range of other applications of the technique in the social sciences. Sociologists are often interested in finding out distributions of objective characteristics such as income, religion, occupational groups, or health conditions. They can also be interested in finding out the range and correlates of particular attitudes in a population. What types of workers, for example, have class-conscious attitudes? Who is most likely to consider himself or herself middle class? Are fundamentalists more likely to be from particular occupation groups?

Case Studies

The basic idea of a field or **case study** is that by examining one example in depth, much can be learned that is generalizable. A thorough examination of one subculture of hard-drug users, for example, might reveal patterns of behavior and interaction that are generalizable to other groups of users. In this particular case, it would be impossible to survey all groups of users or even to establish a random sample from which to generalize results. In-depth focus on one group has the additional advantage of revealing subtleties of interaction patterns that are often missed by statistical summaries.

In field studies, the researcher immerses himself or herself in the group or organization. This can either take the form of the researcher's simply being an identified outside observer, or it can take the form of **participant observation**, in which he or she becomes a member of the group under observation. The researcher takes copious notes on the activities and interactions of interest. The notes then become the data that are analyzed to produce the study's results. Part of the study's report is usually a naturalistic description, which gives the reader a feel for the group's typical interaction patterns, especially those that mark it off from other groups. A novelist's eye for details can be usefully employed. Another part is reserved for theoretically interpreting the meaning of the interaction patterns. The results can be compared with those of similar or related studies, and thereby confirm, refine, or challenge those findings.

Experiments

The basic purpose of an **experiment** in sociology is to gather information on how two or more **variables** (any changeable characteristic) are related under controlled conditions. An experiment, for example, might be designed to study the relationship between exposure to violence on television and violent behavior in children.

Stated technically, social scientists design experiments to test hypotheses of how variables are related. A **hypothesis** is a statement of a suspected, but yet to be proven, relationship between variables. A variable that causes changes in another is referred to as an **independent variable**, while a variable that changes as the result of the effects of another is referred to as a **dependent variable**. Thus, an experiment could be designed to test the hypothesis that exposure to violence on television (independent variable) leads to increases in violent behavior in children (dependent variable).

The classic **experimental design** is based on comparing two groups—an experimental and a control group. Each is given an initial pretest to measure the dependent variable of interest. Then the **experimental group** is exposed to the independent variable of interest, while the **control group** is not. If, as hypothesized, the value of the dependent variable for the experimental group changes (as measured in a posttest), but it does not for the control group, then the direction of causation predicted by the hypothesis is validated. An alternative version of the experimental design compares two or more experimental groups rather than an experimental and a control group.

Social scientists have devised experiments involving small groups of people to test primarily social psychological hypotheses. In these types of experiments, people, usually volunteers, are randomly divided into experimental and control groups and then subjected to exposure or nonexposure to the independent variable of interest. Such small-group experiments may take place in specially constructed laboratory conditions. Rooms may be designed with hidden microphones and one-way mirrors, so that the interaction processes among the participants can be documented and studied.

Experimental or quasi-experimental designs may also be developed to study relationships between variables in normal life settings, but under less controllable conditions. Existing classes of elementary school children, for example, can be separately treated as experimental and control groups in order to measure the effectiveness of a new teaching method. The effectiveness of a new type of public program to, say, decrease drunken driving can be similarly studied by comparing its rates of success before and after introduction or with those of areas where it does not exist.

RIGHTS OF RESEARCH SUBJECTS

By its very nature, social research involves human subjects who cannot be treated in the same way as the nonhuman subjects of research in the physical and natural sciences. The norms of social research thus differ in important respects from those governing the physical and natural sciences. Subjects of research have recognized rights, but often those rights are not completely unambiguous.

Well-being

In no case should subjects of research be intentionally placed in conditions of bodily or psychological danger. A researcher, for example, should not design an experiment to compare the effectiveness of different methods of torture or the effects of different types of frightening experiences. This is probably the most unambiguous ethical norm of social research, though there have been numerous instances of its being violated.

Respect of Privacy

One can imagine research that would result in obvious invasions of privacy through wiretapping of telephone conversations, electronic eavesdropping, hidden cameras, and the like. The ethical problems involved in this type of research are clear, and it is not widely practiced by social scientists. But invasions of privacy do occur in many participant observation types of research. When researchers gain entry into a group in order to study it by posing as full participants, they are, in effect, able to observe and study people without their consent. In this instance, the distinction between justifiable social research and intrusive invasion of privacy remains ambiguous.

Protection from Deception and Manipulation

Many types of social research have employed deception in order to obtain valid results. If subjects in a survey or experiment knew, for example, that they were being tested on prejudice, they might tell the researcher what they thought was the most socially acceptable answer, as opposed to their true feelings. Thus, the sociologist would probably develop a research design in such a way as to hide its true purpose. But the need for scientific validity in this type of instance interferes with the rights of human subjects to not be manipulated and deceived. Like the right to privacy, the distinction between ethically justifiable subterfuge in order to obtain valid results and unjustifiable deception and manipulation of subjects remains ambiguous and a dilemma in social research.

Confidentiality

Social science researchers collect information from individuals about their personal lives and attitudes. It is a generally accepted ethical norm that they may use that information as a basis for analytical conclusions, but that they may not reveal the personal identities involved. In general, researchers cannot release the names of sources of information if that release would prove harmful to the subject in question and therefore a violation of the confidence with which the information was given. The results of a survey of sexual practices, for example, might prove embarrassing if informants were identified. How far the principle of confidentiality can be extended, though, is not clear. Researchers of most illegal behavior have an ethical responsibility not to become police informants. But the principle of **confidentiality** cannot be so absolute as to permit a researcher to knowingly allow, for instance, life-threatening child abuse to continue. Ethical norms can hence come into conflict with each other, putting the researcher in the often-difficult position of having to decide which takes precedence.

ANALYSIS OF RESULTS

To analyze something means to break it down into its constituent parts and determine how they are interrelated. Similarly, to analyze a research problem similarly means to break it down into its constituent parts and specify the nature of interrelationships. Thus, the first task of **analysis** is to categorize the different parts of the research problem. Depending on the nature of the problem, its different parts will be conceptualized in different ways. A study of the origins of industrialism might develop an initial analysis in terms of causes and effects. A study of the causes of high school dropout rates might categorize its data in terms of variables such as parental income, grade point averages, and types of available school programs.

The next task of analysis is to specify how the internal parts of the problem are interrelated. In the study of industrialism, the researcher would use the information collected to make a plausible argument that particular types of causes were related to particular effects. Such an analysis would be made in essentially qualitative terms. When the data collected are of a quantitative nature, statistical inference can be a useful tool for analyzing interrelationships. If the data can be validly expressed in a quantitative form—such as, the percentage of the unemployed who are minorities—internal relationships can be revealingly represented as statistical relationships. Brenner (1976), for example, in the study cited in Chapter One, found that as rates of unemployment increase, rates of general mortality increase. Unemployed people have less income to spend on health care, and the stressful nature of unemployment stimulates a variety of physical and mental health problems, including alcohol abuse, drug abuse, and suicidal depression. Brenner technically found a **correlation** between unemployment and mortality rates. A correlation exists when changes in one variable (the unemployment rate in this case) are associated with changes in another (the mortality rate).

Correlations, a foundation of statistical inference, are expressed as coefficients that range from –1.0 to 1.0. A correlation coefficient of 1.0 means that there is a perfect positive correlation between the variables: every time there is an increase in one variable, there is a predictable increase in the other. A correlation coefficient of –1.0 would mean that every time there was an increase in one variable, there would be a predictable decrease in the other. A correlation coefficient of 0 means that there is no relationship between the two variables: an increase or decrease in one would not be accompanied by any predictable change in the other. The closer a coefficient is to 1.0 or –1.0, the stronger the relationship between variables. The closer the coefficient is to 0, the weaker the relationship. There are additional statistical inference techniques for elaborately measuring the interactions of multiple variables.

A word of caution about the limits of social research is in order. Skillful analysis of information can help to illuminate vaguely understood areas, such as the nature of drug and other subcultures. It can uncover and bring to light hidden interaction patterns, values, and meanings. Hidden realities can be explored. But social research rarely results in definitive causal proofs. It is a positivistic illusion to believe that sociologists can scientifically accumulate full knowledge of social causes and effects. At best, sociologists can use social research to make a plausible case for this or that causal explanation. Their causal conclusions are always tentative possibilities: if x happens, y is likely to happen. If the rate of unemployment increases, rates of family violence are likely to increase. If a certain amount is invested in a social program to create jobs for inner-city youths, drug-related activity is likely to decrease.

Reason remains our most important tool for understanding the social world that surrounds us. With the human capacity to reason out the problems of our existence, we can construct forms of social research that aid us in that quest. But just as we cannot once and for all develop a full understanding of why we exist as human beings, we cannot design research projects that will tell us the definitive answers to life's most important social questions. What we can do is use social research to help us think through creative humane responses to those questions.

Key Terms and Concepts
(in order of presentation)

Research design	Variable
Interview	Hypothesis
Survey	Independent variable
Universe	Dependent variable
Sample	Experimental design
Generalizable	Experimental group
Randomization	Control group
Case Study	Analysis
Participant observation	Correlation
Experiment	Confidentiality

ENDNOTES

[1] I am indebted to Nick Welchman of Eastern Connecticut State University for advice on this section.

Glossary

Agency: (1) concept associated with Pierre Bourdieu that refers to the decisions that individuals make regarding the actions that they will take. Bourdieu sought to determine the relationship between decisions regarding individual actions (agency) and the structural contexts within which they occurred. (2) In C. Wright Mills's use, agency is the social grouping that a particular ideology assumes will bring about a desired change. Thus, for example, through the pursuit of its interest, the working class, in Marxian theory and ideology, will be the agency that brings about socialism.

Agriculture: from Latin *ager*, or "field," and *cultura*, or "cultivation"; hence "cultivation of fields." Type of technology and stage of technological development characterized by large-scale cultivation of fields. In agriculture, humans use animal energy, such as oxen, to pull plows to cultivate large fields.

Agrarian societies: technological type of society based on farming as the main form of production. Horticulture is the lower and agriculture the higher stage of agrarian societies. See also *Horticulture* and *Agriculture*.

Alcoholism: an addictive condition characterized by a deep-seated compulsion to consume alcohol that results in a significant impairment of the ability to function physically or socially.

Alienation: concept that is used in two different ways in sociology. In the first, which follows from the Marxian tradition, it refers to the objective removal of a condition necessary for human fulfillment and development. In Marx's view, humans needed to perform creative labor and have relations of solidarity with each other in order to fully fulfill themselves.

255

The first condition did not exist for increasingly large proportions of labor forces in capitalist societies. The second did not exist in all class societies. In the second use of the concept, alienation refers primarily to subjective feelings of estrangement, detachment, loneliness, and powerlessness of people within societies.

Altruistic Suicide: type of suicide identified by Emile Durkheim in which people sacrifice their lives for the sake of the groups to which they belong, as when soldiers fall on loose explosives to save the lives of others. *See also* Egoistic Suicide and Anomic Suicide.

Analysis: scientific procedure of breaking down a unit or problem of interest into its constituent parts and determining how they are interrelated.

Anarchism: political ideology that advocates abolition of the state and reorganization of societies into small-scale cooperatives.

Ancient Slavery: *see* Slavery.

Animism: belief system in which all elements of the physical world—humans, animals, rocks, trees, and so on—are thought to have indwelling spirits that give them life. In some cases, the spirits are all different, with each having its own separate identity. In others, the spirits are all emanations from one source that unites all human and other creations in nature.

Anomic Suicide: type of suicide identified by Emile Durkheim in which people take their lives because of losses or lacks of structures for their lives. Durkheim believed that social change was more rapid in modern than traditional societies leading to constant stressful destructuralization that in the extreme resulted in suicide. *See also* Anomie, Egoistic Suicide and Altruistic Suicide.

Anomie: concept developed by Emile Durkheim to describe a stressful social condition that results from the loss of structures to which people were accustomed, as when sudden unemployment disrupts routine patterns of living.

Anthropology: academic discipline that studies contemporary and recent past pre-industrial peoples. Anthropologists seek out the cultural configurations and uniquenesses of each people; hence, "culture" is the basic unit of analysis of anthropology.

Antithesis: *see* Thesis-Antithesis-Synthesis.

Aristocracy: from Greek *aristos*, or "best," and *kratein*, or "rule"; hence, "rule of the best." The self-conception of the feudal landlord class that its rule was based upon natural superiority.

Ascription: attainment of a social position on the basis of birthright rather than achievement.

Asiatic mode of production: *see* State Society.

Authority: as used by Max Weber, refers to the type of rationale used by rulers to justify the issuance of commands and the expectation of obedience by the ruled; hence, rulers claim the authority to rule over the ruled. Among the bases on which rulers can claim authority are legal right and consent of the governed. *See also* Legitimacy.

Belief System: *see* Common Conscience.

Bourgeoisie: *see* Capitalist.

Bureaucracy: a large-scale organization based upon specialization, hierarchy, and management, and/or owner control.

Capital: wealth that is available for investment in profit-seeking activities.

Capitalism: economic type of society characterized by commodity production and private ownership of the means of production. There are, though, no purely capitalist societies since in all there are different degrees of government or state ownership (public universities, for example) and control of distribution of goods and services. All contemporary societies, thus, in that sense have mixed economies, with varying relative weights of private and public sectors. Of developed capitalist societies, the United States has practiced a form of free market capitalism characterized by a large private sector and minimal public welfare spending and programs while Western Europe countries have embraced a type of social capitalism, characterized by much more developed public sectors with extensive welfare states.

Capitalist: a person who derives the majority of income from ownership and investments of capital; an owner of the means of production and an employer of labor in capitalist societies.

Capitalist Class: owners of businesses that are large enough to have significant numbers of employees. Also referred to as the bourgeoisie in Marxist theory.

Capital Wealth: wealth in the form of investments that return incomes, such as stocks, bonds, whole businesses, and rental properties, as opposed to personal wealth.

Case Study: technique for collecting information based on an in-depth study of one organization, subculture, or other unit of interest, as opposed to being based on a survey of a number of units.

Character Structure: personality; the unique way in which a person integrates self-perception and role behavior.

Charismatic Legitimacy: concept associated with Max Weber that referred to legitimacy in which people follow and obey because they believe that their leader has an extraordinary ability to lead.

Chattel Slavery: the most severe form of slavery in which the slave has no more legal status or rights than that of a property.

Clan: a network of interrelated families that functions as a social, political, or economic unit.

Class Consciousness: concept originally introduced by Marx to refer to commonly held ideas and beliefs that are consistent with the objective interests of a class. In Marxian theory, the development of working-class class consciousness is seen as necessarily leading to socialist consciousness.

Class Structure: the way in which economic and social classes are organized within a society. *See also* Economic Class and Social Class.

Class-based Theory: theory mainly associated with Karl Marx and Frederick Engels that economically-dominant classes become ruling classes as modes of production develop. Marx and Engels famously wrote in 1848 in "The Communist Manifesto" that "the executive of the modern state is but a committee for managing the affairs of the whole bourgeoisie."

Colonialism: country whose governance is directly controlled by another country. Major examples have included the British control of India, the French control of Indochina, and the Spanish and Portuguese control of most of Latin America. The term *neo-colonial* is often used to describe indirect foreign domination of a country. The term *post-colonial* refers to those countries that have recently attained independence from colonial control.

Commodification: transferring goods and services from being self produced to being purchased from others. Commodification and expanding market relationships accompany capitalist development as when people begin to buy instead of making clothing for themselves.

Commodity: a product that is bought, sold, or traded through a market transaction. Commodity production is considered to be one of the defining characteristics of capitalist societies.

Common Conscience: concept from Durkheim (1893, p. 79), who concluded that "the totality of beliefs and sentiments common to average citizens of the same society forms a determinate system which has its own life." He called these belief systems collective or common consciences. These commonly held beliefs form systems of thinking that are powerful frames of reference through which individuals largely interpret their experiences. As "determinate systems" they follow semi-autonomous logics of their own.

Communal Society: earliest socioeconomic type of society; characterized by equal access to means of production (such as land and tools) and consumption items (such as food).

Communism: (1) future mode of production predicted by Marx that would be characterized by common ownership of the means of production, social equality, and highly developed forces of production and technology; (2) political ideology that advocates in present conditions the development of socialist modes of production characterized by state ownership of major means of production as a transitional stage leading toward the future development of a communist mode of production.

Concept: intellectual abstraction used to categorize and illuminate essential meanings of real-world occurrences.

Confidentiality: ethical research norm that information collected about particular persons should be used only in ways in which personal identities are not disclosed.

Conservatism: political ideology characterized by advocacy of laissez-faire capitalism; that is, allowing societal development to be determined by unregulated market forces.

Contract Labor: type of temporary slavery in which the laborer agrees to work for a particular employer for a specified period of time during which he or she is not free to seek other positions.

Contradiction: in dialectical logic, a problem to be resolved. *See also* Dialectics, Thesis-Antithesis-Synthesis.

Control Group: in most experimental designs, a group that does not receive the independent variable under study. Changes in its dependent variable or variables are then compared with those of the experimental group to determine whether the administration of the independent variable had any differential effect. *See also* Experiment, Experimental Group.

Cooperative: as used in this text, a type of organization characterized by being small-scale and member-controlled.

Core Countries: *see* World-System Theory.

Correlation: statistical term that expresses the extent to which changes in one or more variables are related to changes in one or more other variables.

Corvée Labor: feudal form of rent payment in which peasants were obligated to work a set number of days in the landlord's fields or perform other such tasks.

Crime Rate: number of reported crimes of all types per 100,000 persons in a population unit.

Crude Death Rate: number of deaths in a given year per 1,000 persons in the population.

Culture: the unique way of life of a society as expressed through its own types of material products and nonmaterial values, customs, and language.

Decision-Making Approach: *see* Power Structure Research.

Democratic Centralism: organizational principle of the Leninist political party. The party is organized hierarchically, with higher bodies making decisions that are binding on lower bodies. Base members participate democratically by electing delegates who represent them in the election of top leaders.

Democratic Legitimacy: consent of the governed achieved through holding elections. *See also* Legitimacy.

Demographic Transition: theory based upon the experience of First World countries which successively moved in stages from an initial period of low population growth rates because high birth and death rates offset each other, to a period of high population growth rates because death rates declined while birth rates remained high, to a final period in which population growth rates declined as birth rates declined. Third World high population growth rates can be interpreted as being in the middle stage of the demographic transition.

Demography: specialization within sociology that studies population growths and distributions.

Dependency Theory: an explanation of Third World underdevelopment that holds that it has been caused by exploitative relationships with First World countries, including colonialism and the slave trade in the past, and multinational corporate investments, foreign loans, and unequal international trading relationships in the present.

Dependent Variable: *see* Independent Variable.

Development: concept used to describe the process by which poor societies improve their economic performances and standards of living. There is considerable controversy over whether development is best indicated by size of gross domestic product per capita or health and other living conditions of populations.

Dialectics: philosophical approach to knowledge embraced by Marx and others premised on the belief that all reality is interconnected and constantly changing. Dialectical approaches attempt to interpret all aspects of reality in terms of their interconnectedness with other aspects and their changing natures. *See also* Thesis-Antithesis-Synthesis, Contradiction.

Dictatorship of the Proletariat: concept first introduced by Marx (1875) and inherited and developed by Lenin as the foundation of socialist states. According to Marx and Lenin, socialist governments had to take the form of dictatorships of the proletariat in order to protect working-class interests and the survival of revolutionary socialism. In practice, the concept of the dictatorship of the proletariat led to the establishment of one-party states in which communist parties monopolized political power.

Discrete: the characteristic of being distinct or unique. In social analysis, categories and measurement scales are based upon discrete criteria if they do not overlap and items can be categorized within only one category. The term discrete is usually contrasted to continuous, which refers to differences of quantitative degree as opposed to qualitative identity.

Distribution of Income: the proportionate share of total national income (wages, salaries, interest, dividends, rents, profits, etc.) received by different groups within a society; usually stated in terms of percentiles, such as the percent of total national income received by the highest 10 percent of income recipients.

Distribution of Wealth: the proportionate share of total national property owned by different groups within a society; usually stated in terms of percentiles, such as the percent of total national wealth owned by the richest 10 percent. *See also* Personal Wealth, Capital Wealth.

Division of Labor: specialization and stratification of individuals and groups within social structures or organizations.

Economic Class: a category of people classified according to their shared role in a given type of economic structure.

Economic Structure: the institutionalized way in which a society produces its necessities. Economic structures are composed of typical configurations of economic and social roles. Societies can be classified according to their type of economic structures: communal, state, slave, feudal, capitalist, or socialist. Comparable to the concept of mode of production.

Economic Surplus: *see* Surplus Product.

Economics: academic discipline that studies the production and distribution of goods and services within societies.

Effective Demand: economic concept that refers to those desires and needs for commodities that consumers can afford.

Egoistic Suicide: type of suicide identified by Emile Durkheim in which people take their lives despite the wishes or rules of the groups to which they belong, as when Protestants and Catholics commit suicide despite the opposition of both religions to it. *See also* Altruistic Suicide and Anomic Suicide.

Elite Theory: theory that most societies are divided between elites and masses with the former monopolizing power. Vilfredo Pareto (1848–1923) and Gaetano Mosca (1848–1923) were major early twentieth century exponents of elite theory. Elements of elite theory are also evident in Max Weber's sociology and C. Wright Mills' *The Power Elite* (1956).

Ethnic Group: a socially defined race or nationality within a society that shares common distinguishing and identifying cultural characteristics.

Ethnocentrism: interpreting other cultures according to the values of your own culture.

Eugenics: nineteenth- and early twentieth-century movement in the United States that sought to strengthen the genetic characteristics of the country's people through restricting the reproduction and immigration of people with supposedly weaker genetic traits.

Exchange Value: in Karl Marx's economic theory, the relative market value of commodities as determined by the amount of labor incorporated in their production. *See also* Labor Theory of Value and Use Value.

Experiment: research design in which relationships between variables are studied under controlled conditions. Experimental designs involve administering or changing an independent variable and then determining if those changes cause changes in one or more dependent variables.

Experimental Design: *see* Experiment.

Experimental Group: in an experimental design, a group that receives the independent variable or variables under study. *See also* Control Group.

Exploitation: in Marx's technical use of the term, the capitalist expropriation of unpaid surplus value from workers. More generally, any expropriation of surplus products from subordinate classes. *See also* Surplus Value, Surplus Product.

Family: a living unit of people who are related by blood, marriage, or adoption.

Fascism: extreme right-wing authoritarianism in the form of movements to conquer state power, or governments that rely on using highly repressive means to maintain order.

Feudalism: precapitalist economic type of society characterized by landlord control and peasant labor.

Fief: income-producing opportunity, usually a land grant, given to subordinates within the feudal ruling classes to secure their loyalty.

First World: see *Three Worlds Theory.*

Flexible Accumulation: term used to describe a current stage in industrial development in the developed countries where factories engage in small-batch production of different products in order to serve increasingly diversified consumer demands.

Fordism: term used to describe a stage in industrial development where factories engage in large-scale production of standardized products patterned after the assembly-line technique pioneered by Henry Ford in the United States. Many analysts argue that Fordism now has been surpassed by flexible accumulation techniques in the developed countries. *See* Flexible Accumulation.

Formal Organization: an organization with an intentionally defined structure and goals.

Formal Rationality: concept associated with Max Weber to refer to a type of rationality characterized by goals that have exactly calculable means for their attainment. Weber believed that bureaucracies were based upon the concept of formal rationality. Weber compared formal rationality to substantive rationality. *See also* Substantive Rationality.

Formal Structure: the intentionally defined division of labor in terms of specializations and levels of authority and power that prevails within an organization. *See also* Informal Structure.

Free Market Capitalism: see Capitalism.

French Revolution: 1789 uprising that resulted in the replacement of the traditional monarchical system in France with modern republican governance in which there was a constitution and head of state. Because the revolution occurred in Europe's most populated country and because its leaders sent armies out to attempt to similarly transform other countries, the influence of the revolution over subsequent European as well as French history was great. Among the lasting influences associated with the revolution are: increasing the spread of rational and democratic ideas; separating church and state; and ending aristocratic privileges, especially in governance.

Functionalism: a theoretical approach to the study of societies in which societies are seen as systems, and their subparts (institutions, families, etc.) are interpreted in terms of what they contribute to the maintenance and survival of those systems.

Generalizable: *see* Universe.

Globalization: term developed to describe increasing integration of world economic production and markets. Antiglobalization critics argue that the integration has been undemocratically directed by large corporate interests.

Gross Domestic Product (GDP): the total value of goods and services produced by residents of a country less that derived from foreign activities.

Gross National Product (GNP): the total value of goods and services produced by residents of a country.

Group: any collectivity of two or more persons that occurs for intended or unintended purposes. Groups such as families, churches, social classes, cities, and societies themselves are the basic sociological units of analysis.

Hegemony: as used by Antonio Gramsci, an early Italian Communist Party leader and major twentieth-century Marxist theorist, it refers to a class establishing leadership over the intellectual life of society through noncoercive cultural means. Gramsci argued that the capitalist class's hegemony over intellectual life enabled it to rule mainly without having to resort to force. In a parallel manner, if the working class were to assume power and govern effectively, it would have to first establish its hegemony over the intellectual life of a society.

Herding: *see* Pastoralism.

History and Prehistory: according to this categorization of world history, history begins with literate societies with the earlier period being prehistorical.

Horticulture: from Latin *hortus*, or "garden," and *cultura*, or "cultivation"; hence, "garden cultivation." Type of technology and stage of technological development in which societies subsist through cultivation of small plots of land. In horticulture, humans use their own muscles as sources of energy and hand-held hoes as tools to cultivate garden-sized plots of land.

Human Being: member of the subspecies *homo sapiens sapiens* that emerged from a long line of evolutionary antecedents approximately 100,000 years ago. While there is general agreement over the essential physiological characteristics of the subspecies, there is considerable disagreement in the history of social thought over whether there are essential psychological characteristics and, if so, what their importance is for how societies develop.

Hunting and Gathering: earliest type of technology and stage of technological development in which societies subsisted by hunting animals and gathering wild fruits and vegetables.

Hydraulic Civilization: label used by some scholars for a form of ancient society in which the state came into being in order to direct the construction of and oversee the maintenance of irrigation and other systems of controlling major rivers.

Hypothesis: a statement of a suspected causal relationship between variables.

"I" and "Me": distinction originated by George Herbert Mead to indicate that one part of the self, the "me," is formed socially through interaction with others, and the other part, the "I," results from the person's own internally generated actions and reactions.

Imperialism: in general use, concept that refers to any empire in which one country dominates others. Lenin (1916, p. 737). In a more restricted use, identifies modern imperialism as occurring when monopolies "play a decisive role in the economic life" of powerful countries from which they derive surplus capital, which is then invested in weaker, dependent countries.

Indentured Servitude: type of temporary slavery in which the laborer is owned by another for a defined period of time.

Independent Variable: a variable that is thought to cause change in one or more other dependent variables.

Industrial Revolution: period between 1760 and1840 in which a surge in technological innovations in industry produced wide-ranging economic, social, and political changes in Europe and the United States.

Industrialization: type of technology and stage of technological development characterized by the use of nonanimal sources of energy (electricity, steam, fossil fuels, or nuclear fission) to drive machines in the production process.

Infant Mortality Rate: the number of infants who die before their first birthday per 1,000 live births in a society, city, or other unit.

Informal Structure: regular interaction patterns within organizations that occur outside of those defined and specified by the formal division of specializations and levels of authority and power. *See also* Formal Structure.

Institution: (1) abstract configuration of positions, roles, and norms oriented to the attainment of a type of social need or goal: for example, the economic institution. (2) Any concrete configuration of positions, roles, and norms: for example, Harvard University is an institution.

Institutional Structure: the totality of institutions within a particular area; for example, all of the economic institutions in a country together constitute its economic structure, all of the political institutions, its political structure, and so on.

Intelligentsia: somewhat amorphous concept. In one use it refers to educated people such as writers and artists who produce and explain ideas for the public.

Interview: a meeting in which a researcher solicits information from a respondent.

Iron Law of Oligarchy: concept associated with Robert Michels that indicated that all large-scale organizations, regardless of democratic intentions, tend to be dominated by their leaders.

Kinship: type of interrelationship based on common ancestry or marriage.

Labor Force: persons engaged in the production of goods or services within a society.

Labor Theory of Value: central tenet of Karl Marx's economic theory. He concluded that the exchange value of commodities is determined by the amount of labor incorporated in their production. *See also* Exchange Value.

Landlord: feudal class based upon control of landed estates and collection of rent from peasants.

Left Wing: political ideological term associated with liberalism, socialism, communism, and anarchism. It originated in the nineteenth century when oppositional parties to standing governments sat on the left side of parliaments. Its original meaning was thus associated with opposition to governing parties. By the end of the nineteenth century, though, the meaning shifted to ideological opposition to unregulated capitalism and promotion of more state regulation or wholesale change of the economic system to socialism communism, or anarchism. Left-wing is also association with promotion of lower and working-class interests. *See also* Right Wing.

Legal-Rational Legitimacy: concept associated with Max Weber. Type of legitimacy in which people obey because they believe that their leaders have been selected through rationally designed constitutional procedures.

Legitimacy: acceptance by the ruled of rulers' claims of authority. *See also* Authority.

Liberalism: political ideology characterized by advocacy of public regulations and programs to bring about reforms in capitalist societies.

Looking-Glass Self: concept originated by Charles Horton Cooley to indicate that judgments and reactions of others largely influence a person's sense of self, self-esteem, and self-worth.

Lower Class: in most uses, the poor in a society.

Lumpen Bourgeoisie: economic class term for the lowest levels of Third World small-business owners, such as street peddlers and service providers.

Magic: belief system in which supernatural means are used to control natural phenomena. The communal practitioner of magic invokes a chant or uses an object assumed to be invested with supernatural powers to attain a naturalistic end, such as to ensure success in a hunt, to make it rain, or to cure a sick person.

Marginalized Population: Latin American social science term for unemployed and underemployed people who gain incomes outside of the regularly employed labor force.

Marxism-Leninism: approach to Marxism originally developed in the Soviet Union that followed Lenin's views regarding imperialism, the formation of revolutionary organizations and strategies, and the establishment of one-party dictatorships of the proletariat in socialist societies.

Materialism: philosophical approach to knowledge that starts from the principle that directly experienced reality exists and develops according to its own immanent—as opposed to spiritual or metaphysical—causes.

"Me": *see* "I" and "Me."

Means of Production: tools, raw materials, and land used by labor to produce goods.

Mechanical Solidarity: concept associated with Emile Durkheim that refers to the form of social cohesion within past societies with simple divisions of labor. In those societies, according to Durkheim, cohesion and solidarity were produced by a unifying ideological force, which in most cases was a single religion such as the medieval Catholic church. Solidarity was produced mechanically, in the sense that it was the result of an external energy source. Durkheim contrasted mechanical and organic solidarity. *See also* Organic Solidarity.

Membership Association: as used in this text, a type of large-scale organization that is formally controlled by its members.

Middle Class: social class concept that refers to people who identify themselves as being between the upper class, on the one hand, and the working and lower classes, on the other.

Mixed Economy: a contemporary economy that contains both significant private and state ownership of major means of production.

Mode of Production: *see* Economic Structure.

Modernism: *see* Postmodernism.

Modernization: The concept of modernization in sociological theory encompasses the great shifts in social development that occurred by the end of the nineteenth century in the developed countries, including the transition from feudalism to capitalism in Marxian theory, the development of complex divisions of labor (Durkheim), and the development of formal-rational work structures (Weber). In a more restricted meaning, the concept of modernization identifies an approach to Third World development espoused by the International Montetary Fund, the World Bank, and a number of sociologists. According to this approach, premodern values and institutions are the basic obstacles to development in Third World countries. Consequently, development can only occur when Third World countries promote and adopt more modern values and institutions.

Monopoly Capitalism: stage of capitalist development beginning in the twentieth century in the most developed countries in which one or a few corporations dominate the markets in which they operate. Monopoly capitalism developed after nineteenth century competitive capitalism in which most markets were not dominated by one or a few corporations.

Multinational Corporation: a corporation that owns plants or has investments in more than one country. Also known as a transnational corporation.

Nation: a people with a common language and culture that has evolved historically in a commonly occupied territory.

Nationality: a group that constitutes a nation or national minority. *See also* Nation and National Minority.

National Minority: a nationality that exists within a territory where one or more other nationalities make up the majority. There are two types of national minorities. (1) Immigrant national minorities are made up of peoples, such as the overseas Chinese, who have migrated from their home to a new territory where one or more other nationalities predominate. (2) Indigenous national minorities are made up of peoples, such as Native Americans in the Americas or Aborigines in Australia, who have lost majority status within their own territories due to large-scale immigrations of other peoples.

Neo-colonialism: *see* Colonialism.

Neo-Malthusianism: contemporary views that overpopulation is the cause of major societal or world problems. Neo-Malthusians endorse the conclusion if not all of the reasons of English parson and political economist Thomas Robert Malthus (1766-1834) that as history develops the production of necessities will not be able to keep up with population growth, portending a massive overpopulation crisis.

New World Slavery: *see* Slavery.

Nouveau Riche: French term for first-generation capitalists whose fortunes have been newly acquired. They are often portrayed as lacking the upper-class refined culture of the old rich; that is, of people born into and raised within the upper class.

New Middle Class: economic class made up of employed professionals and middle-level managers.

Nomads: peoples who continually move residence locations in order to hunt, gather, or cultivate new lands.

Norm: rule or value governing the performance of a role.

Nuclear Family: family unit made up exclusively of parents and their children.

Objective Social Life: observable interaction that takes place between people. *See also* Subjective Social Life.

Old Middle Class: *see* Small-Business Owners Class.

Organic Analogy: view that societies are like biological organisms, with each being composed of different organs that have specialized functions; for example, the brain, heart, and nervous system in the human body, and the economy, family, and state in the social body. *See also* Functionalism.

Organic Solidarity: concept associated with Emile Durkheim. The type of cohesion between persons that exists in modern societies with complex divisions of labor. Order and cohesion are based upon interdependence of roles. Durkheim contrasted organic solidarity to mechanical solidarity. *See also* Mechanical Solidarity.

Organizational Environment: the surrounding conditions that managers must take into consideration when guiding organizations or researchers investigate when studying how organizations function.

Participant Observation: technique of information collection based on the researcher becoming an active member of the group under observation and then recording information about it.

Pastoralism: type of technology and stage of technological development characterized by producing food and other necessities from domesticated herds of animals, such as goats, cattle, and sheep.

Patriarchy: literally, "rule of the father." Concept used to refer to male domination over females.

Peasant: economic class made up of rural laborers who work and live off cultivation of a small plot of land. In some uses, restricted to rural laborers who produce primarily for their own consumption, as opposed to for a market. Also used as a social class concept for the rural poor, who can be made up of subsistence farmers, market farmers, and laborers.

Peasant Communities: as used in this text, the first type of agrarian-based socioeconomic structure in world history, characterized by small peasant villages that farm with horticultural methods.

Peonage: system of debt slavery that is based on creditors claiming the right to control the future labor of debtors as payment.

Peripheral Countries: *see* World-System Theory.

Personal Wealth: wealth in the form of properties that are used for the consumption needs of the owner, such as a house that is lived in, as opposed to capital wealth. *See also* Capital Wealth.

Petite or Petty Bourgeoisie: *see* Small-Business Owners Class.

Pluralism: theory that power is or ought to be distributed among multiple groups without being monopolized by any one group.

Political Science: academic discipline that studies political processes and how governments function.

Politics: the struggle for power over governance of organizations, communities, and countries.

Popular Classes: Third World term for members of the social working and lower classes who often make up absolute majorities of populations.

Population Density: demographic concept that indicates the average number of people who live within a square mile or kilometer within a particular country. It is determined by dividing total population by total square miles or kilometers.

Positional Approach: *see* Power Structure Research.

Positivism: approach to sociology originated by Auguste Comte, which advocates using methods of research developed in the physical and natural sciences.

Post-colonial: see *Colonialism*.

Postmodernism: thought movement with manifestations in the social sciences, art, literature, architecture, and other areas. Postmodernists identify rationalization and standardization with modernism, which they see as oppressive and destructive of human values. In place of the modernist concepts of progress, standardization, rationalization, and universal truths, they stress the concepts of relativism, diversity, quality, and pluralism.

Power Structure Research: research aimed at determining the nature and holders of power in communities and countries. The three major techniques of power structure research have been positional, reputational, and decision-making. In the positional approach, the occupants of what are assumed to be powerful positions, such as boards of directors of major corporations and high political offices, are determined. In the reputational approach, persons assumed to be knowledgeable are interviewed and asked to list who they think are powerful individuals. In the decision-making approach, Key decisions of a government, organization, or other unity of interest are studied in order to determine who has power.

Prehistory: *see* History and Prehistory.

Primary Research: type of research in which the researcher generates data that had not existed previously, such as by administering a survey or carrying out direct observations.

Progressive Taxation: method of taxation in which higher-income groups are taxed at higher rates than lower-income groups. Progressive taxation is used to redistribute some income from upper to lower levels within societies.

Proletariat: Marxian term for the working class. *See* Working Class.

Proportional Representation: system of governance in which legislative seats are awarded according to the percentages of votes received by political parties. In a pure proportional representation system, a party that received 15 percent of national votes cast would receive 15 percent of the legislative seats. In contrasting "winner-take-all" systems minority parties do not receive representation.

Protestant Work Ethic: the belief among early Protestants that hard work in economic pursuits obeyed God's will. Max Weber in a classic theory argued that the Protestant work ethic stimulated the accumulation of capital that financed early capitalist development.

Push and Pull Factors: causes of migration away from and toward particular locations. Demographers analyze migration patterns in terms of what causes people to leave particular locations and attracts them to others.

Quitrent: form of feudal rent payment in which peasants give the landlords proportions or set quantities of their harvests. Also called rent in kind.

Race: concept that has had various meanings in terms of groups identified from the sixteenth century onwards. By the nineteenth century, races became increasingly identified as populations with fixed biological characteristics (skin color, type of hair, etc.). But because attempts to develop a scientific taxonomy of different races have failed, race is no longer used as a scientific concept. Nevertheless, the terms "race" and "racial" continue to have important social meanings and references attached to them. Race in this latter sense refers generally to people who share the same range of skin color.

Racism: ideology based on belief in the biological inferiority and superiority of different races.

Randomization: statistical technique for ensuring that the characteristics of a sample are likely to match those of the universe of ultimate interest. A random sample exists when each member of the universe has an equal chance of being included in the sample. *See also* Universe.

Rationality: what is perceived to be true and valid in a culture. Max Weber argued that there is no universal standard for rationality. Rather, it is culturally variable. What is perceived to be rational in one culture is not necessarily viewed the same way in another culture. See also *Substantive Rationality* and *Formal Rationality.*

Rationalization: redesigning work and other environments according to particular goals. Rationalization is most identified with Max Weber's theories of bureaucracies and rationality.

Redistribution of Wealth and Income: usually a politically designed attempt to alter a given distribution of wealth (such as through land reform) and/or income in a society in order to achieve particular goals, such as social justice or economic development. Redistributions of wealth and income can be designed in the interests of lower, middle, or upper levels of the population.

Religion: belief system in which prayers or other supernatural means are used to obtain supernatural ends.

Rentier: French term for a nonworking capitalist who receives an income from the ownership of stocks, bonds, and other investments.

Reputational Approach: technique used in power structure studies in which powerful individuals are identified through surveys of knowledgeable informants and then studied.

Research Design: a plan of how to collect new information for a research project. Research designs involve selecting one or more techniques for collecting new information, such as through use of existing sources (government statistics, books, etc.), interviews, surveys, case studies, and experiments.

Right-wing: ideological term associated with conservatism and fascism. It originated in the nineteenth century when governing parties sat on the right sides of parliaments. By the end of the century it became associated with support for free market capitalism. Right-wing is also often identified with promotion of upper-class interests. *See also* Left Wing.

Role: the behavior expected of people who occupy particular social positions.

Sample: *see* Universe.

Sanction: social reward to encourage conformity to a norm, or punishment to discourage nonconformity.

Scientific Management: school of managerial consultants and studies founded by Frederick Taylor that developed such research techniques as time and motion studies to find ways to increase worker productivity.

Second World: *see* Three Worlds Theory.

Secondary Research: technique of research based on the analysis of preexisting data, such as from government and business statistics.

Self: a person's sense of her or his own being.

Self-esteem: the positive or negative evaluation that one holds of personal worth or self.

Semi-peripheral Countries: *see* World-System Theory.

Setting: the physical or social location within which social interaction takes place.

Single-Parent Family: family unit composed of a single parent—due to death, divorce, or separation of the other parent—and children.

Slave: a laborer whose labor power is owned by another.

Slave Society: economic type of society based upon the predominant use of unfree or slave labor to produce surplus products.

Slavery and slave societies: a socioeconomic structure in which the central classes are slave owners and slaves. It is based upon the predominant use of unfree or slave labor to produce surplus products. The two major periods of slavery in world history have been Ancient Slavery (ancient Greece and Rome from the fifth century B.C. to the fifth century A.D.) and New World Slavery, from the sixteenth to nineteenth centuries in the Americas.

Small-Business Owners Class: economic class made up of individuals and families who derive their primary incomes from the ownership and operation of businesses that do not have significant numbers of hired employees. The working owner is the primary producer in the business, not a hired labor force.

Social: any interpersonal situation in which a person orients her or his actions to one or more others.

Social Being: the idea in social thought that the identities of human beings are inevitably influenced by their social relationships and interactions.

Social Capitalism: *see* Capitalism.

Social Class: groups of people who share common standards of living and perceive themselves as social equals different from classes above or below them.

Social Democracy: political ideology characterized by the advocacy of an evolutionary, gradual development of socialism, mixed economies of both private and state ownership, and political pluralism.

Social Mobility: stratification concept that refers to intergenerational and intragenerational movements of people up and down class hierarchies.

Social Position: the place occupied by a person engaged in social interaction.

Social Structure: the grand total of all institutions within a society.

Social Survey: technique for collecting data in which respondents are asked to answer questions.

Social Theory: a systematic concept-based explanation of how social life functions and changes.

Social Wage: indirect income received by workers in the form of state-subsidized services, such as free education, health care, and the like. Contrasted to individual wages, or income received directly from employers.

Social Work: profession that renders assistance to individual victims of a variety of social problems, such as poverty, homelessness, alcoholism, and domestic violence.

Socialism: (1) economic type of society characterized by common, public ownership of the major means of production (businesses), cooperation, and social equality; (2) political ideology, of which there are a number of varieties, that advocates development of socialist types of economies.

Socialization: concept used in three different manners in sociology: (1) the process by which individuals learn and adopt the values, norms, and roles of particular societies; (2) the process by which governments take over ownership of businesses, as in "the socialization of the means of production"; (3) the process by which individuals engaged in production within modern societies become increasingly interdependent as divisions of labor become more specialized, extensive, and global, as in, "the increasing socialization of production relations."

Society: a population that shares a common territory (usually), government, and period of existence.

Socioeconomic Structure: as used in this text, typical fusions of economic and class structures that have occurred in world history; that is, a feudal economy with landlord and peasant classes, or a capitalist economy with capitalist and working classes.

Sociological Imagination: concept developed by C. Wright Mills (1961) in an influential book by the same title. Possession of a sociological imagination, according to him, was necessary for determining how personal lives were influenced by the social structures and historical periods within which people lived. That would enable people to understand the relationships between their personal problems and social issues.

Sociology: from Latin *socia*, or "society," and Greek *logos*, or "knowledge" or "study"; hence, the "study of society"; the scientific study of societies and social life.

State: the political governing power of a society. As used by Max Weber (1918), "a human community that (successfully) claims the monopoly of the legitimate use of physical force within a given territory."

State Society: early economic type of society in which the state was the major owner or controller of land and other means of production and collected tax or tribute payments from the surplus products of subjects. Comparable to the concepts of the Asiatic and tributary modes of production.

Status: concept used in two different ways in sociology: (1) the prestige attached to a person or his or her social position; (2) any position within a social hierarchy.

Status Inconsistency: sociological concept that refers to situations in which a person does not have equal levels of educational achievement, occupational position, and income, as when a person with low educational achievement occupies an occupational position that requires great skill, or when a highly educated person occupying a professional position receives relatively low pay.

Stepfamily: family unit in which there exist children and parents who are not biologically related.

Stratification: specialization in sociology that studies social inequality due to class, gender, nationality, racial, or other types of positions within societies.

Stone Age: earliest stage of hunting and gathering societies characterized by reliance on stone tools and weapons. The first advances beyond the stone age began around 9000 B.C. in southwestern Asia.

Structural determination: the extent to which economic, social, political, and other institutional structures are responsible for causing human behavior.

Subculture: the unique way of life of a regional, class, nationality, or other type of subgroup within a society, as expressed through its own particular types of material products and nonmaterial values, customs, and language.

Subjective Social Life: how people think and feel about themselves, others, and what they do, as it is affected by their interaction in society; internal thinking processes that are oriented toward interactions with others.

Subsistence Production: production of only basic survival necessities; absence of surplus products.

Substantive Rationality: concept associated with Max Weber that defines rationality in terms of qualitative goals whose attainment may or may not be calculable. Weber compared the substantive concept of rationality to the more limited concept of formal rationality. He believed that the cultural drift of the West favored a shallow formal concept of rationality at the expense of substantive considerations. *See also* Formal Rationality.

Surplus Product: production in excess of survival necessities. Surplus products are available to be accumulated or traded.

Surplus Value: in Marxian economic theory, the amount of new value that is created by labor in each step of a production process. Surplus value is the remainder after the cost of production is subtracted from the value of the product. Marx maintained that workers produced but did not receive surplus value. Rather, capitalists expropriated the surplus value produced by workers and used it to form new capital and as the source of their own incomes.

Survey: technique for collecting information in which questionnaires soliciting particular types of information, such as attitudes, income, or religious affiliation, are administered to samples of respondents and the responses are tabulated.

Symbolic Interactionism: microsociological approach that investigates the interaction processes between individuals and their social surroundings. Its key postulate is that social interaction is carried on through symbols—language and gestures—and that individuals are involved in ongoing processes of interpreting and reinterpreting these social symbols. It follows, according to this school, that social reality is continually being transformed through the changing meanings that individuals attach to the social symbols that they receive.

Synthesis: *see* Thesis-Antithesis-Synthesis.

Taylorism: pejorative term for attempts to increase productivity by treating workers mechanistically as factors of production without due regard for their specifically human needs. *See also* Scientific Management.

Technology: from Greek *techne*, or "techniques," and *logos*, or "knowledge"; hence, "knowledge of techniques" (especially of production). Social scientists distinguish the following stages of technological development: hunting and gathering, pastoralism, horticulture, agriculture, and industry.

Terrorism: as used in this text, a tactic of states (state terrorism) or opposition groups that uses violence to spread fear among a civilian population for political goals. There is no universally agreed upon definition of terrorism.

Theory: logically consistent explanation of causes and interrelationships that occur in reality.

Thesis-Antithesis-Synthesis: stages or moments of dialectical development. According to one dialectical approach, all changes in reality proceed through these stages. In the thesis stage something exists as is. A contradiction emerges within it, forcing the change of its original condition; it is now in the antithesis stage. The contradiction is resolved in the synthesis stage, which is simultaneously the thesis of a new round of triadic development. *See also* Dialectics, Contradiction.

Third World: *see* Three Worlds Theory.

Three Worlds Theory: post World War II journalistic and social science convention that divided the world into first, second, and third world countries. The first world (Western Europe, the United States, Canada, Australia, New Zealand, and Japan) countries were economically developed, prosperous, capitalist, and aligned to the United States in the Cold War. Second World (the Soviet Union and its allies) were developed, less prosperous and socialist. Third World countries were developing, poor and unaligned in the Cold War. China was variously considered to be a second and a third world country.

Traditional Legitimacy: concept identified with Max Weber. Type of legitimacy in which people obey a ruler or rulers out of long-standing habit, as opposed to reason.

Two-Stage Theory of Revolution: theory originally associated with V.I. Lenin that maintains that revolutions go through two stages. The revolutionary's strategic goal in the first stage, around which broad unity can be developed, is to overthrow an old unpopular regime. The strategic goal of the second stage is to develop a radical new government to take its place.

Around this goal less unity is possible. Hence, a struggle ensues over the direction that the revolution is to take.

Two-Wage-Earner Family: family unit in which both the principal male and female adults pursue full-time income-producing occupations outside of the home.

Type: a classification of objects that have a distinguishing characteristic or characteristics that unite them as belonging together and different from others.

Typology: a classification scheme in which different types are determined by interrelating two or more variables.

Universe: term used to refer to the ultimate population that a research project is attempting to understand. The term is usually used in conjunction with the concept of a sample, the unit or group from which information is actually collected. Presumably, the distribution of the characteristics of the sample are generalizable; that is, they approximately match those of the universe of ultimate interest.

Upper Class: in most uses, the rich in a society.

Urbanization: long-range trend in domestic migration characterized by the movement of people from rural areas to cities.

Use Value: in Karl Marx's economic theory, the importance that a commodity has for its consumer. A consumer buys a coat in order to keep warm. Use value is contrasted to exchange value, which is the relative market costs of commodities as determined by the amount of labor incorporated in their production. A coat costs more than a hat. See also *Labor Theory of Value* and *Exchange Value*.

Vanguard Party: concept originally associated with Lenin. Refers to political parties made up exclusively of leaders who see and agree with the need for revolutionary changes. The concept is based upon the observation that in revolutionary periods populations generally divide into those opposed, those in the middle, and a vanguard in favor of radical changes.

Variable: concept most often used in quantitative research that refers to changeable and measurable characteristics, such as rates of unemployment, sizes of family incomes, or years of education completed. It can also be used to refer to any changeable condition, regardless of whether it can be expressed in exact quantitative terms. Thus, something so general as the development of capitalism could be considered a variable.

Village Communities: Early horticulturally based peasant villages.

Working Class: economic class made up of persons who sell their labor to employers. Also used as a social-class concept to refer to people who identify themselves as working people who are above lower-class and below middle-class people.

World-System Theory: contemporary social science theory that holds that that there is a network or system of economic relationships between the world's societies and that location within this network or system largely influences the character of a domestic economy. World-system theorists distinguish three locations in the world-system: core, semi-peripheral and peripheral. Core countries and areas, including the United States, Western Europe, and Japan, are the most powerful and peripheral countries—most developing countries—are the least powerful. Semi-peripheral countries are in between in power.

Appendix

Countries of the World: By Type of Society and in Order of United Nations Human Development Index (HDI)

HDI (Rank)	Population (in millions)	GDP per capita (PPP US$)	Infant mortality rate (per 1,000 live births)	Life expectancy at birth (years)
DEVELOPED CAPITALIST				
a. High human development				
1 Iceland	0.3	36,510	2	81.5
2 Norway	4.6	41,420	3	79.8
3 Australia	20.3	31,794	5	80.9
4 Canada	32.3	33,375	5	80.3
5 Ireland	4.1	38,550	5	78.4
6 Sweden	9.0	32,525	3	80.5
7 Switzerland	7.4	35,633	4	81.3
8 Japan	127.9	31,267	3	72.3
9 Netherlands	16.3	32,684	4	79.2
10 France	61.0	30,386	4	80.2
11 Finland	5.2	32,153	3	78.9
12 United States	299.8	41,890	6	77.9
13 Spain	43.4	27,169	4	80.5
14 Denmark	5.4	33,974	4	77.9
15 Austria	8.3	33,700	4	79.4

HDI (Rank)	Population (in millions)	GDP per capita (PPP US$)	Infant mortalityrate (per 1,000 live births)	Life expectancy at birth (years)
16 United Kingdom	60.2	32,119	4	78.8
17 Belgium	10.4	32,119	4	78.8
18 Luxembourg	0.5	60,228	4	78.4
19 New Zealand	4.1	24.996	5	79.8
20 Italy	58.6	28,529	4	80.3
22 Germany	82.7	29,461	4	79.1
24 Greece	11.1	23,381	4	78.9
28 Cyprus	0.8	22,699	4	79.0
29 Portugal	10.5	20,410	4	77.7
34 Malta	0.4	19,189	4	77.7

b. Unranked

x. Andorra	0.07			
x. Liechtenstein	0.04			
x. San Martino	0.03			

FORMER COMMUNIST

a. Developed, high human development

27 Slovenia	2.0	22,273	3	77.4
32 Czech Republic	10.2	20,538	3	75.9
36 Hungary	10.1	17,887	7	72.9
37 Poland	38.2	13,847	6	75.2
42 Slovakia	5.4	15,871	7	74.2
43 Lithuania	3.4	14,494	7	72.5
44 Estonia	1.3	15,478	6	71.2
45 Latvia	2.3	13,646	9	72.0
53 Bulgaria	7.7	9.032	12	72.7
60 Romania	21.6	9,060	16	71.9

b. In Transition, high human development

64 Belarus	9.8	7,918	10	68.7
66 Bosnia and Herzgovina	3.9	7,032	13	74.5
67 Russian Federation	144.0	10,845	14	65.0

HDI (Rank)	Population (in millions)	GDP per capita (PPP US$)	Infant mortality rate (per 1,000 live births)	Life expectancy at birth (years)
68 Albania	3.2	5,316	16	76.2
69 Macedonia	2.0	7,200	15	73.8
b. In Transition, medium human development				
73 Kazakhstan	15.2	7,857	63	65.9
76 Ukraine	46.9	6,848	13	67.7
83 Armenia	3.0	4.945	26	71.7
96 Georgia	4.5	3.365	41	70.7
98 Azarbaijan	8.4	5.016	74	67.1
109 Turkmenistan	4.8	3,838	81	62.6
111 Moldova	3.9	2,100	14	68.4
113 Uzbekistan	26.6	2.063	57	66.8
116 Kyrgyzstan	5.2	1.927	58	65.6
122 Tajikistan	6.6	1.356	59	66.3
c. Other, medium human development				
114 Mongolia	2.6	2,107	39	65.9
d. Unranked				
xx. Montenegro	0.6	...	...	74.1
xx. Serbia	9.9	...	...	73.6
COMMUNIST				
a.. High human development				
51 Cuba	11.3	6,000	6	77.7
b. Medium human development				
81 China	1,313.0	6,757	23	72.5
105 Vietnam	85.0	3,071	16	73.7
130 Laos	5.7	2,039	62	63.2
c, Unranked				
xx. North Korea	23.6	...	...	66.8

HDI (Rank)	Population (inmillions)	GDP per capita (PPP US$)	Infant mortality rate (per 1,000 live births)	Life expectancy at birth (years)
DEVELOPING				
a. High Human Development				
30 Brunei Darussalam	0.4	28,161	8	76.3
31 Barbados	0.3	17,297	11	76.0
33 Kuwait	2.7	26,321	9	76.9
35 Qatar	0.8	27,664	18	74.3
38 Argentina	38.7	14,280	15	74.3
39 United Arab Emirates	4.1	25,514	8	77.8
40 Chile	16.3	12,027	8	77.9
41 Bahrain	0.7	21,482	9	74.8
46 Uruguay	3.3	9,962	14	75.3
48 Costa Rica	4.3	10,180	11	78.1
49 Bahamas	0.3	18,380	13	71.1
50 Seychelles	0.1	16,106	12	...
52 Mexico	104.3	10,751	22	74.9
54 Saint Kits and Nevis	(.)	13,307	18	...
55 Tonga	0.1	8,177	20	72.3
56 Libya	5.9	10,335	18	72.7
57 Antigua and Barbuda	0.1	12.500	11	...
58 Oman	2.5	15.602	10	74.2
59 Trinidad and Tobago	1.3	14,603	17	69.0
61 Saudi Arabia	23.6	15,711	21	71.6
62 Panama	3.2	7,605	19	74.7
63 Malaysia	225.7	10,882	10	73.0
65 Mauritius	1.2	12,715	13	72.0
70 Brazil	186.8	8,402	31	71.0
b. Medium human development				
71 Dominica	0.1	6,393	13	...
72 Saint Lucia	0.2	6,707	12	72.5

HDI (Rank)	Population (in millions)	GDP per capita (PPP US$)	Infant mortality rate (per 1,000 live births)	Life expectancy at birth (years)
91 Tunisia	10.1	8,371	20	73.0
92 Fiji	0.8	6,049	16	67.8
93 Saint Vincent and the Grenadines	0.1	6,568	17	70.6
94 Iran	69.4	7,968	31	69.5
95 Paraguay	5.9	4,642	20	70.8
97 Guyana	0.7	4,508	47	63.6
99 Sri Lanka	19.1	4,595	12	70.8
100 Maldives	0.3	5,261	33	65.6
101 Jamaica	2.7	4,291	17	72.0
102 Cape Verde	0.5	5,803	26	70.2
103 El Salvador	6.7	5,255	23	70.7
104 Algeria	32.9	7,062	34	71.0
106 Palestine	3.8	...	21	72.4
107 Indonesia	226.1	3,843	28	68.6
108 Syria	18.9	3,808	14	73.1
110 Nicaragua	5.5	3,674	30	70.8
112 Egypt	72.8	4,337	28	69.8
115 Honduras	6.8	3,430	31	68.6
117 Bolivia	9.2	2,819	52	63.9
118 Guatemala	12.7	4,568	32	69.0
119 Gabon	1.3	6,954	60	56.8
120 Vanatu	0.2	3,225	31	68.4
121 South Africa	47.9	11,110	55	53.4
123 Sao Tome and Principe	0.2	2,178	75	64.3
124 Botswana	1.8	12,383	87	46.6
125 Namibia	2.0	7,586	46	51.5
126 Morocco	30.5	4,555	36	69.6
127 Equitorial Guinea	0.5	7,874	123	49.3
128 India	1,134.4	3,452	56	62.9
129 Solomon Islands	0.5	2,031	24	62.3

HDI (Rank)	Population (inmillions)	GDP per capita (PPP US$)	Infant mortality rate (per 1,000 live births)	Life expectancy at birth (years)
131 Cambodia	14.0	2,727	98	56.8
132 Myanmar	14.8	1.027	75	59.9
133 Bhutan	0.6	...	65	63.5
134 Comoros	0.8	1,993	53	63.0
135 Ghana	22.5	2,480	68	58.5
136 Pakistan	158.1	2,370	79	63.6
137 Mauritania	3.0	2,234	78	62.2
138 Lesotho	2.0	13,335	102	44.6
139 Congo	3.6	1,262	81	53.0
140 Bangledesh	153.3	2,053	54	62.0
141 Swaziland	1.1	4,824	110	43.9
142 Nepal	27.1	1,550	56	61.3
143 Madagascar	18.6	923	74	57.3
144 Cameroon	17.8	2,299	87	49.9
145 Papua New Guinea	6.1	2,563	55	56.7
146 Haiti	9.3	1,663	84	58.1
147 Sudan	36.9	2,083	62	56.4
148 Kenya	35.6	1,240	79	51.0
149 Djibouti	0.8	2,178	88	53.4
150 Timor-Leste	1.1	...	52	58.3
151 Zimbabwe	13.1	2,038	81	40.0
152 Togo	6.2	1,506	78	57.6
153 Yemen	21.1	930	76	60.3
154 Uganda	10.9	1,454	79	47.8
155 Gambia	1.6	1,921	97	58.0
b. Low human development				
156 Senegal	11.8	1,792	77	61.6
157 Eritrea	4.5	1,109	50	55.2
158 Nigeria	141.4	1,128	100	46.6
159 Tanzania	38.5	744	76	49.7
160 Guinea	9.0	2,316	98	53.7
161 Rwanda	9.2	1,206	118	37.5

HDI (Rank)	Population (in millions)	GDP per capita (PPP US$)	Infant mortality rate (per 1,000 live births)	Life expectancy at birth (years)
162 Angola	16.1	2,335	154	40.1
163 Benin	8.5	1,141	89	44.7
164 Malawi	13.2	667	79	41.8
165 Zambia	11.5	1,023	102	39.5
166 Côte d'Ivoire	16.6	1,648	118	45.5
167 Burundi	7.9	699	114	47.4
168 Congo (Dem. Rep)	58.7	714	129	45.0
169 Ethiopia	79.0	1,055	109	50.7
170 Chad	10.1	1,427	124	50.5
171 Central African Rep.	4.2	1,224	115	43.3
172 Mozambique	20.5	1,242	100	44.0
173 Mali	11.6	1,033	120	51.8
174 Niger	13.3	781	150	54.5
175 Guinea-Bissau	1.6	827	124	45.5
176 Burkina Faso	13.9	1,213	96	50.7
177 Sierra Leone	5.6	806	165	41.0
.d Unranked				
Afghanistan	25.1	...	...	42.9
Iraq	28.0	...	...	57.7
Kirbati	0.09	4,597	...	...
Liberia	3.4	3,442	...	44.7
Marshall Islands	0.07	...	...	...
xx. Nauru	0.01	...	...	...
xx. Palau	0.02	...	...	...
xx. Somalia	8.2	...	...	47.1
Tuvalu	0.01	...	...	...

HDI (Rank)	Population (in millions)	GDP per capita (PPP US$)	Infant mortality rate (per 1,000 live births)	Life expectancy at birth (years)
Developed Capitalist	884.6	33,082	6	78.4
Former Communist	407.8	9,527	22	69.6
Communist	1435.8	6,408	22	64.7
Developing	3,786.6	5,282	57	50.7
World	6,514.8	9,543	52	68.1

Sources: UNDP (2007, Tables 1, 1a, 5, and 10).

Notes: Classifications primarily based on United Nations (2008, p. xxx). The Human Development Index (HDI) of the United Nations is composed of measures of education, health, and economic standard of living. High, Medium, and Low human development are U.N. categories based on HDI rating. Purchasing Power Parity (PPP) is a measure of average income that controls for differences in costs of living between countries. The table includes member countries only of the United Nations.

Bibliography

ACEP (American College of Emergency Physicians). 2005. http://www.acep.org/ 1.391.0_html.

ACS, GREGORY and SANDI NELSON. 2003. "Changes in Family Structures and Child Well-Being: Evidence from the 2002 National Survey of America's Families." Washington, DC: The Urban Institute.

AMIN, SAMIR. 1980. *Class and Nation: Historically and in the Current Crisis* (Susan Kaplow, tr.). New York: Monthly Review Press.

ANDERSON, PERRY. 1974a. *Passages from Antiquity to Feudalism.* London: Verso.

ANDERSON, PERRY. 1974b. *Lineages of The Absolutist State.* London: New Left Books.

ANDREWES, ANTONY. 1967. *The Greeks.* London: Hutchinson.

BALLANTINE, JEANNE. 1993. *The Sociology of Education: A Systematic Analysis*, 3rd ed. Englewood Cliffs, NJ:Prentice Hall.

BARAN, PAUL. 1957. *The Political Economy of Growth.* New York: Monthly Review Press.

BARCLAY, WILLIAM, JOSEPH ENRIGHT, and REID T. REYNOLDS. 1970. "Population Control in the Third World." *NACLA Newsletter,* Vol. 4, no. 8 (December), pp. 1–18.

BARKIN, DAVID. 1990. *Distorted Development: Mexico and the World Economy.* Boulder, CO: Westview.

BERRY, RALPH E., Jr. and JAMES P. BOLAND. 1977. *The Economic Cost of Alcohol Abuse.* New York: Free Press.

BLAUNER, ROBERT. 1964. *Alienation and Freedom: The Factory Worker and His Industry.* Chicago: University of Chicago Press.

BLOCH, MARC. 1933. "Feudalism, European." *Encylopedia of the Social Sciences.* New York: Macmillan.

BLOCH, MARC. 1940. *Feudal Society* (L.A. Manyon, tr.). Chicago: University of Chicago Press, 1961.

BOGGS, JAMES. 1963. *The American Revolution: Pages from a Negro Worker's Notebook.* New York: Monthly Review Press.

BRAVERMAN, HARRY. 1974. *Labor and Monopoly Capital.* New York: Monthly Review Press.

BRENNER, M. HARVEY. 1976. "Estimating the Social Costs of National Economic Policy." United States Congress: Joint Economic Committee.

BRUNDENIUS, CLAES. 2002. "Whither the Cuban Economy after Recovery." *Journal of Latin American Studies* 34 (part 2, May).

BRUNT, P.A. 1971. *Social Conflicts in the Roman Republic.* New York: Norton.

CASTRO MARTIN, TERESA and LARRY L. BUMPASS. 1989. "Recent Trends and Differentials in Marital Disruption." *Demography*, Vol. 26, no. 1, pp. 37–51.

CENTERS, RICHARD. 1949. *The Psychology of Social Classes: A Study of Class Consciousness.* Princeton, NJ: Princeton University Press.

CIA (Central Intelligence Agency). 2005. "The War on Terrorism," http://www.cia.gov/terrorism/faqs.htm

COMMONWEALTH FUND. 2008. *Why Not the Best? Results from the National Scorecard on U.S. Health System Performance, 2008.* New York: The Commonwealth Fund, July 2008.

COOLEY, CHARLES HORTON. 1902. *Human Nature and the Social Order.* New York: Schocken Books, 1964.

DAHL, GUDRUN. 1979. "Ecology and Equality: The Boran Case." In *Pastoral Production and Society.* Cambridge: Cambridge University Press.

DANIEL, P. 1972. *The Shadow of Slavery: Peonage in the South 1901–1969.* Urbana: University of Illinois Press.

DAVIE, MICHAEL. 1987. *Titanic: The Death and Life of a Legend.* New York: Alfred A. Knopf.

DAVIS, F. JAMES. 1991. *Who Is Black? One Nation's Definition.* University Park: Pennsylvania State University Press.

DAVIS, KINGSLEY and WILBERT E. MOORE. 1945. "Some Principles of Stratification." *American Sociological Review*, Vol. 10, pp. 242–249.

DEEVEY, EDWARD S., Jr. 1960. "The Human Population." *Scientific American*, Vol. 203, no. 3 (September), pp. 195–204.

DeNAVAS-WALT, CARMEN, ROBERT CLEVELAND, and BRUCE H. WEBSTER, Jr. 2003. Current Population Reports, P60-221. *Income in the United States: 2002.* Washington, DC: U.S. Government Printing Office.

DeNAVAS-WALT, CARMEN, BERNADETTE D. PROCTOR, and JESSICA SMITH, 2007. Current Population Reports, P60-233. *Income, Poverty, and Health Insurance Coverage in the United States: 2006.* Washington, DC: U.S. Government Printing Office.

DOMHOFF, G. WILLIAM. 1967. *Who Rules America?* Englewood Cliffs, NJ: Prentice Hall.

DOMHOFF, G. WILLIAM. 1983. *Who Rules America Now?* Englewood Cliffs, NJ: Prentice Hall.

DURKHEIM, EMILE. 1893. *The Division of Labor in Society* (George Simpson, tr.). Glencoe, IL: Free Press, 1964.

DURKHEIM, EMILE. 1897. *Suicide* (J.A. Spaulding and George Simpson, trs.). Glencoe, IL: Free Press, 1964.

EGAN, DANIEL and LEVON A. CHORBAJIAN. 2004. *Power: A Critical Reader.* Upper Saddle River, NJ: Prentice Hall.

EISENSTADT, S.N. 1966. *Modernization: Protest and Change.* Englewood Cliffs, NJ: Prentice Hall.

ENGELS, FREDERICK. 1884. *The Origin of the Family, Private Property and the State.* Moscow: Progress Publishers, 1948.

ESPINOSA MARTINEZ, EUGENIO. 1999. "The Cuban Economy in the 1990s: From Crisis to Recovery." In José Bell Lara, ed., *Cuba in the 1990s.* Havana: Ed. José Martí.

FAO (Food and Agricultural Organization). 2002. *World Agriculture: Towards 2015/2030.* New York: United Nations.

FINLEY, M.I. 1980. *Ancient Slavery and Modern Ideology.* New York: Viking.

FRANK, ANDRE GUNDAR. 1969. *Capitalism and Underdevelopment in Latin America.* New York: Monthly Review Press.

FREUD, SIGMUND. 1930. *Civilization and Its Discontents.* New York: W.W. Norton, 1962.

FREUD, SIGMUND. 1933. *Why War?* Paris: International Institute of Intellectual Cooperation, League of Nations.

FURSTENBERG, FRANK F., Jr. and ANDREW J. CHERLIN. 1991. *Divided Families: What Happens to Children When Parents Part?* Cambridge, MA: Harvard University Press.

GELLES, RICHARD J. 1985. "Family Violence: What We Know and Can Do." In Eli H. Newberger and Richard Bourne (eds.), *Unhappy Families: Clinical and Research Perspectives on Family Violence.* Littleton, MA: PSG Publishing.

GERTH, HANS H. and C. WRIGHT MILLS. 1953. *Character and Social Structure.* New York: Harcourt, Brace and Company.

GILBERT, DENNIS. 2008. *The American Class Structure in an Age of Growing Inequality.* Los Angeles, CA: Pine Forge.

GIRARD, CHRIS. 1993. "Age, Gender, and Suicide: A Cross-National Analysis." *American Sociological Review,* Vol. 58, no. 4 (August), pp. 553–574.

GODELIER, MAURICE. 1969. *Sobre el modo de producción asiático.* Barcelona: Ediciones Martínez Roca.

GODELIER, MAURICE. 1978. "The Concept of the Asiatic Mode of Production." In D. Seddon (ed.), *Relations of Production.* London: Frank Cass.

GOTT, RICHARD. 2005. *Hugo Chávez and the Bolivarian Revolution.* New York: Verso.

GRALL, TIMOTHY S. 2007. *Custodial Mothers and Fathers and Their Child Support: 2005.* Current Population Reports P60–234. Washington, DC: U.S. Census Bureau.

GRAMSCI, ANTONIO. 1985. *Prison Notebooks: Selections.* New York: International Publishers.

GULLIVER, P.H. 1955. *The Family Herds.* London: Routledge & Kegan Paul.

HAGAN, E.E. 1962. *On the Theory of Social Change.* Homewood, IL: Dorsey.

HAMPER, BEN. 1991. *Rivethead: Tales from the Assembly Line.* New York: Warner Books.

HARDY, CHARLES. 2007. *Cowboy in Caracas: A North American's Memoir of Venezuela's Democratic Revolution.* Willimantic, CT: Curbstone Press.

HART-LANDSBERG, MARTIN and PAUL BURKETT. 2004. "China & Socialism." *Monthly Review,* Vol. 56, no. 3 (July–August).

HARVEY, DAVID. 1989. *The Condition of Postmodernity.* Oxford, UK: Basil Blackwell.

HERRNSTEIN, RICHARD J. and CHARLES MURRAY. 1994. *The Bell Curve: Intelligence and Class Structure in American Life.* New York: Free Press.

HESSE-BIBER, SHARLENE NAGY and GREGG LEE CARTER. 2005. *Working Women in America.* New York: Oxford University Press.

HOFFERTH, S., et al. 1991. *National Child Care Survey, 1990.* Washington, DC: Urban Institute.

HOROWITZ, IRVING LOUIS. 1966. *Three Worlds of Development.* New York: Oxford University Press.

HUNT, KATHLEEN. 1988. "Subduing the Lion Killers," *The New York Times Magazine,* December 18, p. 42.

HUNTINGFORD, G.W.B. 1953. *The Southern Nilo-Hamites.* London: International African Institute, 1969.

HUXLEY, ALDOUS. 1958. *Brave New World Revisited.* New York: Harper and Row.

JUBILEE USA. 2003. "Are IMF and World Bank Economic Policy Conditions Undermining the Impact of Debt Cancellation?" (policy paper). Washington, DC: Jubilee USA Network.

KAGARLITSKY, BORIS. 1988. *The Thinking Reed: Intellectuals and the Soviet State, 1917 to the Present* (Brian Pearce, tr.). London: Verso.

KAMMEYER, KENNETH C.W. and HELEN GINN. 1986. *An Introduction to Population.* Chicago: The Dorsey Press.

KLEIN, HERBERT S. 1986. *African Slavery in Latin America and the Caribbean.* New York: Oxford University Press.

KRADER, LAWRENCE. 1975. *The Asiatic Mode of Production.* Assen, The Netherlands: Van Gorcum & Comp, B.V.

LEAR, MARTHA WEINMAN. 1988. "The New Marital Therapy." *The New York Times Magazine,* March 6.

LEBOWITZ, MICHAEL A. 2006. *Build It Now! Socialism for the Twenty-First Century.* New York: Monthly Review Press.

LEMBCKE, JERRY. 1988. *Capitalist Development and Class Capacities.* Westport, CT: Greenwood Press.

LEMBCKE, JERRY. 1993. "Classical Theory, Postmodernism, and the Sociology Liberal Arts Curriculum." *The American Sociologist,* Vol. 24, nos. 3–4 (Fall–Winter), pp. 55–68.

LENIN, V.I. 1902. *What Is to Be Done?* In V.I. Lenin. 1970. *Selected Works in Three Volumes.* Moscow: Progress Publishers.

LENIN, V.I. 1916. *Imperialism, The Highest Stage of Capitalism.* In V.I. Lenin. 1970. *Selected Works in Three Volumes.* Moscow: Progress Publishers.

LENIN, V.I. 1917. *The State and Revolution.* In V.I. Lenin. 1970. *Selected Works in Three Volumes.* Moscow: Progress Publishers.

LENIN, V.I. 1918. "The Proletarian Revolution and the Renegade Kautsky." In V.I. Lenin. 1970. *Selected Works in Three Volumes.* Moscow: Progress Publishers.

LENSKI, GERHARD and JEAN LENSKI. 1982. *Human Societies,* 4th ed. New York: McGraw-Hill.

LIVI-BACCI, MASSIMO. 1992. *A Concise History of World Population*. (Carl Ipsen, tr.). Cambridge, MA: Blackwell Publishers.

LORD, WALTER. 1955. *A Night to Remember.* Mattituck, NY: Amereon House, 1987.

MADDOX, BRENDA. 1976. *The Half-Parent*. New York: Signet.

MALTHUS, THOMAS ROBERT. 1798. *An Essay on the Principle of Population*. New York: Macmillan, 1894.

MANNHEIM, KARL. 1936. *Ideology and Utopia*. New York: Harcourt, Brace.

MARCUSE, HERBERT. 1955. *Eros and Civilization*. Boston: Beacon, 1966.

MARX, KARL. 1858. *Grundrisse: Foundations of the Critique of Political Economy* (Martin Nicolaus, tr.). Harmondsworth, Middlesex: Penguin, 1973.

MARX, KARL. 1859. *A Contribution to the Critique of Political Economy*. Moscow: Progress Publishers, 1970.

MARX, KARL. 1865. "Wages, Price and Profit." In Karl Marx and Frederick Engels. 1970. *Selected Works in Three Volumes*. Moscow: Progress Publishers.

MARX, KARL. 1867. *Capital*, Vol. I. Moscow: Progress Publishers, n.d.

MARX, KARL. 1871. *The Civil War in France*. In Karl Marx and Frederick Engels. 1970. *Selected Works in Three Volumes*. Moscow: Progress Publishers.

MARX, KARL. 1875. "Critique of the Gotha Program." In Karl Marx and Frederick Engels. 1970. *Selected Works in Three Volumes*. Moscow: Progress Publishers.

MARX, KARL and FREDERICK ENGELS. 1846. *The German Ideology*. Moscow: Progress Publishers, 1976.

MARX, KARL and FREDERICK ENGELS. 1848. "The Communist Manifesto." In Karl Marx and Frederick Engels. 1970. *Selected Works in Three Volumes*. Moscow: Progress Publishers.

MASS, BONNIE. 1976. *Population Target: The Political Economy of Population Control in Latin America*. Brampton, Ontario, Canada: Charters.

MEAD, GEORGE HERBERT. 1934. *Mind, Self, and Society*. Chicago: University of Chicago Press.

MEYER, MICHAEL C. and WILLIAM L. SHERMAN. 1987. *The Course of Mexican History*. New York: Oxford University Press.

MICHELS, ROBERT. 1911. *Political Parties*. New York: Free Press, 1967.

MILES, ROBERT. 1989. *Racism*. London: Routledge.

MILLS, C. WRIGHT. 1953. *White Collar*. New York: Oxford University Press.

MILLS, C. WRIGHT. 1956. *The Power Elite*. New York: Oxford University Press.

MILLS, C. WRIGHT. 1961. *The Sociological Imagination*. New York: Grove Press.

MOYNIHAN, DANIEL P. 1965. *The Negro Family: The Case for National Action*. Washington: U.S. Department of Labor.

O'CONNOR, JAMES. 1973. *The Fiscal Crisis of the State*. New York: St. Martin's Press.

OECD (Organization for Economic Co-operation and Development). 2008. *OECD in Figures 2006-2007*.

PELTON, LEROY H. 1981 "Child Abuse and Neglect: The Myth of Classlessness." In Leroy H. Pelton (ed.), *The Social Context of Child Abuse and Neglect*. New York: Human Sciences Press.

PETERS, GARY L. and ROBERT P. LARKIN. 1983. *Population Geography*. Dubuque, IA: Kendall/Hunt.

PETRAS, JAMES and HENRY VELTMEYER. 2001. *Globalization Unmasked: Imperialism in the 21st Century*. London: Zed.

PHILLIPS, PAUL. 1990. "The Debt Crisis and Eastern Europe." *Monthly Review*, Vol. 41, no. 9 (February), pp. 19–27.

PIÑEIRO HARNECKER, CAMILA. 2005. "The New Cooperative Movement in Venezuela's Bolivarian Process." *Monthly Review* (online publication *MRzine,* May 12). http://mrzine.monthlyreview.org/harnecker051205.html

POPE, WHITNEY. 1976. *Durkheim's Suicide: A Classic Reanalyzed*. Chicago: University of Chicago Press.

PORTER, JOHN. 1965. *The Vertical Mosaic*. Toronto: University of Toronto Press.

REYNOLDS, LARRY T. and LEONARD LIEBERMAN. 1993. "The Rise and Fall of 'Race.'" Race, Sex & Class, Vol. 1, no. 1 (Fall), pp. 109–127.

RHOADES, LAWRENCE J. 1981. A History of the ASA, 1905–1980. Washington, DC: American Sociological Association.

RODNEY, WALTER. 1972. *How Europe Underdeveloped Africa*. London: Bogle L'Overture.

ROSS, ROBERT J.S. 2004. *Slaves to Fashion: Poverty and Abuse in the New Sweatshops*. Ann Arbor: University of Michigan Press.

ROSTOW, WALT W. 1960. *The Stages of Economic Growth*. Cambridge: Cambridge University Press.

RUSSELL, JAMES W. 1989. *Modes of Production in World History.* London: Routledge.

RUSSELL, JAMES W. 2006. *Double Standard: Social Policy in Europe and the United States*. Lanham, MD: Rowman & Littlefield.

RUSSELL, JAMES W. 2009. *Class and Race Formation in North America*. Toronto: University of Toronto Press.

RUSSELL, PHILIP L. 1994. *Mexico Under Salinas*. Austin, TX: Mexico Resource Center.

RYAN, MARY P. 1979. *Womanhood in America: From Colonial Times to the Present*, 2nd ed. New York: New Viewpoints.

SAHLINS, MARSHALL. 1972. *Stone Age Economics*. Chicago, Aldine.

SANEY, ISAAC. 2004. *Cuba: A Revolution in Motion*. Blackpoint, Nova Scotia: Fernwood Publishing.

SCHUMPETER, JOSEPH A. 1927. *Imperialism and Social Classes*. New York: Augustus M. Kelley, 1951.

SHANNON, THOMAS RICHARD. 1989. *An Introduction to the World-System Perspective*. Boulder, CO: Westview Press.

SIMMEL, GEORG. 1922. *Conflict & The Web of Group Affiliations*. New York: Free Press, 1964.

SIMPSON, GEORGE EATON and J. MILTON YINGER. 1985. *Racial and Cultural Minorities*, 5th ed. New York: Plenum.

SIMPSON, MILES E. and GEORGE H. CONKLIN. 1989. "Socioeconomic Development, Suicide, and Religion: A Test of Durkheim's Theory of Religion and Suicide." *Social Forces*, Vol. 67, no. 4 (June), pp. 945–964.

SINGH, GOPAL K. and MOHAMMAD SIAHPUSH. 2006. "Widening Socioeconomic Inequalities in U.S. Life Expectancy, 1980–2000." *International Journal of Epidemiology. 2006* Volume 35, no. 4 (August), pp.969–979.

SPALTER-ROTH, ROBERTA and JANENE SCELZA. 2008. *How Des Our Membership Grow? Indicators of Change by Gender, Race and Ethnicity.* American Sociological Association Research Brief, February.

SPRUIT, INGEBORG P. 1982. "Unemployment and Health in Macro-Social Analysis." *Social Science and Medicine*, Vol. 16, no. 22, pp. 1903–1907.

STARK, EVAN and A. FLITCRAFT. 1988. "Violence Among Intimates: An Epidemiological Review." In V.B. Van Hasselt, et al. (eds.), *Handbook of Family Violence*, pp. 293–319. New York: Plenum Press.

STARK, RODNEY and WILLIAM S. BAINBRIDGE. 1982. "Toward a Theory of Religious Commitment." *Journal for the Scientific Study of Religion*, Vol. 19, pp. 114–128.

STEFANSSON, CLAES-GöRAN. 1991. "Long-term Unemployment and Mortality in Sweden, 1980–1986." *Social Science and Medicine*, Vol. 32, no. 4, pp. 419–423.

STEWART, SUSAN D. 2007. *Brave New Stepfamilies: Diverse Paths Toward Stepfamily Living.* Thousand Oaks, CA: Sage.

SUBSTANCE ABUSE AND MENTAL HEALTH SERVICES ADMINISTRATION. 2007. *2006 National Survey on Drug Use and Health.* Washington, DC: U.S. Department of Health and Human Services.

SWEEZY, PAUL M. 1953. *The Present as History.* New York: Monthly Review Press.

SWEEZY, PAUL M. 1980. "Post-Revolutionary Society." *Monthly Review*, Vol. 32, no. 6 (November), pp. 1–13.

SWEEZY, PAUL M. and HARRY MAGDOFF. 1990. "Perestroika and the Future of Socialism." *Monthly Review*, Vol. 41, no. 10 (March), no. 11 (April).

SZYMANSKI, ALBERT. 1983. *Class Structure: A Critical Perspective.* New York: Praeger.

TUMIN, MELVIN. 1953. "Some Principles of Stratification: A Critical Analysis." *American Sociological Review* 18 (August), pp. 387–394.

TURNER, JONN KENNETH. 1910. *Barbarous Mexico.* Austin: University of Texas Press, 1969.

UNDP. 2007. *Human Development Report 2007/2008.* New York: United Nations.

UNICEF. 1994. *Crisis in Mortality, Health and Nutrition.* Economies in Transition Studies Regional Monitoring Report, No. 2. Florence, Italy: UNICEF International Child Development Centre.

UNICEF. 2001. *A Decade of Transition.* Regional Monitoring Report, No. 8. Florence, Italy: UNICEF Innocenti Research Centre.

UNICEF. 2004. *Innocenti Social Moniitor 2004.* Florence, Italy: UNICEF Innocenti Research Centre.

UNICEF. 2004a. *The State of the World's Children 2005.* New York: UNICEF. Report, No. 8. Florence: UNICEF Innocenti Research Centre.

UNICEF. 2007. *Progress for Children*, No. 6, December.

UNITED NATIONS. 2004. *World Economic and Social Survey 2004.* New York: United Nations.

UNITED NATIONS. 2008. *World Economic and Social Survey 2008.* New York: United Nations.

United Nations High Commissioner for Refugees (UNCR). 2008. *Global Trends: Refugees, Asylum-seekers, Returnees, Internally Displaced and Stateless Persons, 2007.* Geneva: UNCR.

U.S. CENSUS BUREAU. 2003. *Statistical Abstract of the United States*. Washington, DC: Government Printing Office.

U.S. CENSUS BUREAU. 2007. *Current Population Survey. 2007 Annual Social and Economic Supplement*. Washington, D.C.: Government Printing Office.

U.S. CENSUS BUREAU. 2007b. *America's Families and Living Arrangements: 2007*. Current Population Survey. March 2007, Table C3. Government Printing Office.

VOGT, JOSEPH. 1975. *Ancient Slavery and the Ideal of Man* (Thomas Widemann, tr.). Cambridge, MA: Harvard University Press.

WALLERSTEIN, IMMANUEL MAURICE. 1974. *The Modern World-System: Capitalist Agriculture and the Origins of the European World-Economy in the Sixteenth Century*. New York: Academic Press.

WALLERSTEIN, IMMANUEL MAURICE. 1984. *The Politics of the World-Economy: The States, the Movements, and the Civilizations*. New York: Cambridge University Press.

WALLERSTEIN, JUDITH and SANDRA BLAKESLEE. 1989. *Second Chances: Men, Women and Children a Decade after Divorce*. New York: Ticknor & Fields.

WARNER, W. LLOYD, M. MEEKER, and K. EELS. 1949. *Social Class in America*. Chicago: Social Resarch Associates.

WEBER, MAX. 1905. *The Protestant Ethic and the Spirit of Capitalism*. New York: Scribners, 1948.

WEBER, MAX. 1918. "Politics as a Vocation." In Hans H. Gerth and C. Wright Mills (ed. and tr.). 1958. *From Max Weber: Essays in Sociology*. New York: Oxford University Press.

WEBER, MAX. 1921. "Structures of Power." In Hans H. Gerth and C. Wright Mills (ed. and tr.). 1958. *From Max Weber: Essays in Sociology*. New York: Oxford University Press.

WEBER, MAX. 1922. *Economy and Society*. New York: Bedminster Press, 1968.

WESTERMANN, WILLIAM L. 1955. *The Slave Systems of Greek and Roman Antiquity*. Philadelphia: American Philosophical Society.

WILLIAMS, ERIC. 1944. *Capitalism & Slavery*. New York: Capricorn Books, 1966.

WITTFOGEL, KARL A. 1957. *Oriental Despotism: A Comparative Study of Total Power*. New York: Oxford University Press.

WORLD BANK. 1988. *World Development Report 1988*. New York: Oxford University Press.

WORLD BANK. 1994. *World Development Report 1994*. New York: Oxford University Press.

WORLD BANK. 2006. *World Development Indicators 2006*. Washington, DC: The World Bank.

WORLD BANK. 2007. *World Development Report 2008*. Washington, DC: The World Bank.

WORLD BANK. 2007a. *World Development Indicators 2007*. Washington, DC: The World Bank.

WORLD HEALTH ORGANIZATION. 2005. *The World Health Report 2005*. Geneva: World Health Organization, 2005.

ZEITLIN, MAURICE, KENNETH LUTTERMAN, and JAMES W. RUSSELL. 1973. "Death in Vietnam: Class, Poverty, and the Risks of War." *Politics and Society*, Vol. 3, no. 3 (Spring), pp. 313–328.

Index